Lorenzo Sears

The History of Oratory

From the Age of Pericles to the Present Time

Lorenzo Sears

The History of Oratory
From the Age of Pericles to the Present Time

ISBN/EAN: 9783337338541

Printed in Europe, USA, Canada, Australia, Japan

Cover: Foto ©ninafisch / pixelio.de

More available books at **www.hansebooks.com**

THE
HISTORY OF ORATORY

FROM THE

AGE OF PERICLES TO THE
PRESENT TIME

BY

LORENZO SEARS
PROFESSOR IN BROWN UNIVERSITY

S. C. GRIGGS AND COMPANY
1896

TO

CYRUS NORTHROP, LL. D.,

PRESIDENT OF THE UNIVERSITY OF MINNESOTA,

AND SOMETIME

PROFESSOR OF RHETORIC AND ENGLISH LITERATURE

IN YALE COLLEGE,

THIS VOLUME IS INSCRIBED

IN PLEASANT MEMORY OF ACADEMIC YEARS.

Great thanks might justly be given to our days, most excellent Ammæus, for an improvement in other branches of culture, and particularly for the signal advance that has been made by the study of Civil Oratory.—*Dionysius of Halicarnassus, on the Decline and Revival of Oratory.*

PREFACE.

IF Oratory is what the ancients called it, "The Art of Arts," it should have a history of its own, like the arts of painting, sculpture, and architecture, of music, poetry, and the drama. If, also, it is a science, as Aristotle and his successors have shown, its fundamental principles must have been derived from a series of experiments whose record becomes historical. Again, if there is a philosophy of public discourse, referring its laws to methods of mental and moral action, such reference is the better established and confirmed the farther back observation extends and the more complete the account becomes of such successes and failures as attend any continuous endeavor. Furthermore, if modern methods of study are to be applied to the art, the science, or the philosophy of public address, something like a connected narrative of its beginning and growth, its decadences and revivals is requisite.

These phases of the subject cannot, of course, be formally separated from each other in its historical treatment. As in ordinary discourse itself they are mingled in varying proportions, so in any continuous account of it these several elements must appear in solution rather than as precipitated or crystallized with exact formality;

Great thanks might justly be given to our days, most excellent Ammæus, for an improvement in other branches of culture, and particularly for the signal advance that has been made by the study of Civil Oratory.—*Dionysius of Halicarnassus, on the Decline and Revival of Oratory.*

PREFACE.

IF Oratory is what the ancients called it, "The Art of Arts," it should have a history of its own, like the arts of painting, sculpture, and architecture, of music, poetry, and the drama. If, also, it is a science, as Aristotle and his successors have shown, its fundamental principles must have been derived from a series of experiments whose record becomes historical. Again, if there is a philosophy of public discourse, referring its laws to methods of mental and moral action, such reference is the better established and confirmed the farther back observation extends and the more complete the account becomes of such successes and failures as attend any continuous endeavor. Furthermore, if modern methods of study are to be applied to the art, the science, or the philosophy of public address, something like a connected narrative of its beginning and growth, its decadences and revivals is requisite.

These phases of the subject cannot, of course, be formally separated from each other in its historical treatment. As in ordinary discourse itself they are mingled in varying proportions, so in any continuous account of it these several elements must appear in solution rather than as precipitated or crystallized with exact formality;

a process which has sometimes followed the other. Nevertheless, notice may with propriety be taken of such analytic and synthetic methods when they occur in the history of public speech.

Such considerations have led to the preparation of the following chapters, in the failure to find the fortunes of oratory, during a period of about twenty-four centuries, traced in any single work.

The treatment of the subject within the compass of one volume has its obvious limitations. To do this as exhaustively as Professor Jebb, following German and English scholars, has treated the one section, from Antiphon to Isæus, would require several volumes. The immense body of oratorical literature, and of biographical and historical material related to it, imposes a constant necessity of selection and condensation. In view of this it has been attempted to give only a brief account of each typical orator's place in the long succession, to note the rhetorical principles that he exemplified, and to observe the trend of eloquence in the several periods which may be designated as the Greek, Roman, Patristic, Mediæval, Reformation, Revolution, Restoration, Parliamentary, and American.

It should be added that the substance of these chapters was originally delivered in a course of lectures, and that the principal changes have been made in the way of abridgement. It is also due to the writer, as well as to the reader, to say that if in the course of composition the possibility of publication had been clearer, references might have been kept to authorities which are now beyond immediate recall. Still, the sources of helpful material have been indicated with tolerable fulness in the text. The editions of orations and speeches are, likewise, so many and various that no attempt at reference to volume and page has been considered desirable in the relatively few citations made. If, however, some notion shall be conveyed of the elevations and depressions of eloquence through many centuries, and some facts recalled which contribute to a just appreciation of its higher achievements; above all, if any impulse shall be imparted to the study of oratory, in which there are present indications of revived interest, especially among students; if these results shall be in any degree attained, the purpose of this sketch will be accomplished.

The author appends his grateful recognition of valuable assistance rendered in the reading of proof by his friend, Mr. Harry Lyman Koopman, Librarian of the University.

BROWN UNIVERSITY, PROVIDENCE, R. I.
DECEMBER, 1895.

CONTENTS.

I.—TRACES OF ORATORY IN EARLY LITERATURE.

The beginnings of literature itself in primitive verse concerning Nature; in later poetry regarding human life; succeeded by philosophic prose. Appearance of the first recorded rhetorical precept. Prose in history. Oratory in the episodes of Herodotus' history. The speeches of his characters. Thucydides also incorporated speeches with his history. Oratory in the drama. Poetry and oratory mingled by the dramatists and their successors. The speeches finally predominate in the play. Theodectes, tragedian and orator, marks the transition. Oratory triumphs as a literary art. Public address in biblical ages.

II.—FORENSIC ORATORY IN SICILY.

Sicily Hellenic in character. Syracuse a resort of literary men in the fifth century B. C. Empedocles. Aristotle's estimate of him as a rhetorician. The art of methodical speech is Hellenic. Favored by language, literature, and philosophy, in fifth and sixth centuries B. C.; and finally by a democratic government in Syracuse. Practical character of early forensic oratory. In theory every citizen his own advocate. Leads to delegated argumentation. Corax the first instructor in legal oratory. His five rules. Their anticipations of later treatises. Their foundation in unchanging principles. Summary.

III.—PROFESSIONAL SPEECH-WRITERS.

The occasion of their appearance. Antiphon marks the transition from the rhetorical school to the law-court and the assembly. Formulated briefs. His topic of general probability. Becomes the pioneer of political, legislative, and deliberative discussion. Develops former principles. His style. Gorgias. His methods of instruction. Plato's *Gorgias*. Practical and teachable, useful and scientific rhetoric, the orator and the rhetorician. Lysias. Marks the transfer of the science to Greece. Socrates' mention of him. His rhetorical education. A wealthy manufacturer. Business troubles force him into professional speech-writing. Adapts his arguments to the characters of his clients. Versatility of style. Master of prose-writing. His success. Isocrates. Socrates' prophecy concerning his future. Loss of fortune drives him into professional labors. His school at Athens. His illustrious pupils. His improvements upon the methods of his predecessors. Exalted themes. Oratorical and ethical purpose. Results of his instructions. The character of his professional work. The extent of his literary influence. The pecuniary value of his services and productions. Not a mere rhetorician. His advancement of Greek oratory. The anomalous character of this period. Its contributions to the art and science of rhetoric. The logographer's place in the growth of forensic and deliberative oratory.

IV.—ATTIC ORATORS.

Andocides. Orator of natural ability, so-called. His faults. Lack of clearness and orderly arrangement, of proportion and precision in illustration, and of earnestness, charged by Hermogenes. Plutarch's uncharitable criticism. Illustration of the obverse and reverse sides of rhetorical criticism. Faults might have been less if he had been less natural and self-sufficing. Isæus. Suffers from his position between Lysias and Demosthenes. Transmits results of former efforts to a greater successor. Catches the excellencies and not the faults of his models. Clear, brief, and graphic in diction; flexible, vigorous, animated, and earnest in style. Rapid in movement and skilful in arrangement. Cumulative reasoning crowned with appeal. Advances his profession by limiting it to private causes. Adapts arguments to clients. A master of forensic discussion. Instructor of Demosthenes. Bondage to conventionalisms his mistake. Review of the progress of forensic oratory. Leading traits of principal orators.

V.—POLITICAL ORATORS.

Forensic oratory leads to deliberative. Four orators of the best period. Lycurgus, the conservative. Characteristics. Hyperides, the progressive patriot. Qualities of his oratory. Estimates by Hermogenes and Longinus. Æschines. Natural gifts and acquired accomplishments. Drawbacks. Demosthenes, the culmination of Attic eloquence. Its earlier types. Elements in his phenomenal achievement. Necessity of effort through loss of inheritance. Shares in prosecution of his guardians. Training under Isæus. Obstacles and hindrances. Apprenticeship at speech-writing. Legal, historical, and political studies. Beginning of professional career. Championship of Athens. Manner and tone of early speeches. Their pervading principle. Labor in composition. Characteristics of argument and style. Recognition of his genius. Its highest achievement. Variety and versatility. The task imposed upon his oratory. The patriot soldier's indorsement of his own speech. His primacy among ancient orators.

VI.—ARISTOTLE, THE RHETORICIAN.

A century's growth of oratory, under Greek criticism, civil liberty, and literary contests develops Attic excellencies. Material accumulated for a science of rhetoric, in compositions of various styles and values. The power to analyze and classify these is found in Aristotle. Favoring circumstances and qualifications. Literary and scientific habits. Acquaintance with orators and their methods. Reduction of particular modes to general principles of speech. Substitution of laws for rules and precepts. His estimate of predecessors. His definition of rhetoric. Division of the subject. Proof in his system. Comprehensiveness and minuteness of his analysis. Example in his division of *Deliberative Oratory*. Other examples. Not a minute philosopher merely. Develops and exhausts the subject in a large and manly way. The father of rhetorical science. Permanent value of his work. His style. His analytic methods useful to writers. Lack of emotive element alleged. His theory and art of composition. His philosophy of rhetoric.

VII.—EARLY ROMAN ORATORS.

Slow development of Latin literature. Its indebtedness to Greek inspiration. Diffusion of the Greek language. Persistence of the Latin. Prose composition favored by the Roman character. A rugged speech natural to the Latin race. A sturdy and martial oratory precedes other forms of literature. Which in turn antedate the maturity of eloquence. Cato the Censor and his vigorous prose. Contemporaries of Cato. Scipio Africanus Major and Minor. Sulpicius Galba. Rutilius Rufus. The Gracchi. Tiberius and Caius. Other orators. Greek influence and culture. Mark Antony. Crassus. Cicero's opinion of him. Hortensius. His Asiatic style.

VIII.—RHETORICAL SCHOOLS.—CICERO, THE RHETORICIAN.

Conflict of literary tastes. The Attic and Asiatic controversy. Its causes. Criteria of style. Quintilian's dictum. The law of diversity. Rhetorical study becomes retrospective and imitative. Hellenic teachers of oratory at Rome, and Roman youth at Athens. Rhetoric a remunerative profession. The exalted position of oratory in ancient education. The rhetorical works of Cicero. A digest of previous treatises with his own additions. His division of the subject. With Aristotle he emphasizes invention as the foundation of the art. The *De Oratore*. Qualifications of an orator. Symposia. The *De Claris Oratoribus* and *Orator*. His rhetorical position as affected by his philosophical and moral codes. Philosophical studies contribute to oratorical. The ethical element in his system. His eloquence affected by his times. Resumé of influences and oratorical examples.

IX.—CICERO, THE ORATOR.

His life outlined. Fidelity to his own rhetorical system. Details of construction and argumentation. Variety of method. Adaptation. Latinity. Diction. Harmony of sound and sense. Examples. Excellencies. Strictures. Overbalancing merits. Compared with Demosthenes. In comprehensiveness; multitude-moving power. Demosthenes' singleness of aim. Cicero's broader culture. Pleasantry; sobriety. Cicero's advantage of living in a later age. Differing motives and methods of address. Contrasting styles. Rapidity of movement. Demands of modern taste. Values of concise and copious expression. Roman taste pleased by stately splendor. Cicero's ethical sentiments illustrated in his eloquence. His struggles between the desire to please and to do right. Quintilian's summary of his virtues.

X.—CICERO'S SUCCESSORS AND QUINTILIAN.

Oratory declines in vigor and advances in finish. Becomes servile with the loss of liberty. Reactions and Asian tendencies. Neglect of deliberative oratory under tyrants. Public speech restricted to the courts; and to rhetorical schools. Ends in mere declamation. Rare exceptions. Mostly "sound and fury." Temporary revival under Nerva. The highest literary ambition. Pliny the Younger as an advocate. Tacitus, the historian, as an orator. Weight, force, and dramatic character of his eloquence. Return of downward tendencies. Pedantry and affectation. Culminate in Fronto's praise of dust and smoke. Quintilian. Early training. Imperial favor. Champion of the Ciceronian style. The training of an orator. Ethical element. Follows Aristotle. Wide reading. Elocution. Critical estimates of Cicero, Cæsar, and contemporary orators. Generosity of his criticism. A ripe scholar before he began to write. Literary modesty. Exhaustive character of his *Institutes of Oratory*. Outline of his system. Its comprehensiveness. Relation to his own and subsequent times.

XI.—Patristic Oratory — Greek.

Revival of Greek literature in the second century. Medley of dogmas. Finally a new philosophy, literature, and oratory. The new faith and its preacher. St. Paul at Athens and Rome. Constantine makes speech free. Character of the emancipated oratory. Conflicts of opinion. Nicene controversy. Athanasius. Characteristics of his eloquence. Singleness of purpose. Recognition at Alexandria. Literary labors. His logic and rhetoric. Chrysostom. Legal training. Seclusion. Popularity. Power. Character of his eloquence. Bishop of Constantinople. Unsparing denunciations of evil. Reaction. Martyrdom. Basil of Cæsarea. Greek education. His eloquence. A central idea. Practical preaching. Religion and science. Examples. On vanity. Pagan doings. Larger themes. Divine science. Gregory of Nazianzum. His tribute to eloquence. His estimate of the ethical element. Eulogy on Basil. Resumé. A stormy age. Formative and reconstructive. Importance of issues. Its oratory compared with that of Greek statesmen. Inspiring motive and ruling ideas in each.

XII.—Patristic Oratory — Latin.

The Christian religion Greek at first. Its prestige transferred to Rome. Tertullian of Carthage and African theology. His gloomy and aggressive spirit. Ridicule of pagans. Strictures on the laxity of believers. Creator of a Latin ecclesiastical literature. Ambrose. Apostle of the Western Church. Rhetorician and lawyer. Governor and bishop. Fame of his preaching. Last struggles of paganism. Eulogy on Gratian and Valentinian. Ambrose. His oratory. Denunciation of vice and vanity. Augustine. Professor of Rhetoric in Carthage, Rome, and Milan. Eloquence as a preacher. Rhetoric in the fifth century. His writings. Influence upon subsequent times. Leo the Great. Eloquence and administrative methods. Speech of Leo wards off barbarian hordes. Builds a new empire upon the ruins of imperialism. The greatest man in Rome.

The pulpit his vantage ground. His apostolic preaching. Its cardinal doctrines. Personal humility and official arrogance. Influence of the pulpit then. Comparison of the new oratory with the old in manner, motive, and results. The later life breathed into the earlier forms.

XIII.—MEDIÆVAL PREACHERS.

Decline of pulpit eloquence. Exaltation of papacy and ritual. State of learning. Oratory ecclesiastical. Preaching of Paulinus. Bede. His preaching. Learning in Britain. Sermon on the Celestial Country. Monastic oratory. Rhetorical instruction. Boniface. Mission preaching. Homilies. Adaptation to a simple people. Transition from ancient to mediæval oratory. Examples of contemporary discourse. Rabanus' sermons. Damian's expositions. Ignorance and illiteracy of the *Sæculum Obscurum*.

XIV.—PREACHERS OF THE CRUSADES.

The passing of the millennial year. Signs of revival. Rise of the universities. Peter of Amiens. Described by William of Tyre. A natural orator with scanty outfit. Impassioned oratory. Demonstrative. Effect on auditors. Drives Europe to Palestine. Finally fights for the cause he has proclaimed. His eloquence cannot be criticized by later standards. Anselm. Metaphysician and preacher: expository style. Ivo of Chartres. Bruno of Aste. Mystical preaching. Hildebert. Guarric. Adam Scotus. Peter Cellensis. Peter of Blois. Bernard of Clairvaux. Contests of papacy and chivalry. Bernard's commanding eloquence. A peacemaker. Preaches a crusade. Inspiring oratory. Marvelous power. Antony of Padua. Followed by multitudes. Mystical and imaginative. Type of his times. Mediæval oratory ends "without grace or glory."

XV.—ECCENTRIC ELOQUENCE.

Low estate of oratory in fourteenth century. Artificial and overstrained. Graphic and grotesque. Exceptions. Gabriel Biel; thoughtful and direct. John Raulin, satirist. Fables for clergy and people. Literary tastes of the age. Philip von Hartung's vigor and originality. De Barzia's strong points. Transition from expository to topical discourse. Beza's devices to enliven long sermons. Vehement and picturesque. Value of such discourse to after ages; to our own time.

XVI.—SAVONAROLA.

His ascetic life. Disorders of his day. A prophet to an evil generation. First sermons didactic. Florentine indifferentism. His antagonisms of style and manner. Denunciations of vice. Critical audiences. Discouragements. Mariano, his popular rival. Meditations and visions. Message to a corrupt age. Responsive hearers at Brescia and Genoa. Recalled to Florence. St. Mark's thronged. Prophetic warnings. Popularity. Courted and beneficed. Growth of his oratory. Disadvantages from lack of rhetorical training. Sincerity and ardor. Restoration of genuine eloquence. The house of Borgia. More visions and prophecies. Effects of his eloquence. Fulfilment of predictions. The burden of his message. The day of his triumph. Persecutions and martyrdom. His place among orators.

XVII.—ORATORY OF THE REFORMATION.

Martin Luther. Monastic and university preaching. Freedom and fearlessness, freshness and vigor. Eminence as an orator. His appearance. Mental qualifications. Temperament. Characteristics of his speech. Self-criticism. What his oratory did for the Reformation. Bucer. Lecturer in Cambridge. Earns the title of "the eloquent." Oratory becomes submerged in controversial writing. Hugh Latimer. Pungent and indefatigable. Learned and original. His versatility, wit, and drollery. His pulpit anywhere. Boldness. Quaint English. Examples of his similitudes. Colloquies with his audience. Last words. John Knox, the irrepressible. Politics and religion. Preaches a crusade against monasteries. Tirades in Edinburg. Denunciation of St. Bartholomew massacre.

XVIII.—THREE FRENCH ORATORS IN REIGN OF LOUIS XIV.

Tributary influences. Previous literary achievements. Poetry, chronicles, romance, biography. Early criticism and philosophy. Literary age of Louis XIV. Bossuet. His early education. Precocity. A member of the Academy. Distinction in Paris. Patristic studies. Three periods of his career. Attitude toward royalty, the common people, and the truth. Natural eloquence. Lamartine's estimate of it. The manner of the man. His funeral discourses. Bourdaloue. Argumentation his strong point. Voltaire and Vinet's opinions. Thought and expression. Suggestive logic. Sermon before the king. Extracts. Massillon. His felicitous exordiums. Grace and elegance of diction. The king's commendation. The oration at the funeral of Louis the Great. Characteristics of the three great preachers. Which was greatest?

XIX.—ORATORY OF THE FRENCH REVOLUTION.

Abnormal conditions produce a singular style of eloquence. Long-suppressed freedom of speech became wild with its restoration. Its purpose and its necessity. Mirabeau. Early years. Pamphleteering first, and then spokesman of a moderate party. His immense activity. His employment of helpers in composing. His assimilative and recreative powers. Characteristics of his oratory. Examples. His extemporaneous speech. Independent attitude toward king and people. Danton. Jacobins and Girondists. Inspirations of the time. Vergniaud on the Jacobin conspiracy. Danton stands for the whirlwind as Mirabeau has stood for the gathering storm. Napoleon's censorship. Military addresses. Intuition. Motives which he appeals to. Examples of his harangues to troops. His farewell. His oratory as contributing to his success.

XX.—Orators of the Restoration.

De Serre's brief but successful career. Points of excellence. General Foy. His good sense and knowledge of the time. Sensational but approved. Methods of preparation for extemporaneous speech. Benjamin Constant. Writer and orator by turns. Rostrum and press. Variety of treatment. Other qualities. Adroit and artful speech. Royer Collard. Elaborate and erudite. Aphoristic. Manuel. His patient explication. Subtlety of his dialectics. Improvisations. Art of delaying debate. Parliamentary tactics. Lafayette. His speech dignified conversation addressed to the understanding. "French grace, American indifference, Roman placidity." Odillon Barot, the staid and philosophic theorizer. Dupin, the versatile and impetuous advocate. Lamartine, the Gorgias of France. Poetic, imaginative, and flowing speech. Guizot. The writer contrasted with the speaker. Lucidity of thought and expression. Too cautious to be eloquent. His panegyric on the Constitution of 1789 compared with similar passages in ancient and modern oratory. Thiers, historian and orator. Readiness, disorder, and precipitation. Amusing and convincing. Range of his information. Discordant elements in the oratory of the age.

XXI.—British Parliamentary Oratory.

The importance of the period. Lack of obvious causes for its eloquence. Association of genius in groups. State of national affairs. Harmony at home and ambition to extend dominion. A time of dangerous prosperity demanded wise counselors. Deliberative oratory of a high order appears. The ambition and the possessions of the government. Discussion of policy toward American colonies. Orators of the seventeenth and eighteenth centuries. Elliot, Strafford, Belhaven, Walpole, Chesterfield. William Pitt. Early oratorical studies. Macaulay's sketch of him. Integrity in office. Political triumph. Estimation of his rank among orators. Natural powers. Cultivation of them. Personality. Resources. His treatment of themes. Style. His best speeches. Extracts. Prophetic words.

XXII.—MANSFIELD.—BURKE.

Mansfield's precocity. Study of ancient orators. Practice of extemporary speech. Contests in debate with Pitt. Story's tribute to him. Judicial oratory. His clear statement of a case. Examples. Burke starts with Chatham's commendation. His preparation. His reading in ancient oratory and poetry. Philosophical spirit. The period of his greatest eloquence. Contemporary opinion of his first speech on conciliation. His independence. Second speech on conciliation with America. Value of his speeches to political students and orators, and as literature. Characteristics of diction and style.

XXIII.—SHERIDAN.—FOX.

The succession of Irish orators. Sheridan's literary career. Gibbon's estimate of his eloquence. Tributes from Pitt and Fox. His progress from the stage to Parliament. Disadvantage of a literary reputation to members of Parliament. Sheridan's early failures. Diligent cultivation of native abilities. His methods of preparation. The great speech of his life. Structure of this speech. Testimony of contemporaries to its effects. Personal traits. Asiatic style. Diction. Fox. Early influences. Classical training. Espouses the cause of popular rights. The inspiring cause of his eloquence. Ambition to become a powerful debater. Argumentative character of his speeches. Straightforwardness and sympathy. Oratorical methods. Strong language from strong feeling. His illustrations. Fairness toward an adversary. His most finished speech. His ablest.

XXIV.—COLONIAL ORATORY.

Allied to that of Great Britain. Interest in parliamentary discussion. Its influence upon colonial thought and expression. Samuel Adams. His sturdy speech. Characterization. Address to colonial governor. Its force and brevity. His practical speech. To be measured by what it accomplished. James Otis. His rank as an orator of the Revolution. Appearance and characteristics. Effects of his eloquence. Speech against taxation. Fisher Ames. Preparation for forensic speaking. Political writings. Debater in Congress. Appreciation at home. His style. Patrick Henry. Meager opportunities. Legal venture. Success as an advocate. Power over juries. In the House of Burgesses. Incendiary eloquence. Popularity. States-rights advocate. Frequency of speeches. Their climax. Dramatic effects. Professional labors. Care in preparation of arguments. Forensic triumphs. Methods of attack. Descriptions and estimates. Other orators of this period in the South; and in the North.

XXV.—CONGRESSIONAL ORATORY.

John Randolph. Marks the transition between colonial and congressional periods. Violence of his early speeches. Their popularity. Characteristics and manner. His forecast of national troubles. Emancipation suggested. Henry Clay. Lack of early advantages. The Richmond debating-club. Law in Lexington. Practice in daily reading and speaking. Campaign speech. In Congress. Speaker of the House, and other positions. Elements in his oratory. Sincerity and honesty of conviction. Clearness of statement to the common intelligence. Unconstraint. Earnestness. Majestic presence. Enthusiasm of his audiences. Rank as a parliamentary orator. Qualities of his eloquence. John C. Calhoun. Limited opportunities. Extemporary speaking in the law school. In politics early. Contemporary issues. The ruling element in his speeches. Logic. Persistence. Massiveness and breadth. Manner and method of his oratory. His greatest efforts. Characterization and comparison with Clay and Webster.

XXVI.—DANIEL WEBSTER.

Difficulties of oratorical criticism. His early struggles. Productive causes. Early proclivities. Promising boyhood. College performances in speaking. Fourth of July orations. Exuberance of style. Later studies. Legal companions and instructors. The value of perspicuous state-

CONTENTS. 19

ment. Effective diction. Lucidity of statement. His manner with a jury. Their confidence in him. The Kenniston and White trials. Skill in discovering vital points. Dartmouth College case. Emotional element. Major and minor points in argument. In Congress. Improvement in style. Statesmanship. Deliberative oratory. Replies to Hayne. Occasion. Question at issue. Exordium. Method of argumentation. Oratorical principles exemplified and illustrated. Literary skill. Lofty spirit. Exposition of the Constitution. Fairness to opponents. Kinds of argument employed. Analytic power and grasp of principles; earnestness of conviction; force of appeal; general adaptation. Ethical element. His place in the history of oratory.

XXVII.—OCCASIONAL ORATORY.

Definition. Edward Everett. Literary attainments. Professor of Greek in Harvard. Beginning of oratorical career. His services to the cause of letters. Qualities and characteristics. Bequest of classic eloquence in the demonstrative manner. Rufus Choate. At Dartmouth College in a forensic age. Later studies. In Congress. Deliberative oratory in the fervid style. Legal argumentation. Skill in arrangement. Imagination and humor. Literary tastes and studies. Style in construction and manner in expression. Occasional addresses.

XXVIII.—CHARLES SUMNER.

Antecedents. Studies and companions. First occasional oration. Its wealth of allusion. Recognition. Eulogy upon Pickering, Story, Allston, and Channing. Succeeding orations. Classicism and stateliness. Development of anti-slavery sentiments. Their unpopularity. Personal unconcern. Determination and opposition. Attacks upon slavery. Leader in the final struggle in Congress. Singleness of devotion. Ethical power.

XXIX.—WENDELL PHILLIPS.

Early influences and position. The mob in broadcloth. Speech in Fanueil Hall on the Alton mob. A reputation made. The eloquent agitator. Lyceum platform discussions throughout the North. Characteristics of his addresses. Methods of composition and delivery. Estimate of his work and rank as an orator.

XXX.—GEORGE WILLIAM CURTIS.

The orator and editor. Represents a transition period. Platform and press complements of each other. Curtis' first important speech both academic and political in character. The scholar in politics. The Philadelphia and Chicago speeches illustrate his moral courage. War speeches. Eulogies on Sumner. Phillips, Bryant, and Lowell. The extent of Curtis' influence. Honors. Characteristics. Unmentioned orators, past and present. Prospect. The present condition of oratory. The issues of a reconstructive and commercial period as affecting eloquence. Its revival one of the repetitions of history. Indications of renewed interest. In colleges. Retrospect. The horizon line. Its elevations and depressions. Principal names. Oratory and liberty go hand in hand. Phases of expression in different centuries. Conformity to universal laws.

THE HISTORY OF ORATORY.

I.

TRACES OF ORATORY IN EARLY LITERATURE.

PLATO makes the orator Gorgias say, in the dialogue bearing his name, that in discoursing of his art he can be as long as he pleases or as short as he pleases. Socrates begs him to reserve his length for some other occasion, and in this conversation to be as brief as possible. In consequence, his replies for some time are simply—"Yes," "No," "Certainly," "Very true," "That is evident," and others equally curt, until his interlocutor cries out, "By Here, Gorgias, I admire the surpassing brevity of your answers." Some minutes later, after a question about the art which Polus had called "the noblest," joined with another concerning the greatest good, Socrates gets the following rejoinder: "I should say that the art of persuasion, which gives freedom to all men, and to individuals power in the State, is the greatest good;" and then, after a little more of conciseness in reply, Gorgias is drawn out into a fuller and longer exposition of his theory of public discourse.

A historical treatment of this subject induces a constant balancing between these two moods of Gorgias. However, on the one hand it is hardly desirable to adopt the brevity he assumed after he had been warned to be short by the son of Sophroniscus, while on the other the temptation to be long is as great as the literature of eloquence is vast. In such a dilemma the probable interest in the topic assigns a limit so moderate that a representative presentation of the phases of oratory in different centuries and countries is compelled, and a comprehensive view of the diversities in its fortunes.

It will doubtless be admitted that in a survey which is at all comprehensive, some inquiry should be made for remote records and for the beginnings of a growth which at length became wide-spread and vigorous.

Such investigation will necessarily meet with much that is foreign to the immediate object of search. As an abundance of material is encountered which is not the vein of gold that is traced, so the vestiges of eloquence are imbedded in other forms of literature in such intricate ways as to be well-nigh obscured. It is possible, however, that it may antedate them all, as speech precedes writing, and prose poetry in ordinary composition. For if the latest conclusion of evolutionists be accepted, supported as it is by ethnic examples, it will appear that the germ of oratory is found in the primitive laudation of a conqueror returning with the spoils of war, a brief and simple proclamation of victory at first, developed later into eulogistic speech. However this may be, it is evident that the orator left his mark upon primeval literatures along with the poet and the historian, the philosopher and the dramatist. In the compositions of such writers themselves public address often appears here and there like a continuous thread running through the fabric which primitive artisans were weaving. Protoplasmic eloquence may not be found in early folk-songs to Spring and to Autumn, to Apollo, Adonis, and Tammuz, or in the verses of bard and minstrel, in epic, elegiac, and choral poetry; but there were brave speeches in the Epos which underlay our present Iliad that were not composed by Æolic poets and rhapsodists without the living model in their memory. Neither is it promising ground to look for eloquence in the philosophic prose which next follows; still it is in the beginning of a treatise of Diogenes of Apollonia that the following rhetorical precept is found entombed like a trilobite in limestone: "It appears to me that every one who begins a discourse ought to state the subject with distinctness and to make the style simple and dignified."

It is, however, when the domain of history is reached that public address takes a definite place in literature. Especially in the episodes of Herodotus appear numerous examples of formal speech; for into the historical narrative, and to enforce certain dominant ideas, particularly concerning the envy of the gods and the danger of pride, Herodotus has introduced speeches, which he puts into the mouths of one and another of his characters. Being somewhat of a theologian and poet, as well as historian, his speeches have a lyric rather than a dramatic part to perform; that is, they set forth the composer's own thoughts and feelings, rather than the external circumstances and events of the story. They are the author's meditations and reflections upon the course of time, the choral song which succeeds the dialogue in the tragedy. As to the ethical character of these reflections it has been remarked that they resemble the writings of the Old Testament both in matter and in the oriental manner of their expression, as might be expected from the historian's acquaintance with Persian affairs.

Thucydides also diversified his historical narrative with imputed oratory—speeches of his heroes at important crises, in which he exhibits their motives and their thoughts as if he had seen them through and through. And although he was criticised by contemporaries for leaving the domain of history, his example was followed by subsequent writers, who gave to Greek and Roman history a rhetorical flavor. There are forty-one such speeches in his first seven books, panegyrical, judicial, and deliberative. Fourteen are from generals to soldiers, short and to the point. Others are obscure through too great condensation and compression, and are faulty through certain mannerisms, as repetitions of "nominally" and "really," "in word and in deed," needless definitions and distinctions; and in one place the mistake is made of attributing a spirit of niggardly detraction to his audience in the very opening of a speech ascribed to Pericles. But there is much in these speeches to illustrate the methods of the time, and as Grote remarks, "The modern historian strives in vain to convey the impression which is made by the condensed, burning phrases of Thucydides." There is not so much a crowding of ideas, as of aphorisms about an idea, which we may best understand by reading a page of Carlyle or Emerson. Expounding an obvious or familiar thought he betrays a tendency to astonish the reader by the new and strange way in which it is developed.

In accordance with the training which epic poetry had given the Greeks, they expected the account of a man's bodily deeds to be accompanied by his spoken words, as an indication of his mental character. Historians, therefore, could not satisfy their readers with the record of any hero's achievements without giving some report of his intentions or reflections as revealed by his public utterances. Accordingly, the speeches of generals and counselors are often incorporated with plain narration of events. The artless simplicity with which Thucydides makes the following admission in regard to such speeches is creditable alike to his honesty as a historian and his ability as a rhetorician. He says, "As to the speeches made on the eve of war, or in its course, I have found it difficult to retain a memory of the precise words which I had heard spoken; and so it was with those who brought me reports. But I have made persons say what it seemed to me most opportune for them to say in view of each situation; at the same time I have adhered as closely as possible to the general sense of what was actually said." His frankness recalls the naïveté of an artist whose portraits of certain distinguished persons were charitably criticized by a brother artist as "Beautiful productions, but not remarkable for their resemblance to the originals." "But," replied the undaunted idealist, "don't you know that is just how they ought to look?"

Thucydides' ingenuous confession might be made with reference to much that has been set down in type as the veritable utterance of many orators, both ancient and modern. This accounts for the uniformity of style in which his generals addressed their troops, and his counselors their auditors. One exception, however, is prominent in the general Thucydidean host, namely, Pericles, to whose eloquence the historian had listened so often and so eagerly that, consciously or unconsciously, he caught a distinctive manner and transferred it to his reports of that orator's eloquence.

But in all these speeches Thucydides finds a place to incorporate his own views, sentiments, and opinions. As a relator of facts he is exact and faithful in the body of his narrative; but when he comes to making a speech for one of the generals or ambassadors, he finds an excellent opportunity to give the impression which the course of events has made on the mind of Thucydides as a philosophical historian, and not Thucydides the chronicler, like Herodotus who was a very Froissart of Greece.

Any sketch preliminary to the study of oratory would be incomplete without the mention, at least, of its place in the Greek drama. Indeed, dramatic poetry and oratory were so near one another from the beginning "that they often joined hands over the gap which separates poetry and prose." Accustomed to listen to long speeches in their assemblies, the Athenians tolerated a large interpolation of them in their tragedies, and so kindly that the oratorical element outgrew the others, and the speeches at length became the chief business of the play. But as they lacked the reality of daily life, their rhetoric resembled the speaking of the Sophists rather than the genuine eloquence of the Attic orators, and accordingly the people at last demanded the genuine oratory instead of the dramatic speech.

The transition took place in the person of one Theodectes, dramatist and rhetorician, orator and tragedian. It was at the famous funeral of Mausolus that Theodectes produced both a panegyric and a tragedy; and although Theopompus carried off the prize from all the orators on that occasion, Theodectes so hit the taste of his age that he obtained eight victories in thirteen contests. Even Aristotle found material in Theodectes' tragedies to illustrate his Rhetoric. The time had come when the drama was to yield the first place to oratory, the play itself being largely made up of affecting speeches, based on skilful argumentation and paradoxical assertions closely maintained. Dramatic style approximated more and more to prose, as a lofty poetical tone ill became the subtleties of argument and the labyrinthine reasoning which had become the staple of tragedy. Finally, there followed the separation and establishment of oratory as a distinct form of expression, and its eventual triumph over other phases of literary art in the Hellenic states.

In any attempt to discover the origins of eloquence it should not be assumed that there were no "speaking men" before the middle of the fifth century B. C. That faculty which, more than reason itself, distinguishes man from beast could not have remained unemployed during the existence of empires which were old when Greece was young. The earliest documentary testimony we possess brings to view first the poet and then the prophet, speaking before kings and people of the welfare and the woe to a nation which was to be carried into captivity by one of the oldest powers of which there is any written or monumental record. The prophecy of Isaiah is an example of what human speech had attained to six generations before the age of Pericles. Passing over contemporaries and successors during this period, and turning backward for indications of eloquence, it is not impossible to find them here and there in the historical documents of the Hebrews. They grow fainter with every receding century, as might be expected, until the first far-off fragment of the earliest recorded human address is reached—the boastful defence of Lamech for the crime of homicide.

To the question, was it originally spoken in verse? it may be as difficult to reply as to say whether the audience consisted of Adah and Zillah only.

One corroborative instance in this retrospect toward the primal age occurs in connection with what Herbert Spencer might call a germ-occasion of oratory, when Miriam goes out to celebrate the victory of "Jehovah, the man of war," over the Egyptians. The song of triumph is attributed to her brother Moses, the poet-prophet, whose prose orations as literary compositions are of similar excellence. As a speaker, however, he confesses that he "is not eloquent, but slow of speech, and of a slow tongue." In reply he is assured by divine authority that his brother Aaron "can speak well, and he shall be thy spokesman unto the people."

Once more, what sort of speakers had the author of the book of Job listened to that he could build upon their suggestive words the dignified and sublime discourses which fill his masterly dialogue?

To make a characterization of primeval public speech from its meagre records would be more difficult than to portray a mastodon from a few bones found in a deposit of the tertiary period. Collateral helps make the latter achievement possible, while there is a great deficiency of them in the instance of oratorical address. From the few available specimens that have survived, together with what can be inferred from the constant quality of human nature, modified by diversities of experience and cultivation, it is safe to say that strength, plain honesty of sentiment, and directness of diction belonged to the primitive man who spoke to an assembly of his fellow men. At the same time there is a corresponding lack of such amenities of discourse as might not be essential in rude and uncritical ages. Homeric speakers do not hesitate to boast of their own virtues, while Thucydides, who ought to have known better, makes his favorite orator violate the first principle of persuasion in offending his audience at the outset of his address, and certainly the Hebrew orators uttered the weightiest words in their exhortations and maledictions.

In general, primitive speech, like prehistoric man, was unadorned and without much art, unpretentious and lacking later refinements; but though crude in form it was direct in purpose, vigorous in manner, unmistakable in expression, and often productive of marvelous results.

II.

FORENSIC ORATORY IN SICILY.

NOT the least important of the islands that have been famous in history is the ancient Trinacria, the three-cornered. On the map Italy seems to have crowded it down towards Africa, to lie in the track of the East on its way to the West through the Mediterranean. Greek navigators, sailing the Ionian Sea, would not fail to wonder at a cloud of smoke in the horizon, and steering westward would descry the ashy cone of Ætna rising from the waters like a beacon, beckoning them toward Sicily. So far as relates to the subject of oratory, interest centers in the city of Syracuse on the eastern coast, nearest Greece. Here the old Greek drama of government appears to have been re-enacted, very much as at home, with varying fortune. Oligarchies, despotisms, and a sort of republicanism prevailed by turns. In the year 478 B. C. a despotism happened to be the dominant order, but with a strong leaning toward the humanities. Hiero's patronage of literature made Syracuse a famous resort for men of letters, and thither came Greek poets and dramatists, among them Æschylus and Pindar, Epicharmus and Sophron. Such a literary culture was soon to find more than one mode of expression, and poetry became the precursor of philosophy and oratory.

The figure which stands out clearest in this transition period is EMPEDOCLES, a native of the island, born at Agrigentum, on the south shore. Priest and poet, physician and philosopher, he received that adoration from his contemporaries which easily passes into semi-deification and canonization among posterity. Marvelous traditions of his powers have come down from an almost mythical time, and he will always occupy the borderland between fact and fable as something more than human, if less than divine. On the other hand, he did not allow an impressible populace to diminish their awe of him when he appeared in public, attended by a retinue of servants, with a crown upon his head, sandals of brass upon his feet, and a branch of laurel in his hand. He knew the value of appealing to the imagination of an imaginative people. Notwithstanding his vanity there was much of which Empedocles might be vain, even in the literary age in which he lived. Plato found his doctrines worth developing in the *Dialogues*, and Aristotle calls him a " Homeric spirit, personifying and deifying everything, robing himself in symbols and mystery." He may have been one of the early contributors to the tradition of Dr. Faustus.

The same high authority for everything relating to the science and literature of his predecessors, Aristotle, also speaks of him as "the Father of Rhetoric, a master of expression, and especially skilled in the use of metaphor." Although the fragments of his works which remain indicate that most of his compositions were in verse, according to the fashion of the time—tragedies, hymns, and epigrams—it is hardly possible that a man who was by no means of a retiring disposition should not have found it convenient to address the populace among whom he moved in such majestic state. Leader of the popular party, opposing the restoration of a tyranny, and saving the republic from a dangerous conspiracy, we cannot imagine that he did not sometimes do as modern heads of parties do—make speeches to an enthusiastic crowd, although these later party leaders may not always imitate him in refusing supreme power, or even political office when offered them, as he did. In the main Aristotle must have been as near right as usual· No doubt that Empedocles was the "Father of Oratory," in spite of his laurel crown and his sandals of brass.

It is to later times and more cultured nations that we must look for the cultivation of the art of methodical speech for definite ends and purposes. And among the nations there was none so completely equipped for this work as the Greek.

Before considering Greek oratory in detail certain conditions should be noted which greatly favored the attainment of phenomenal excellence. In the first place the Hellenic language was eminently adapted to the expression of thought and feeling. The perfection of structure, which it had acquired in the tenth century before the Christian era, implies a long period of previous culture, which was continued in subsequent centuries in the usual order from poetry to prose until the highest form was reached in the famous hundred years between the middle of the sixth and the middle of the fifth centuries B. C. For convenience let the year 500 be taken as a point about which may be loosely grouped the great lyric poet Pindar, and the dramatists Æschylus, Sophocles, and Euripides, all between 525–480 B. C.

To this period also belong the prose compositions of Herodotus, 484, the first great historian, and Thucydides, 471, the first writer of philosophical history, and Xenophon, 447, the graceful narrator of events and graphic delineator of Greek life. Philosophy followed history as history had succeeded to poetry, and Socrates, 468, teaches it to Plato, his junior by forty years, whose pupil, Aristotle, appears forty-four years later, establishing the Peripatetic school in imitation of Plato's academy.

It is with such advantages of preparation that oratory begins to appear as an art. The treasures of poetry in its epic, lyric, and dramatic forms were spread out before the imagination; history had accumulated the records of the past, philosophy had gathered the harvest of reflection, and all things were ready for that form of composition which draws from every source to convince, to please, and to persuade. It was the natural outcome of all that had gone before in the literary life of the Greeks. Of course we must move our grouping centre on a little, but not far, if we take into account the speeches and orations which had already been reported by the historians; for Solon, Miltiades, Pisistratus and Pericles, Aristides and Themistocles were orators as well as legislators, generals, and counselors. Pericles, 495, contemporary with Empedocles, may possibly share with the Sicilian the credit of being the first orator at Athens, as the other was at Agrigentum, cultivating oratory while he adorned his mind with the teachings of philosophy and general literature. He was followed by an illustrious company of Athenian orators of whom something will be said further on.

But for the rise of the rhetorical art in its technical character we must return to Sicily, and this time observe its growth in Syracuse.

As has been observed already, King Hiero's patronage of letters had brought to this city many literary men whose writings naturally paved the way for the highest expression in oratory. Still, other conditions besides a literary atmosphere were necessary to its freest development; for this form more than any other demands favorable surroundings. Poetry may flourish in days of adversity as among the captive Hebrews by the waters of Babylon, or in disordered England when Milton wrote his great epic. Sad prose may be written within prison walls, like Sir Walter Raleigh's famous apostrophe to death, but eloquence has never been successfully cultivated in captivities or under despotisms. It is in free states and under popular governments alone that oratory can flourish. The art of persuasion is valuable only as the people can be appealed to on the subject of public affairs, and where their judgments can be enlightened for the enforcement of political measures, and their feelings aroused sufficiently to lead them into personal activity and sacrifice; and where eloquence and freedom go hand in hand the most remarkable exhibitions of human ability occur.

It was when this rule of the people was fairly established in Sicily that oratory as an art began to be taught and practiced there. Nor was it for political purposes, as might be surmised, under the new and popular form of government. There was something of more importance to be attended to first than elections and candidacies for office. For under Thrasybulus, estates had been confiscated and bestowed upon favorites of the tyrant, and now, the despot being disposed of, the original holders and owners of landed property came forward with their claims to estates which had been alienated, and the law courts were full of citizens demanding their rightful possessions. It is also probable that, as is usually the case in disturbed times, there were also some pretended claims whose validity would be questioned, and, accordingly, legal processes with proofs and pleadings would have to be instituted with due forms of law. But up to this time all such arguing of cases appears to have been in the hands of the original parties without the intervention of an advocate. Each citizen, therefore, according to the Greek notion of citizenship, would have to conduct his own affairs in court, stating his claim and arguing his case. Immense differences of ability would of course occur then as now, if, in a similar state of things, one man and another should appear in court to reclaim their titles. The plausible and talkative citizen might secure his rights while his diffident and tongue-tied neighbor might get no redress.

It was this inequality in speech and the general lack of forensic skill in Syracuse that led one CORAX to set up for an instructor in the arts which avail most in legal tribunals. Undoubtedly there was some information given upon points of law, but the first purpose of his teaching seems to have been to render the ordinary citizen capable of arguing his own cause before the courts. Some Timoleon, for example, knowing of a suburban estate out toward Plemyrium could say that it was his by inheritance from his father, who owned it before the usurpation of Thrasybulus. All this might be strictly true, and justice be on his side, but such a statement would be about as effective with the judges as for a citizen now-a-days to go into the courts and attempt to establish a title to real estate which had been confiscated, sold, and given away several times since war broke out in 1861. Accordingly Corax, for some reason or consideration, undertook to assist the rightful claimants in the orderly and proper presentation of their cases, arranging the details of procedure, collecting documents, and sifting evidence. Chiefly, however, he instructed his clients in the art of forensic oratory, and of speaking so as to appeal to the sense of justice and of right which is, or ought to be, predominant in the judge. Moreover, the average man of that age was susceptible to the power of the spoken argument to a degree much beyond the impressibility of the modern, for causes which will be mentioned in their proper place.

In this oratorical method which Corax taught, five rules are observable, arising from the similarity of causes to be argued. They are the beginnings of rhetorical art, and take their rise from necessity and nature. At the same time it is remarkable that this writer of the primer of rhetoric should have anticipated so far the more elaborate treatises of subsequent authors. The five divisions which he thus early makes of the plea—to use the word in its secondary meaning—are under the heads of Proem,

Narration, Argument, Subsidiary Remarks, and the Peroration. A better division it would be hard to find, either in the days when great elaboration has been studied, as in New England in the last century, for example, or in the less formal age in which we are living. The Proem, as the word signifies, is an opening strain, giving the pitch of the piece. The Narration was a plain statement of facts and circumstances; the Argument was a fair induction from those facts. Subsidiary Remarks gathered up the reasons which were auxiliary and additional, and the Peroration was a persuasive and fitting close to the whole. Thus early did rhetoric formulate itself into a method which, with some artificial deviations, has through all the centuries preserved its essential character. This circumstance is also an early testimony to the truth that the science of speaking is based upon common laws of our nature, the same unchanging fact from age to age.

One most interesting feature of the beginning of the art is to be noticed here, that is, that its origin was intensely practical. It was not "art for art's sake," as the modern phrase goes, but for the sake of rightful possession of lands and houses and homes. Unlike the arts of music and painting it did not attempt to please for the sake of giving pleasure. It was simply and professedly for regaining what had been wrongfully alienated. The very divisions which Corax established grew up from a perception of that form of conviction and persuasion which is most effective with the reasonable mind. Facts were established, and then the legitimate deduction of moral obligation was drawn. It is the same practical necessity that has prevailed in the making of much of the best literature, both in prose and verse—Shakespeare writing for his daily bread and to purchase Stratford New Place; Scott throwing off page after page of manuscript to purchase Abbotsford or to discharge a debt of honor; and so, if the secret could be discovered, of many an ancient and many a modern classic.

The impression which is left by this earliest record of methodical oratory, so far as it can be gathered from fragmentary memorials, is, that while there must have been speaking men in all antiquity, like Aaron at the court of Pharaoh, there was in this fifth century before our era, in a Grecian province, and as the fruit of prolonged literary cultivation, a sudden development of forensic oratory, due largely to an unexpected acquisition of freedom—the essential condition of genuine eloquence. Before this time oratory had a somewhat irregular character and a natural and spontaneous utterance, as is indicated by the very uniformity of the speeches which Thucydides puts into the mouths of his generals; but now oratory is reduced to a system, for practical purposes, and begins to have the scientific characteristics which poetry and narrative prose had already acquired.

III.

PROFESSIONAL SPEECH-WRITERS.

THE demand for forensic argument, which was created by litigation consequent upon the return of landholders who had been exiled, was met at an early day by men who made the composition of legal arguments a business. Corax instructed citizens of Syracuse in the general principles of forensics, but it naturally followed that some preferred to have arguments written out for them by another and to pay for the service, perhaps with a goodly share of the restored estate, rather than to learn the five principles and construct a brief. This substituted argumentation was an early example of division of labor, and an indication of the advance of civilization.

Only a few, however, became famous in this department of vicarious composition. Of these ANTIPHON is the first, 480 B. C. He marks the transition from the technical to the practical stage of oratory, from the school of rhetoric to the court and the assembly. Four of his Tetralogies are extant, in which he formulates examples of prosecution and defence according to the almost uniform necessities of a large class of similar cases arising under the restoration of estates mentioned above, estates which had been alienated by Hiero, Gelo, and Thrasybulus. With a change of names and a filling in of blanks an argument could be put in a client's possession as readily as a deed or mortgage is now drawn in a lawyer's office. And, for all we know to the contrary, the furnished argument was as effective in the tribunals of Sicily as modern efforts are in our own courts. In any case, it was a paying profession, which is the best proof at this distant day that this sort of composition and pleading by proxy answered an important purpose for the property-holder, besides encouraging several men of note to enter the profession.

Antiphon's strong point in argument was the topic of General Probability. "Is it likely that such and such a thing would have occurred?" "Would this little man have been likely to attack this big one; or if he did, would he not have known beforehand that the presumption would be against him?" This topic of general probability was the favorite weapon of the earliest Greek rhetoricians. Aristotle himself gives it an important place in his great treatise, in which he formulated the principles that had prevailed in the usage of the early orators.

But Antiphon did not confine himself to the construction of legal arguments. He marks the first departure from the courts to the assembly, and becomes the founder of political oratory, with its cognate branch of legislative and deliberative discussion. Moreover, he reduced the art of public speaking to more definite rules than the five principles which Corax had inculcated, developing particularly, as has been mentioned, the doctrine of the probable. The strictness, however, with which he adhered to his vocation of writing and teaching is exemplified by the fact that while he composed many speeches for others he never addressed the people himself until he made his own defence in the trial which resulted in his condemnation and death.

His style, as compared with those of other orators of his time, was rugged and sturdy, indicating that he was not a mere writing-master of rhetorical flourishes. Instead, he is dignified in diction, bold but not florid in imagery, with a weight and grandeur of thought which speak plainly for the character of the orator as a man.

In these years GORGIAS, 427 B. C., an orator and rhetorician, came to Athens from Leontini in Sicily to ask succor for the Leontines who had been attacked by the Syracusans. He captivated the Athenians by his eloquent appeals in which florid antithesis played an important part, and having gained such men as Alcibiades, Æschines, and Antisthenes for pupils and imitators, he set up a school of oratory at Athens. His methods differed from those of his contemporaries in that he taught rhetoric by having prepared passages learned by heart. Diction was his principal object, without much reference to invention or arrangement of material. It is not strange that such attention to manner merely brought his art into temporary disrepute, and that Plato in his light treatment of rhetoricians should have chosen to give to the dialogue in which he does this the name of *Gorgias*, after this exponent of the new profession that was now springing up.

It may be observed here in regard to this new profession of oratory that, as in the case of other sciences, its principles were first evolved by practice and determined by the demands of different times and communities. The rules to which these principles were reduced then became useful to any who might attempt to attain the success which their predecessors had acquired by many trials and some failures. Accordingly the rhetoric which was called the "useful" or "practical" was soon followed by the rhetoric which was termed the "teachable" or "scientific," and the orator was succeeded by the rhetorician. In some instances both the rhetorician and the orator were combined, as in Gorgias; and in others the rhetorician alone was paramount, as in Antiphon and Isocrates.

The place which Antiphon occupies in the history of rhetoric as an art is held by LYSIAS in the history of oratory. He marks the transition of the science from Sicily to Greece; for although born in Athens, he removed at the age of fifteen to Thurii, on the Italian coast—the site of the ancient Sybaris—where he lived for thirty-three years studying oratory, and then returned to Athens in company with his brother Polemarchus, of whom Socrates speaks in the opening paragraph of the *Republic*. In a house favored with the guests there mentioned Lysias had literary associations that were of the greatest value to him. In the years he was at Thurii he had for his instructor Tisias, who had been a pupil of Corax, the inventor of rhetoric, and for a townsman Herodotus the historian, now in middle life. Political troubles in that disturbed age before long drive him to Athens, as has been remarked, where, with his brother, he appears as a wealthy manufacturer of shields for seven years. Then business reverses follow the doings of the thirty tyrants, and he who had employed one hundred and twenty workmen becomes a laborious speech-writer, his rhetorical education serving him well when his inherited fortune and prosperous business both failed him. For twenty-three years Lysias writes speeches for other men to deliver in the courts of law. The arrangement of them does not greatly differ from that of Corax—introduction, narration of facts, proof, conclusion. Subsidiary remarks only are left out, or more probably incorporated in the topic of proof. Although he was so long a professional writer he possessed the rare gift of concealing his art. Speeches before his time were after a uniform pattern, without much regard to the diversity of clients. Lysias, on the contrary, adapted his argument to the character of the man who was to deliver it in court as presumably his own. Accordingly he abandoned the stiff, uniform, and monotonous splendor of the earlier rhetoricians and introduced the idiom of every-day life, making the ordinary citizen speak in his own character and not as the noble and eloquent Pericles. He could write, however, according to the terminology of the day, in the grand, the middle, or the plain style; but he never made an artisan speak like Antiphon.

Perhaps it was for this reason that out of the two hundred and thirty-three speeches that he wrote for his clients, only two failed to bring a favorable verdict. Thirty-four of these survive as evidence that, as Cicero says of him, he was one of the most perfect masters of Greek prose in his own province—lucid, simple, direct in diction; lively, graceful, entertaining in manner; varying in tone according to the dignity of the subject, with equal command over the periodic and the continuous sentence and paragraph, while through all runs a kindly and genial nature, with a keen perception of character, fine sense of humor, a flexible and graceful intelligence, pervaded by a warmth of friendship and a loyalty to country that stamp him greater than his vocation. All this and more was brought out when he mounted the *bema* and delivered his splendid denunciation of Dionysius, the tyrant of Syracuse, at the Olympic festival, in 388 B. C. But the highest reach of his eloquence was attained when he prosecuted the legal murderer of his brother, the tyrant Eratosthenes; adding to his customary winning introduction and convincing narration of facts a pathos and fire of conclusion unusual with him but irresistible by its moving force and terrific in its execration.

In the *Phædrus* of Plato one of the interlocutors says to Socrates, "But there is a friend of yours who ought not to be forgotten." "Who is that?" "ISOCRATES the fair." "Isocrates is still young, Phædrus; but I think that he has a genius which soars above the orations of Lysias, and he has a character of a finer mould. My impression of him is that he will marvelously improve as he grows older, and that all former rhetoricians will be as children in comparison of him. And I believe that he will not be satisfied with this, but that some divine impulse will lead him on to things higher still. For there is an element of philosophy in his nature. This is the message which comes from the gods dwelling in this place and which I will myself deliver to Isocrates who is my delight, and do you give the other to Lysias, who is yours;" the message being that if the compositions of orators are based on knowledge of the truth and can be defended and proved, then these writers should be called lovers of wisdom or practical culture.

This prophecy of Socrates that Isocrates would surpass his predecessors was abundantly fulfilled, and marks an advance in the study, teaching, and practice of the rhetorical art, as we shall see before his career is ended. He must have been about twenty-six years of age, and seven years the senior of Plato, when the above prediction was uttered. Weakness of voice unfitted him to enter the political assembly and the courts. He was also deficient in the audacity which characterized the Athenian demagogue in the age after Pericles. The loss of his fortune was another reason for taking up the profession of a teacher. The proscription of the thirty tyrants drove him to Chios where he had no remarkable success, being chiefly interested in regulating the political affairs of the island. Returning to Athens he was occupied for ten years in the writer's profession, after which he took new and larger views of rhetorical instruction. Indeed, in subsequent years, he discarded his former business of writing for other men and devoted himself to teaching his clients and pupils to write and speak for themselves, contrasting what he calls the petty concerns of the forensic orator with those larger and nobler themes which engage the politician. Having this high purpose in view he opened a school at Athens at the age of forty-four. His real vocation became apparent from the day that he devoted himself to this work of teacher and writer. Cicero says that this was the school in which the eloquence of all Greece was trained and perfected, and forty-one illustrious pupils are mentioned as foremost among the accomplished writers and debaters of that intellectual age.

It is recorded that at a panegyrical contest instituted by the widow of Mausolus at his funeral and participated in by many orators, there was not one who had not been a pupil in the school of Isocrates. Learners came from every quarter, from Ægean coasts, from the cities of Sicily, the early home of oratory, and from the shores of the distant Euxine; so far had the fame of this great teacher extended. The most eminent men of the day were also frequenters of his school, where they discussed political events and listened to orations which he had spent years in writing. The instruction he gave followed somewhat the rules laid down by his predecessors, but it was signalized by a departure from the artificial methods of style and teaching which had hitherto prevailed, especially in the abandonment of set pieces committed to memory for the sake of communicating grandeur of expression. He began his reform with the Theme, leading the attention of his pupils away from what was of mere local and Athenian interest; at the same time keeping before their minds questions of the day which had a larger consequence and more extended relation to all Greece. He hoped to turn the minds of his townsmen from municipal politics, and neighboring tribes from intestine strifes, to the nobler enterprise of union for the conquest of Asia. He sought to enlarge the mental horizon of his disciples in an age of political pamphleteering, that they might produce something of value to posterity. It may be affirmed that many literary survivals from his day owe their present existence to this worthy ambition of Isocrates. After his exalted themes came his technical teaching in applying rules and principles to composition. Then he revised what had been written. Such instruction produced the foremost orators of a remarkable century, fuller than any other in the political and intellectual life of Greece.

As a professional workman he was the first Greek to give the true definition of rhetoric as the "art of persuasion," and also the first to give an artistic finish to literary composition. He was, moreover, the best builder of the periodic sentence, no longer rigid and monotonous like those of Antiphon, or too terse and compact like those of Lysias, but ample and luxuriant in the rhythm of prose, which, as much as poetry, has metrical laws of its own, recognized and followed by those who have an ear for its music. It was this writer also who gave such form and melody to the standard literary prose of his time that, transmitted to Rome, it became incorporated in the works of her chief orators and writers, and by them was handed on for centuries; so that it has been computed with admitted accuracy that the school of Isocrates lasted over nine hundred years.

It may help to the understanding of the esteem in which public speaking was held to note the terms which such a teacher as Isocrates could command for his instruction in days when money was worth twice what it now is. The extent of his instruction in time, the length and number of his courses, and the degree of proficiency required of his pupils are not easy to determine; but it is on record that his charge for tuition was 1,000 drachmæ, about $250. Even at this rate he had a hundred pupils at a time and a revenue of $25,000. This modest income he was able to piece out with his literary productions, obtaining, for example, from the king of Cyprus twenty talents, $20,000, for a single oration. It was such productions as these, upon which the author sometimes labored for ten years, that were copied and recited in all the countries inhabited by the Greeks. His *Panathenaicus*, a eulogy on Athens, was written after he was ninety-four years old, and at ninety-nine he was still at work, revising and perfecting it with some of his pupils.

That he was something more than a mere rhetorician is shown by the comprehensive views contained in his political essays, in which he advocates a large panhellenic policy. And when at last the cause of Greek liberty seemed to have been forever lost at the battle of Chæronea, his patriotism could not endure the shock, and, refusing food, he ended his life by voluntary starvation. By his teaching Greek oratory had been advanced into a larger science and a nobler art. Freed from its restriction to a few professed artisans of speeches, it was now made the privilege and possession of any who had an aptitude for writing and could be taught the graces of delivery. Isocrates made that democratic which had been oligarchic hitherto, and carried eloquence from the classroom to the *bema*. In addition, he placed rhetorical composition upon a philosophic basis, and formulated principles of study and practice which were so reasonable and sound that they outlasted his own generation, and remained the foundation of other men's systems for centuries. Velleius Paterculus, the Roman historian and critic, goes so far as to say that there was nothing distinguished before Isocrates. It is not strange that this herald of a larger freedom was called by Milton, "The old man eloquent," as Cicero before had named him, "The father of eloquence."

This entire group of professional speech-writers represents a singular epoch in the history of oratory. Such a business could not have been supported in any age that was not primitive in its ideas of the art. The unquestioning spirit, in which one man was allowed to put words into the mouth of another, marks the time of childhood in the intellectual attitude of men. Imagine a plaintiff or defendant in our own courts reciting an argument which his lawyer had written out for him, and a judge, jury, and assembled crowd gravely listening to an argument written by an Antiphon or Lysias for some farmer or artisan, the like of which they heard yesterday and might listen to its duplicate to-morrow. But custom, and the necessities of such procedure, took away all thought of the inconsistency. Doubtless the chief interest lay in the manner in which this bungler and that would present the argument of the artist, or in what Lysias or Isæus would do with the facts in this or that case. What everybody did was a novelty to no one, and causes were adjudged according to evidence and its handling. On the other hand, this custom of speaking by proxy had its valuable place in the progress of forensic oratory. If every man in a rude age had gone into the assembly with his own untutored address and what is called "natural ability," the art of speaking effectively and persuasively would have been confined to one or two in a thousand, to the disadvantage and loss of the many. The practice of an art by the skilled few soon leads to the imparting of it to several; and finally to all who can learn and will learn. Accordingly the "logographer" became eventually the instructor, spreading abroad the knowledge and skill which was once entirely his own, preparing the way for the diffusion of this branch of science, as other branches in similar ways have always been diffused, by those who have found it profitable to lend the key of knowledge.

IV.

ATTIC ORATORS.

THERE were a few orators belonging to the Attic Group who were distinguished, not as the rest for excellence of artistic composition, so much as for some one strong point worth remembrance and perhaps imitation. One of these was ANDOCIDES, the representative of a large class of "natural orators," as they are called; men who have a native ability upon which they rely, despising the aid of rhetorical precepts and methods. Such orators are found both among those classes who are unable to avail themselves of the advantages of education, and also among those upon whom such opportunities are actually forced. The resultant attainment is about the same in either case, if allowance be made for the unrecognized influence of collateral pursuits upon the educated. Other studies in college, for example, will impart something of rhetoric to the youth whose conceit of his native ability permits him to neglect the study itself. This was somewhat the case of Andocides. With the minimum of rhetorical training he combined the largest reliance upon his native wit. As a natural consequence the minimum of attention has been paid him.

As the distinction men gained by excellencies has been noted, it may be worth while to observe first the faults for which Andocides was conspicuous. It will be evident that, for the most part, they were those which a diligent observance of the established principles of rhetoric would have corrected; thus, very likely placing this orator on a plane with some others of the famous ten. Starting with what were recognized in his times as the chief excellencies of forensic speaking—clearness, the stamp of truth, and fiery earnestness, Hermogenes the critic declares that Andocides was deficient in these cardinal virtues. "His arrangement of material is not lucid; he amplifies in an irregular fashion; he tacks on clause to clause, using parentheses to the loss of a distinct order, seeming to some frivolous and obscure. He has little discernment to see where each topic should be introduced, dwells upon irrelevant circumstances, and adds as afterthoughts things that should have occupied an important place." In his figures of rhetoric or of illustration his critic says that this orator did not use precision, leaving them in the rough; and, in general, there was a lack of finish or smoothness in his composition. Worse than all, for a political speaker of that age, he lacked earnestness, a fault fatal to the best eminence. Now, with the exception of the last, all these faults might have been remedied by the same attention to rhetorical study which other orators of the time are known to have paid. For it was a time when the literary merit of an address counted for as much as its oratorical merit. In those days it must read well, and not merely sound well. The modern opinion has embodied itself in the reverse statement that what is good when delivered is pretty sure to be poor reading. If a question should be raised as to which theory is the correct one, it would be safe to side with the ancients, at least for oratory pure and simple, although the printing press might come in as an element to affect modern judgment. If, however, Andocides be judged by the standard of a natural eloquence which does not read well, something may be said in his favor. Plutarch asserts that he was "simple and inartificial in arrangement of thoughts, plain and sparing of figures."

Here is a striking instance of the different view which two critics take of the same qualities, according to the attitude of each. Following the lenient and charitable Plutarch the homely virtues of Andocides begin to appear. What Hermogenes condemned as rough, irregular, and obscure, becomes in the eyes of his later critic simple, plain, and frugal. "His style is plain and easy, without the least affectation or anything of a figurative ornament." He condescends to employ the language of daily life, as the greater Lysias did, but without trying to hide the art. Still less does he attempt the grand style like Antiphon and strive to rise above the common language of the people, borrowing words from far antiquity. While dispensing with figures of language he uses largely those figures of thought which give life to a speech—irony, indignant question, and others which belong to what may be termed the natural oratory of a strong but indolent or self-sufficient speaker.

Again observe the disagreement of critics. What one calls a want of lucidity in arrangement and irrelevance of statement another terms artlessness. "He had a long story to tell and was unable, or did not try, to tell it concisely." One thing, however, seems to be conceded—his keeping in sympathy with his audience, amusing them with stories, putting his arguments in vivid shape, and using abundant illustration. He makes the most of particulars and avoids generalities, and thus carries his audience along with him by the power of an absorbing interest in his narration of facts. His description is lively without straining to be graphic, and his address to judges and opponents is full of rhetorical question and answer. His anecdotes are always amusing or telling, raising a laugh or sneer which, with now and then a truckling to low tastes and sometimes a resort to emphatic abuse, make him a political orator some centuries in advance of his own times, who might find sympathizers and followers in ours.

Naturalness and self-sufficiency are, then, the exceptional features which distinguish Andocides, in an age when high art was worshiped and modesty was no drawback to other virtues and excellencies. With more cultivation of genuine naturalness and considerably less of that conceit which blinded him to his natural defects Andocides would not have needed a stretch of charity to place him on a higher level with his contemporaries. There were several others who had excellencies of their own and a reputation in that age who did not attain the first rank, as Polycrates and Thrasymachus, Alcidamas, Anaximenes, Theodectes, Naucrates, and others.

One other there is, however, among the canonized ten, who, if he had not had the misfortune to be preceded by a great orator, and followed by another greater still, would have been a more prominent member of the classic group. Standing alone Isæus would have had a distinction of his own; but with Lysias on one side and Demosthenes on the other he naturally suffers somewhat by comparison. If the above-named critic, Dionysius—who lived three hundred years later, and judged the Attic orators by the records and traditions of their work—if this critic charges him with imitating Lysias, he also gives him the credit of furnishing the beginnings of eloquence to Demosthenes. In this position he occupies the honorable place of one who, gathering up the teachings of his predecessors, handed them on to a greater successor, as the dramatic productions of Marlowe may have furnished material if not inspiration to Shakespeare. If Isæus was an imitator of Lysias, it was in those respects which make that orator illustrious rather than in the direction of his faults, as is too apt to be the case when a great model is servilely followed. In brevity, combined with clearness, he is equaled by his immediate predecessor only, and in the avoidance of rare or novel expressions by only two, Lysias and Isocrates; while for bringing the circumstances narrated before the eye of the hearer with vivid reality he resembles Lysias. This for his diction. In his composition he marks a farther removal from the uniform, rigid, and antithetical style that had prevailed among the earlier orators. His speech is free from such stateliness, having a movement adapted to the occasion and the circumstances of which he is speaking. Energetic, vigorous, vivacious, he uses figures of thought in a way that indicates his earnestness. He asks the rhetorical question, answering it himself.

He introduces persons as speaking or raising objections which he goes on to refute — "How many payments of war-tax do your books show?" "So many." "What sum was paid on each occasion?" "So much." "Who received the money?" "Persons who are here." "What, do you mean a paid army? I shall be asked." "Yes." By such animated discourse does he keep his audience awake and alive to the issues before them. Another of his strong points was his arrangement of materials, moving his forces with a rapidity and a skill which throw the stress of the assault upon the enemy's weakest point. This is an art which the ancients prized as much in oratory as in war; so much that opposing speakers used to demand of the judges that their own order be adhered to by the speaker who was to follow, as Æschines did when Demosthenes was about to demolish him. Therefore Isæus varies his disposition of arguments according to present need, like a master of arts instead of a servant of rules. Sometimes he drops the introduction altogether and begins with a brief statement of the case with unconventional abruptness. Again he makes the narrative short, or long, as he chooses, combining luminous recital with perspicuous reasoning, going step by step through his argument, satisfied with nothing but a systematic and rigorous demonstration, laying close siege to the understandings of the judges. Sometimes he convinces without persuasion, though he seldom persuades without convincing. His reasoning, based on positive law, iterated verbally, repeated in different forms or summed up in a recapitulation, fall with cumulative weight, increased rarely by an added appeal to the emotions—"I claim, judges, that Euphiletos is our brother and your citizen, and that he has been subjected by the conspirators to injurious and outrageous treatment. Sufficient proof of this has, I think, been laid before you." Thus does he close the argument for one who had been struck off the list of his *deme*. But his usual close is with a keen argument, swiftly thrust home.

Isæus' place among the the orators of his time was that of a professional writer of speeches, but he advanced the profession by narrowing his work to private causes. He comes nearer being an advocate in matters of inheritance and property than a criminal lawyer, or the deliberative orator in the halls of legislation. As such a writer of speeches for other men he too, like Lysias, tries to make it seem as if the client were speaking his own words instead of his lawyer's. It is not easy to imagine at this day what a study of a client's character and manners was involved in such a process of adaptation, but the art from rude beginnings in the time of Corax had been growing more complete and technical and triumphant, until in Isæus we find a man morally persuasive and logically powerful, versatile in arrangement, elaborate and systematic in proof, apt in law, and keen in logic, having and keeping a close grip upon his opponent, with a twist and a trip at last, like a wrestler that throws his adversary. Isæus stands forth as the earliest master of forensic conflict.

But while he ought to be allowed to stand for himself and his own work, he will always be associated with Demosthenes, his greater pupil. Dionysius is the first author of this association, saying that Demosthenes took the seeds and beginnings of his oratorical power from Isæus. Like later judges, however, this critic made his estimate chiefly from a literary point of comparison in which the likeness mainly consists in the blending of terse and vigorous periods with passages of more lax and fluent ease; in vividness and dramatic vivacity, in question and answer, in irony, and other figures of thought; in the unfolding and drawing out of systematic proof, and more than in anything else do the two resemble each other in the energetic struggle with an antagonist. "What, in the name of heaven, are the guarantees of credibility for statements?" asks Isæus. "Are they not witnesses? And what are the guarantees of credibility for a witness? Are they not tortures? Yes, and on what ground are the adversaries to be disbelieved? Is it not because they shrink from our tests? Assuredly. You can see then that I am urging this inquiry and bringing it to the touch of proof; the plaintiff is shifting them to a basis of slanders and hearsays—precisely the course that would be taken by a grasping adventurer!" There is a thrusting home here that comes very near the *argumentum ad hominem*, and *ad hostem* likewise; a plain dealing worthy a modern court, having little of the circuitous refinement of the high art of fifty years before. Forensic oratory was growing practical, and therefore advancing to the highest art, as was soon to be exemplified in the pupil of Isæus, Demosthenes himself, who was already getting hints from his lawyer-friend which would be expanded later into larger principles. Isæus is an example of a man who just missed of great achievement by not daring to forsake the old standards of plainness for which he had little aptitude, and adopting the powerful and expressive style which was natural to him.

Bondage to conventionality, combined with the narrow scope of property-litigation, without the moral and literary courage to follow the impulses of his native ability, perhaps through fear of the critic, made him a compromise when he should have been a departure. It is the old story of the men who in various departments have almost attained the prize that lay within easy reach, but who through lack of courage or faith in themselves have missed at the critical moment and left the discovery, the invention, the success, and the victory to a bolder or later man; some man who did not ask if the times were ripe for the new way, but launching forth led the age to its approval and adoption.

It may be advantageous before passing from forensic oratory to the deliberative to review its growth from Corax to Isæus. The foundation of it, after allowing its grammatical substructure to be laid in the popular dialectic and orthoepy of the eastern sophists, was itself laid in the Sicilian rhetoric, particularly by Corax, who drew up and committed to writing a system of rules for forensic speaking, the earliest Greek treatise on the theory of any art. Arrangement of a speech in five parts and the topic of general probability are the two important features of his system. Tisias, his pupil, develops further the favorite topic of probability; Gorgias bases his method of teaching on the committing to memory of prepared passages with the purpose of inculcating beautiful and effective expression. Rhythmic expression combined with a distinguished air was his secret of power, carrying everything before him among a people who were familiar with the poetry of Homer and the prose of Herodotus. But the people were just emerging from the rhythmic age in which everything to be excellent had to be expressed in verse, into which they fell as easily as children fall into rhymes. Accordingly they were pleased with the poetic Gorgias as they would not have been in subsequent times when the true place of rhythm in prose had been discovered. Then Pericles follows, embalmed in the pages of Thucydides, famous for "the thoughts and moral force which won him such renown for eloquence as no one else ever secured without artistic aids. Tranquil and stately, rapid and yet persuasive, he had the rare art of leaving his words sticking in the memory of his hearers."

In Antiphon appears the first master of the comparatively new art of rhetoric, now becoming indispensable in the courts and in the assembly of the people, which was the legislature of Athens. He represents the primitive ideas and methods of oratory. Hitherto all expressions had been in poetic measures or in common talk. Now a speech was beginning to be evolved which was neither common nor high-flown, but combined the excellencies of both. "Having weight and grandeur rather than life and vivacity, he is ambitious to bring the whole of his thought down upon his hearers with a splendid and irresistible force, dazzling and overawing them." Harsh, stern, or crabbed is the critical term for this style among the Greeks, emphasizing each word, clause, and sentence, employing a rough naturalness while choosing a majestic rhythm, with slow and measured delivery. The nearest modern representation of it is a French gentleman of the old school, superb in decorum and artificial in ostentation.

Lysias should be remembered as the plain speaker as distinguished from the grand styles that preceded him. It was a lawyer's language of sober prose, a lawyer, moreover, who had the daring in an age of stereotyped professional work to adapt himself to the character of his clients. Simple, clear, concise, and vivid, with a peculiar power of seizing and portraying character, blended with an accurate discernment of the properties of the subject, the audience, and the occasion, Lysias added to all what the ancient critics called his "charm," famous but not to be explained, intangible and elusive as the harmony of music and the beauty of a statue. "To write well," says Dionysius, "is given to many men; but to write winningly, gracefully, with loveliness is the gift of Lysias."

Isocrates, it will be borne in mind, was less an orator proper than an artist of a literary rhetorical prose. The stately flow of his periodic sentences was made harmonious by the prose rhythm of which he was the discoverer and developer, although not the perfecter. He regarded melodious prose as much a work of art as poetry, having its sources in the music latent in language and revealed to those who have the ear to hear it and write it. Moreover, he lifted rhetoric out of the courts and the myths of the heroic age to the higher level of state affairs and the interests of Greek citizenship. Still, he is the artist of the school, developing a literary style chiefly for the historians, but not without its advantages to Demosthenes, and later to Cicero, and through him to later times.

Andocides must stand for the natural orator who depends upon his own resources rather than upon what the experience of all ages can give him in the written laws which have been gathered from that experience. His simplicity and inartificiality, with a certain vividness in his narrative and a confident vigor which is apt to go with self-making, rendered his speech effective with men of his own rank.

In Isæus is seen the professional man narrowing, and therefore advancing, the lawyer's business; a specialist in private causes of property and inheritance,. but by the same process narrowing his own ability to seize upon the grand opportunity of becoming eminent in the larger field of deliberative oratory in which Demosthenes, his pupil, was successful.

This brief summary of the characteristics of orators, chiefly forensic, belonging to the first period of Greek rhetoric, may itself be reduced to a more diminutive scale if we say: the solemn and sometimes pathetic Thucydides; the majestic and restrained Pericles; the grave and stately Antiphon; the plain but versatile Lysias; the elegant and artistic Isocrates; the inartificial and self-confident Andocides; the intense and vigorous Isæus. Taken together they represent a marvelous epoch in the history of the high art of public speech, teaching us that excellence in it is not the exclusive property of any one form and method, but that each one's own natural way, improved by that careful study which appropriates the best of others' ways, is the best way for him. That while imitation is fatal, and nature untrained is apt to blunder, natural capacity guided by art will have its own kind of success according to the mental and moral character of the speaker. In this first age of oratory sincerity and earnestness and knowledge of men, finding their expression with skill, vigor, and dignity, are the qualities and methods which told most, and will always tell most, for the speaker with his hearer.

V.

POLITICAL ORATORS.

BY THE orators whose work has been traced thus far an oratorical prose was developed which takes its character largely from the requirements of forensic speech. The eminently practical origin of it cannot be overlooked. It began with the statement of personal rights to what is one's own, which, next to the defence of hearth and home by arms, is the most earnest strife in which men engage. We find, accordingly, a vigorous earnestness in the pleadings of the orator, and directness of statement aided by skill in marshaling arguments and reasons, enforced by appeals to the conscience and heart of persons who have sympathies as well as judgments, emotions as well as intellect. Of necessity, forensic oratory does not cover interests much beyond those of the individual; but these are sacred and the foundation of the larger interests and rights of the state. The discussion of the one prepared the way for the maintenance of the other. It was, therefore, to forensic oratory that the higher art of deliberative speech owed its main excellencies when its masters began to discuss affairs of state. The able lawyer became the successful political orator.

Four men exemplify the best period of political eloquence. LYCURGUS, 396 B. C., the first of these in order of time, was a noble and public spirited patriot, a man of whom his biographer says, "he was outspoken because he was noble." Without great elegance of speech, somewhat harsh in his diction, and inapt in his illustrations, he nevertheless is impressive in his earnestness and majestic mien, and, according to Dionysius, powerful in his denunciation. His literary sympathies are with the elder poets and tragedians, and his moral tone is that of older Athens. Archaic words mingle with the newer dialect, and a lofty religious tone pervades his high discourse. It is as if a statesman and orator, inbued with the spirit of our own early republicanism and puritan respect for religious things, should address the legislative bodies of to-day. "Be sure, judges, that each of you, by the vote which he now gives in secret, will lay his thought bare to the gods. Who is so foolish as, by saving this man, to place his own life at the mercy of cowardly deserters? Who will conciliate the gratitude of his country's betrayer in order to make himself obnoxious to the vengeance of the gods?" It has been said that his character is the best comment on his oratory, and that he was thrice elected to the office of secretary of the treasury is an indication of the esteem in which he was held while fearlessly lifting up his voice against the prevailing apathy and luxury of his times. "By restoring the festivals of the gods, by cherishing a faithful tradition of the great poets against the corruption of texts by actors, by enacting sumptuary laws to restrain extravagance, by prosecuting disloyal citizens," he tried to check the downward drift of his age, and by his earnest and solemn speech to recall his countrymen to the higher rectitude and patriotism of the past.

The second orator of this group was HYPERIDES, 395 B. C., who had begun his career as a professional speech-writer. Unlike Lycurgus he had little love of the former days. He was a man of his own age, a true son of the changed order, yet withal a loyal and intense patriot. In his ordinary life, however, he was governed by his own remark, that "he could not live beautifully until he had learned what beautiful things there were in life." In public affairs he was energetic, but with his zeal and energy there he united an easy and pleasure-loving disposition in social life, which had its influence on his speeches. Catching something from the elevated tone of Isocrates, his master, he was not insensible to the value of tact, wit, delicate allusion, and the use of homely idiom, making a susceptible audience feel that he was in accord with their sprightly life. Crafty beyond others in the disposition of his subject-matter, surpassing in the adornment of his diction, sticking to his subject and emphasizing its strong points with large intellectual resources, seemingly simple, but with much art concealed, he found his way to the popular understanding. Hermogenes, the critic, cannot endure his colloquialisms and quotations from comedy, and says he has little finish; but Longinus thinks that if merits were to be counted instead of weighed, Hyperides would outnumber Demosthenes in his excellencies. He is not so good a specialist, but a better general speaker, better in the range of his voice, and variety of graces. His wit and sarcasm are in keeping with political oratory and in harmony with the exquisite manner of the time. With beauty of style are joined a power of pathos and a facile inspiration that take him smoothly along in his narrative, while he varies his expression with playful grace and graver eloquence. Later estimates place him, for reasons that will appear further on, second to Demosthenes, but second to him alone.

The orator, however, who in modern minds is oftenest associated with Demosthenes, is ÆSCHINES, by reason of his antagonism in the case of the crown ; but properly for no other cause. He was a man of considerable natural gifts of spontaneous eloquence, as distinguished by himself from the laborious methods of his adversary, which, together with a familiarity with the old literature of his country, made him a brilliant speaker. At the same time he imitated the quiet style of the old orators, and his habitual practice of composition and declamation made up somewhat for his lack of art and systematic training. There was in his style an equal want of finish, purity, and rhythm. The old critics said he was blatant and headlong and coarsely abusive, but powerful, and as inartistic as self-educated orators are apt to be.

His best education was acquired on the stage as an actor, where he played showy parts until he stumbled one day, without the happy recovery which William of Normandy made at Pevensey. However he left the disastrous boards with the possession of a magnificent voice, a splendid diction, and a certain vehemence and impetuosity of manner that doubtless engulfed little offences and overbore minute criticism. The chief detraction is, that his speeches are greater than himself, his words than his character. The critic of Æschines' day would have called him inartistic and superficial, lacking in *ēthos* or moral force, and would have said that with a certain theatrical splendor he combined an impudent and unscrupulous smartness.

The culmination of Attic eloquence occurs in DEMOSTHENES. It had taken its rise partly in the dialectics of the sophists and partly in the Sicilian rhetoric of the courts. Early it began to manifest itself in two forms, the dignified and harsh style of Antiphon and Thucydides, and the ornate manner of Gorgias, taken up and corrected later by Isocrates. Between the embellishments of this style and the plain talk of daily life Lysias develops a sober expression, from which to strenuous political oratory a transition is effected by Isæus. Then comes the deliberative oratory of Demosthenes, who continues, combines, and perfects these earlier types. By the concurrent testimony of scholars, statesmen, and orators in subsequent times Demosthenes is conceded to have produced "the greatest results ever attained in this art. This he did without great natural gifts or good voice or commanding presence or ornament or philosophic generalizations, pathos or wit."

In these circumstances and under such unfavorable conditions it is natural to inquire after the elements within the man and the environments around him which contributed to his phenomenal achievements. Fortunately there are ample materials for such an investigation. His very form and attitude as a speaker have been preserved in authentic copies of his statue. The particulars of his life, early and late, are contained in his own speeches, substantiated by the comments and animadversions of his rivals and adversaries. He had the advantage over his predecessors in living nearer the age when literary history began to be extensively written, and was himself the subject of ten different biographies.

The son of a prosperous manufacturer, he did not lack the advantages of wealth and education. At his father's death the boy of seven was left with a prospective fortune of fourteen talents, about $16,500, a fair inheritance for those days, when the legal rate of interest was ten per cent. But, unfortunately, this property was left in the charge of two cousins and a family friend, and as a consequence when Demosthenes came of age he found, instead of the $35,000 to which his fortune ought to have amounted, only $1,166 left.

But there were laws and courts and lawyers and plea-writers in abundance, and Demosthenes was not slow to avail himself of the services of Isæus, the most skilful advocate in the matter of inheritances. With his help he brought action against the main delinquent for ten talents, a third part of the embezzled funds. In the main, however, he composed his own speeches in this litigation for the recovery of his property, and though they are not brilliant they have a directness and force which characterize his later productions. He won his case, but by the law's delays and various pretexts he was put off from time to time, and at last secured less damages than reputation out of the proceedings. This, however, was to be a better capital with which to start in life. As in the case of many a rich young man before and since, the loss of his inheritance threw him upon his own resources and developed faculties that might have lain idle.

Another kindred motive is also to be noticed. The necessity of legal proceedings to right a personal wrong was the beginning of Demosthenes' oratory, as it had been the origin of Grecian oratory at large in the forensic contests of the courts of Sicily. The hard, practical demands of justice and equity came first to make men speak for their rights, and afterward came the development of the highest of arts in deliberative oratory, and its highest attainment in Demosthenes.

In order to this there were first the three years of training under Isæus in the knowledge of law and in the practice of vigorous reasoning with an antagonist at close quarters. Here, too, came the struggle with natural infirmities. Neither strong nor confident in his bodily presence, short-breathed, with defective articulation and clumsy manner, and a voice weak and ill-managed, it is not strange that his first appearance in the assembly was followed by uproarious and derisive laughter. But like a few rare spirits since his day he determined to be heard further on. Demetrius of Phalerum is the authority who says that Demosthenes told him how he recited verses with pebbles in his mouth, declaimed running or walking up hill, and practiced gestures before a mirror. Nor did he despise the instruction and example of actors in a day when a dramatic manner was in vogue.

According to the custom of his predecessors he served an apprenticeship at speech-writing for the courts, perhaps for seven years after his Isæan training and his own law-suit with his guardians. History, law, and politics, with questions of finance, occupied his days and months of solitude, which were relieved by the hearing of law cases and writing briefs and arguments for others. The beginnings of his professional career in public were in civil cases; but gradually he came to the larger discussions of state affairs and "to assert for Athens her proper place in the Greek world, to reform domestic evils, and to rouse the patriotism which he deemed slumbering but not extinct."

In these speeches he illustrates the value of his historical studies by the way in which he reanimates examples and applies the principles they embody to questions of the present with force and heartfelt sincerity. Argument, irony, and indignation close the first of these speeches in a manner unlike the customary Attic form and generally his own, betokening the fervor of the beginner and the moral sense of the uncorrupted youth. In succeeding speeches the moral tone is equally elevated. In one the sacredness of public faith is the prevailing thought, and commercial morality and the good name of the city rather than its riches and its honor, as if it were that of a person; not even the pretext of religion is to justify a dishonesty, and meanness of spirit is always abhorrent. In another he maintains the guardian's responsibility of Athens for other Hellenic states and the dishonor of revenging private wrongs from them and the necessity of individual action, while he opposes an old dream of the visionary about the invasion of Persia by a united Greece and convinces the people of its futility. He was accustomed to insist that states as well as individuals should be controlled by moral motives, and that justice is obligatory upon them by reason of their immortality; that they were to promote harmony, kindly feeling, and the impulse towards duty. The statesman must be sincere, speaking the truth at all costs; he must also be possessed of personal responsibility.

What is honorable may be regarded as the chief motive in the speeches of Demosthenes. Not that which is most easy, pleasant, and profitable, but that which honor and duty demand of the state and the citizen is the burden of the moral teaching which distinguishes him from many of his contemporaries, placing him on the same ethical plane with the modern orator who most resembles him, Edmund Burke. He was above the prejudice of a mere Athenian; the level of his panhellenic patriotism was higher than that of Pericles, and equaled only, if at all, by that of Epaminondas. He had a high moral sense of citizenship and statecraft and comprehensive views of intertribal obligations, making the foundation of his oratory broad and deep. Without these fundamental principles no command of words could be anything more than a display of verbal pyrotechnics. But with them as a substratum on which to stand before a people who were sensible of moral distinctions, even if they did not always follow the right and abjure the wrong, it became an easier matter to win the first place. And yet in that day it was no easy thing to triumph in an artistic way. Sound moral principles were no doubt possessed here and there by one whose name has not been immortalized. Demosthenes' fame rests upon his ability to add to these the graces of the highest oratorical art. How he attained these is a matter of well-known biography, already recounted in part. The slow, careful, painstaking toil for seven years preparatory to his entrance upon public life, the equal diligence in speech-writing for clients in which he puts forth all his skill and strength, the care and labor which until the last he continued to expend upon his speeches, all indicate that toil was a large factor in his genius. He does not resent the taunt of his would-be rivals that his writings smell of the lamp, nor does he aspire to the modern equivalent of inspiration, extemporary speaking. Everything is finished beforehand with special reference to cutting away remorselessly whatever is not absolutely essential to the instantaneous apprehension of his meaning by the hearer. There were no long and close trains of reasoning, no observations so profound that they were obscure, no remote allusions, but rather a series of plain remarks bearing directly upon his subject, mingled with striking and stirring appeals to the moral sense and patriotism of his audience. Clearness combined with terseness was the demand of the Athenian hearer, and adaptation to the subject the first requisite of any speech. Consequently his style is now accepted as the type of all that is simple, direct, and forcible.

Somewhat stately and elaborate in his early efforts his mature eloquence becomes more varied and abundant. Conversational vivacity mingles and alternates with dignified periods, and popular idiom with artistic expression. Every-day phrases are combined freshly and naturally without seeming commonplace, and similes, sparsely introduced, are forcible in their apt homeliness, while his metaphors are often vivid in their condensation into a single word. But in all this artistic skill, severe and restrained, there is a directness of purpose which is seemingly unconscious of rhetorical effort. However he may throw light upon his subject, now from this side and again from that, there is the same focal point of which he never loses sight. "His aim is to keep the whole subject before his audience all the time by means of rapid turns, ingenious retrogression, anticipations, and constant recapitulation." He does not apparently follow a plan closely; much less, strongly marked subdivision. He passes to and fro, combining apology and invective, argument and narrative by transitions which stand in the place of the ordinary orator's numbers and heads of discourse. Narrative, repetition, proof, exhortation, invective, are blended or separated according to the requirements of the case. And yet there is no haphazard confusion. Certain main-building ideas have ordered the whole arrangement, but with reference to a single purpose, and the details are like those of a temple or cathedral, understood by the master-builder in the aggregate, rather than by the observer at one point.

Therefore he became a recognized adviser and leader of public opinion, one whose aim was to organize a panhellenic league with Athens at the head. As a reward of his efforts he beheld himself the supreme director of the state for two years. It is by the record of these years that he claims to be judged. Unfortunately the record of his eloquence fails at the point when its highest successes are achieved, no speeches of this stirring period being preserved. Eloquence ended in immediate action, the highest testimony to its supreme efficiency. Its highest flight that has been transmitted to us is the famous Crown-oration, unless the third Philippic be excepted, which, according to the opinion of Lord Brougham, is even more varied and pathetic. But that on the Crown has the mournful distinction of being his last speech, and by the general judgment of all subsequent ages is considered to be the noblest monument of ancient eloquence extant.

It is not possible to sum up genius in a single epithet, but there is one phrase which is so inclusive that it comprehends many characteristics and qualities of illustrious talent. It is true of the great in every department of activity that their resources are not limited to narrow and stereotyped forms, and also that they are able to see the needs of each occasion and adapt themselves to it. It is true of great generals and statesmen and of great dramatists and orators as well. They go out of themselves to be the men for their time and opportunity. Shakespeare's "infinite variety" was anticipated by Demosthenes, so far as the limitations of his art would allow. It is this that made him first among a race of speaking men. He borrowed something from every school and master, but also added more than he took. He was quick to discern the character of every occasion, and also able to bring out its greatest possibilities and its hidden powers. He had entrancing display for the high festival, exposition and logic for the courts, and appeal to the moral sense in the deliberative assembly. He could so use a common word as to give it an uncommon effect, or create a phrase which thenceforward should have an immortality in literature. His sentences and periods were slow-moving and spacious at one time, at another close and compact; his language grave and dignified, or colloquial and vivacious and even exclamatory. It was in these directions that he went beyond the strict canons of contemporary criticism; but he also carried the public with him in his intense and energetic action on the *bema*, and finally the critics followed the throng, confessing that the new and vehement style of the young politician had great and enduring merit. Yet there was a peculiar restraint of emotion which only provoked the more demonstration in his auditors. He knew how to make his facts carry their own pathos without wearisome detail; a brief clause, a single word, and the wrong and the woe fell like a shadow upon the land. Thought and feeling, reason and emotion, are fused by the force of an intense personality, too fervid to trifle, but also too keen in its sense of what is true and fitting to violate the unalterable principles of that high art, which is a near approach to nature at its best. Therefore it is that Longinus says, "One might as soon face with steady eyes a descending thunder-bolt as to oppose a calm front to the storm of passions which Demosthenes can arouse."

The task imposed upon his oratory is the best proof of its power. For thirteen years his eloquence was pitted against the resources and diplomacy of an absolute monarch. The nation awoke at last to his call, but too late to avail itself of his counsel and to avert the calamity against which his warnings had been uttered in heedless ears.

The orator went down in the ruins, after giving the indorsement of a private soldier in the ranks to the words uttered on the *bema;* and if clouds gather about his last days we must remember the disasters of a troubled time, and imagine what would have been had his countrymen been as loyal and as high-minded as he in the time when they might have prolonged the glory of Greece. His own oratorical fame, however, is not tarnished, and will outlast the memory of much that was once considered of greater value. All in all he will stand as the first orator of the ancient world. We may not be able to see why, living under different skies, in a distant age and a differing civilization; but as the standards of true art are restored, or exemplified, it will be seen that Demosthenes has approached nearest to perfection in the high art of communicating thought and emotions from man to men.

VI.

ARISTOTLE, THE RHETORICIAN.

FOR a hundred years oratory had been practiced and taught among Hellenic people. Thucydides had given its first efforts a definite form in his history, and the speech-writers had taken care to put their own productions into manuscript for their clients and for posterity. A gradual growth towards the perfection of the best naturalness had been going on under the criticism of a people whose keen perception of the true, the useful, and the beautiful has never been equaled. In an age of marvelous creative power individual capacities had been exercised under the most favorable conditions, and one style after another had been developed with freedom and judged without reserve by a cultivated people whose exquisite discrimination and high relish of rhetorical excellence were combined with their susceptibility to the strongest emotions. It was truly observed by Cicero that the most ordinary assembly has a far better taste than it generally gets credit for; but when to ordinary common sense and intelligence are added a surpassing quickness of wit and liveliness of understanding, it can be imagined that what was ill-timed or uncouth or inharmonious would be reviled by a people whose tongues were as lively as their wits, and upon whom the remotest allusion was never lost. On the other hand, when it is remembered what an important place public speech played in all Greek civic life, and that every citizen was a member of an assembly which debated and decided great issues, the value to each citizen of correct and persuasive oratory becomes apparent. When to this is added the fact that the business of the Greek audience was to criticise, approve, and disapprove, the power of its influence upon the orator in the preparation and delivery of his compositions can be imagined, especially in the case of those literary contests at the Olympic games, when the public of universal Hellas, an august congress representing the total civilization of the earth, sat in judgment upon the productions of its best writers. All this tended to produce a painstaking care in the elaboration of their compositions, which is compared by Dionysius of Halicarnassus to the fine chasing of gold or chiseling of sculpture. Isocrates, for example, employed more years in refining his panegyric on the Persian war than Alexander took to conquer all Asia, and Plato continued correcting his dialogues up to his eightieth year. By a note-book found after his death it was discovered that he had written the first sentence of the *De Republica* several times over with different arrangements. As it now stands it reads, " I went down to the Piræus yesterday with Glaucon, the son of Ariston, that I might offer up a prayer to the goddess; and also because I wanted to see in what manner they would celebrate the festival of Bendis, which was a new thing." Of course it is difficult for us to see through the medium of a translation as faithful as Professor Jowett's even, how Plato, whose diction has been termed gorgeous and magnificent, should have turned this sentence over and over, succeeding at last in making it loose instead of periodic. But the judgment of antiquity is not to be reversed by a single example, and repeated trials only will show whether or not it can be further improved. Moreover it must always be remembered that the Attic writers endeavored to be perspicuous first of all, and the simple grandeur of their best authors is like the perfect proportion of their best architecture and sculpture, beautiful in its expression of the true.

With this century of writings accumulated from Herodotus to Demosthenes an opportunity was offered for the beginnings of a science of rhetoric. Different minds had expressed themselves with a freedom which belongs to a creative age, before many or great models had been set before the youthful intellect, by which it might be consciously or unconsciously moulded. Consequently there was an individuality which came from fidelity to each writer's own cast of mind, which may not be found among an equal number of authors in any hundred years since. Indeed it is this distinctive expression which has done much to give a permanent value to the literary survivals of that intellectual age; for as we have seen there were greater and lesser lights among the immortals, and of course there were some distinguished writers and speakers in those days who have fallen into the obscurity of mere mention by contemporaries, and doubtless there were others of considerable promise and notoriety in their day who have sunk into utter oblivion. But out of the diverse individuality of expression among at least ten strong writers enough material could be gathered to formulate a system or science of the art which had been practiced with success and distinction. In order to such analysis and classification a mind was needed with the analytic and inductive faculty developed to a high and rare degree. Such an intellect, fortunately, came upon the scene at the close of the first great period of intellectual activity in Greece, gathering up and classifying its productions, and laying the foundations of rhetorical science so broad and true that they have never needed relaying. The man to do this, the only man who could do it, was the great master of all ancient science, the philosopher, ARISTOTLE, 384 B. C. The expression of thought was interesting to him as a part of that domain of nature in which he was everywhere at home.

Preëminent, however, as Aristotle is among rhetoricians, there were natural causes which contributed to his surpassing primacy. The Periclean glory had faded in the sixty years since that great statesman's death, but the thoughts and words he uttered had lived in the bright afterglow as the inspiration of the Greek mind and tongue down to Xenophon's time. Plato's Academy was opened in season for Aristotle's instruction after two years of study by himself, and the great teacher at once bestowed the title of "The Reader" upon his distinguished pupil. Young, rich, and ambitious, every advantage of that intellectual age lay within his reach. Keen and witty, logical and learned, a brilliant talker in a city of talkers, no new and no old knowledge was likely to escape him. Upon a mass of tradition, history, and discovery he brought to bear the strong light of a mind which searched it through and through, separating every ingredient from its alien elements and assigning every particle to its congenial sphere. For seventeen years he walked and conversed and studied with Plato, and for twenty in all he moved about the streets of Athens, discoursing of affairs and men; of life, vegetable and animal; of nature, terrestial, human, and divine. Treating of every subject in the range of ancient thought he essayed to take up and carry out to scientific accuracy all that the intellect of his countrymen had attempted. The high art of public speech which he saw exemplified daily all around him would not escape his contemplative and analytic method. As Sir William Hamilton says of him, "His seal was upon all the sciences and his speculations have determined those of all subsequent thinkers." Accordingly after logic and the laws of thought, and dialectic as the first law of expression in conversation between man and man, it was natural that he should take up rhetoric as the law of address from one man to an assembly of his fellowmen. He had seen Isocrates and his disciples upholding the renown of Athenian eloquence; had heard the comments of his townsmen favorable and unfavorable; had made his own criticisms and drawn his own comparisons; saw wherein they agreed in certain respects on all occasions and what idiosyncracies caused variations from the general custom. He found that a few general principles could be applied to the almost uniform action of human thought and speech at their best, and that exceptions belonged to phases which were inferior in their character.

Out of the methods which speakers employed to

move the reason or the emotions of their hearers he derived rules by which any orator of ability might be able to do the same without stumbling his way to success, losing much time and meeting with failure, early or late, for want of proper guidance. This direction had hitherto been furnished personally by the great masters of the art from Corax to Isæus; but the system of each was the system of one man modified by one or two more antedating him. A science which should formulate universal laws of expression, founded upon the nature of universal experience, was what Aristotle aimed to substitute for the primitive and partial methods which were the outcome of limited practice and observation. One writer alone, before Aristotle, had attempted anything like a technical treatment of the subject, and this one, Anaximenes, succeeded in a practical, rather than in a scientific way, indulging in sophistical tricks which brought his system into disrepute. Other treatises, inferior to his even, had been composed by writers who are known only by report. As might be expected the science of rhetoric which Aristotle formulated was largely analytic. In his definition of it he takes occasion to rank the art of expression side by side with the faculty of thought, logic; perhaps with an eye to Plato's slurs upon rhetoric in comparison with his own favorite dialectics, which was not logic exactly, but rather the larger art of conversation, which the ancients cultivated as a science and of which logic was one element. Having assigned rhetoric its honorable place among the mental sciences, and disposed of his predecessors by remarking that such as had compiled systems of oratory hitherto had executed a very trifling part of it, by reason of their neglect of the factor of "proof," he comes to his own definition of it as "A faculty of considering all the possible means of persuasion on every subject." And after contrasting the extension of this art with other arts, such as medicine, which is restricted to matters of health, and mathematics to numbers, he emphasizes the length and breadth and depth of the rhetorical art and science by adding, that it is "able to consider the means of persuasion on any given subject whatsoever." Not much can be added by way of extension to this definition. It covers the whole field of human knowledge, and claims for rhetoric the ability to deal in one way and another with whatever is found there. It becomes the authorized interpreter of every voice and every speech and every language in the universe.

Starting with this broad definition of the rights and powers of rhetoric as prince of all the provinces of literature he begins to ramify from this trunk. Great branches divide into smaller, and these into lesser still, these again into twigs and stems, until a division is reached which, in its amplification and logical derivation, resembles nothing so much as the clear tracery of a leafless tree against a winter sky. There is no foliage to adorn and beautify. The language is plain, sometimes jagged and uncouth, but there is no indefiniteness about it, no mistaking the lineage of each minor and major proposition. It is a science of expression constructed upon scientific and logical principles.

It is natural, therefore, that this master of all sciences

should lay more stress upon proofs than upon mere appeals to anger, fear, envy, pity, or other affections and emotions of his hearers. These he regards as additional and supplemental to the real sphere of rhetoric; and about them he says his predecessors had busied themselves most mightily. Such emotions, he adds, do not appertain to a case, but to the judge, and it is not right that an orator should bias him by winning with anger or pity or jealousy, making that crooked which should be straight and upright. A pleader's business is nothing more than to prove the matter of fact, either that it has or has not happened. And because all men in some sort attempt to prove their accusations or excuses, some by chance and some by method, this method may be discovered and taught as an art for all to use who will learn.

So much for definition. Now, to return to the beginnings of his division of the subject, he first states that there are three kinds of orations, deliberative, judicial, and demonstrative, relating to the future, the past, and the present, respectively as to their proper times. They have their proper offices also. To the deliberative belong exhortation and dissuasion; to the judicial, accusation and defence; to the demonstrative, praise and blame. Certain ends or purposes also belong to each. To the deliberative, the expedient or inexpedient; to the judicial, the just or the unjust; to the demonstrative, the honorable or the dishonorable. And the orator in these several cases must have appropriate proof based upon the common opinions men have formed, and also other principles upon which to base his argument according to the greater or less importance of facts in the case.

To illustrate Aristotle's minute analytic method let us trace his division and subdivision of the first branch of the general subject of oratory, the deliberative. In this kind he says there are to be considered the subject and the object of speech. The subjects on which men deliberate are nearly all included in five, namely, finance, peace and war, safeguard of territory, imports and exports, and legislation. Take the last as an example of his subdivision. To the making of laws is necessary so much political philosophy as to know what are the several kinds of governments; by what means each is preserved or destroyed, from without or within. This knowledge is obtained partly by observing the several governments in times past, by history, and partly by observing governments in the present, by travel. Such is the subdivision of the topic of legislation, under the theme deliberative, under the general subject of oratory. A similar division is given of the ends of deliberative oratory. Happiness in some sort is such an end proposed by the orator; and is to be obtained by such things as we call good, as follows: nobility, riches, honor, health, and nine other things enumerated.

Furthermore in deliberative oratory the principles from which the orator is to draw proofs, that is, the common opinions concerning good and evil, are absolute or comparative; of the absolute again there are two kinds, the disputable and the indisputable. Of the last he draws out twenty-seven particular examples, and of the disputable twenty-two; making forty-nine under the topic of principles or elements, under the theme deliberative, of the general subject of orations.

There is something in these commonplaces that reminds one of Bacon's *Essays*.

Bearing in mind, now, that this enumeration of particulars relates only to the subdivision of the first branch of a preliminary division of the large subject of rhetoric it will be readily seen what a ramification is likely to follow the mention of the judicial and demonstrative branches in the lay-out of this analytic treatise in Book I. The same minute yet logical partition prevails in Book II. about principles of belief, as related to the speaker and the hearer; and in Book III. about elocution and disposition. In the last, under the chapter on the topic of crimination and purgation, fourteen specifications of ways in which this may be done are given, as for example, to cite the fifth, "I did one thing, but meant another;" or the third, "I did him harm, but withal I did him honor." Such suggestions, no doubt, were a great help in carrying out Aristotle's idea that ordinary men could be made effective orators by a careful study of a complete science, and lest they should fail he has put into their hands directions for almost every imaginable exigence that might arise in the ordinary life of his times. For that matter it might be said that he has furnished material that is available in any age if men would take pains to quarry it.

But aside from his accurate, logical, and analytic treatment of the art of expression, as a great scientist should treat it, Aristotle in a large and manly way develops all the various points which an orator must keep in view, and indicates the kinds of knowledge which he must acquire to be master of his profession. In this treatment he exhausts the subject, leaving hardly anything of consequence for subsequent writers to add by way of original and fresh material. His treatise would hardly be acceptable to modern students on account of its extreme analysis and its dry statements and seeming remoteness from present modes of thought and style. Add to this the importance which he lays upon evidence and such proof as is required in courts of law, and his equal neglect of whatever affects the sympathies or the aversions of an audience, and a further reason is found for his withdrawal from our curricula of study. Nevertheless he must be recognized as the father of rhetorical science, and as the man who in an age of orators compassed the whole scale of their practice. It has been observed that in the most perfect example of persuasive oratory on record—the creation of the greatest genius among the English speaking race—Shakespeare's speech of Mark Antony, the rationale of it all had been set forth by the great Greek scientist eighteen centuries before. So uniform and permanent are the principles which underlie all effective expression, that genius in every age, one in one way, another in another, gives them kindred forms. Accordingly eminent moderns have ranked Aristotle's great work as the very foremost in point of psychological knowledge which pagan literature has left us, determining the main lines on which subsequent writers have treated the science of rhetoric.

To understand its value it should be read from beginning to end. He who does this will find amidst much that is tedious many suggestions embedded in a style that is without graces in the original, which translation has not improved. But ideas and principles are there which will remain in the memory of the reader after he has forgotten the angularity of the style. Aristotle at least followed his own definition of the first excellence of style, clearness, without being below or above the dignity of the subject.

Perhaps the chief criticism to be passed upon his treatment of the subject is that it is better for analyzing a speech than for showing how to make one. But it must be remembered that one of the most helpful processes for any writer is the careful analysis of standard compositions, together with the attempt to reconstruct the same afterward in one's own way and words, followed by a comparison of the result with the original. Again it has been urged that his system places too little emphasis on the part the emotions have to play in dealing with an audience. This may be due to the known scientific habit of mind in the writer, and perhaps to the circumstance that the ordinary reader has been satisfied or wearied by the first book, to the neglect of the second and third. Furthermore it is sometimes forgotten that different occasions require different distribution of proof and of exhortation, and that the permanence of the impression may be inversely in proportion to its vividness after the mind comes back to its normal states. For the place which emotions occupy in the art of persuasion, the chapters on Anger and Reconciliation should be read, and those on Fear and Assurance, Envy and Emulation, Pity and Indignation, the Manners of Youth, Middle Age and Old Age, of the Rich and the Noble, and of Men in Power.

So also Book III. furnishes many practical instructions under the chapters on the Choice of Words, of Similitudes, of Purity of Language, of its Amplitude, of Things that Grace an Oration and, most salutary of all, of the Things that Make an Oration Flat.

On the whole there is no better groundwork for the philosophy of rhetoric than that which the great philosopher of antiquity laid, broad and deep as the foundations of the temples which he looked upon as he walked and talked, and some of whose massive blocks may have served as his writing table while penning this immortal treatise. At all events the book has survived the edifices, and while their fair proportions can only be guessed from remaining fragments, the perishable scroll which fluttered at their base has been treasured and reproduced by admiring generations until it has to-day the promise of a renewed immortality.

VII.

EARLY ROMAN ORATORS.

THE classical literature of Greece closes with Aristotle, who in his own attention to literary style in his youth and in his inattention to it in his mature age symbolizes the transition from the better to the worse in Greek oratory which followed his time. After an age of original production always comes one of criticism, and after Athens came Alexandria. Unapproachable models in the works of the older masters furnished abundant materials for second-rate orators, historians, and dramatists, but the age of originating anything new and grand had passed, making way for critical and scientific tendencies, which found a congenial atmosphere for their growth beyond the limits of Greece.

Unlike Athens Rome came slowly and late to a literary attainment that can be called classic. It had been founded five hundred years without exhibiting anything more than the rudest germs of composition, or producing a single author in poetry or prose. About two hundred and fifty years before Christ conquest made the Romans acquainted for the first time with Greek art and literature, and first directed to the pursuit of intellectual cultivation a people who had been more ambitious of military renown than of mental improvement. Roman literature was therefore an imitation of the Greek, and while the copy is excellent, the inspiration of the living original is often wanting.

The language, too, like the people, was sturdy, solid, and energetic, expressing the thoughts of an active and practical, but not an imaginative people; while the Greek speech in its flexibility readily adapted itself to every form, and remained comparatively unchanged from age to age. Demosthenes and his friends were at home with Homer, and the early Christian fathers wrote and spoke the language of Plato. Early Roman historians even were compelled to write in Greek, because their own language could not so well express their thoughts. As late as the times of Cicero Greek was the foundation of a liberal education, and Athens was the university-town to which Roman youth resorted to study literature and philosophy. Like modern French the language was well-nigh universal in Europe and the East, the favorite dialect of literary men and the vehicle in which the doctrines of a religion destined to spread over the earth were given to the world. So late as the middle of the fifteenth century the language of Plato and Aristotle was spoken at the court of Constantinople with a dignity and elegance which characterize the purest writers of the classical ages. It is said that to-day a well-educated modern Greek finds less difficulty in understanding the writings of Xenophon than an Englishman would experience in reading Chaucer, or perhaps Spenser. But what Latin lost in grace and delicacy it made up by a certain weight and persistence in fastening itself upon conquered nations, leaving its impress and stamp ineffaceable upon barbarous and provincial dialects. The

Gracchi fastened it upon the Iberian of Spain, Cæsar upon the Gaul of France, and Trajan upon the jargon of the Scythian tribes. Accordingly if Greek still lives in its own narrow peninsula with somewhat of purity, Latin exists in the grain and fibre of the many Romance dialects all over Europe, and in our own English and American speech. And yet the best Latin scholar would not understand Dante or Tasso, nor would a knowledge of Italian enable one to read Horace and Virgil.

But prose was far more in accordance with the genius of Romans than poetry. "The literature which tended to statesmanship" had a charm for them which no other literature possessed. History, jurisprudence, and oratory engaged their attention, and were studied with a view to their utility, in a scientific rather than an artistic spirit. The graces of composition came late and, with the exception of Caius Gracchus, the earliest orators spoke with a rude and vigorous eloquence. Erudition rather than originality and invention characterized their style, which always had a look backward in historical retrospect. Jurisprudence and statesmanship also entered into the oratory of the Romans, to make the man more efficient as a legislator and a citizen. Even the great captain of soldiers could not do without a rude and shrewd oratory. Still the early features of Roman eloquence were vigorous common sense, honest truthfulness, and indignant emotion. The Latin race was hard, practical, and unimaginative, with good sense rather than a luxuriant fancy. War, politics, legal and political rights were their ruling ideas, without much reflection or introspection. The intellectual life of Greece had been reflected in its poetry first, and afterward in an oratory almost as graceful and rhythmical. The robust and practical Roman demanded common sense enforced with vehemence. Where Athens looked for glory or freedom, Rome sought for increase of domain and the majestic sway of the laws.

It is not so true, therefore, that Rome was late in coming to an appreciation of oratory as that its eloquence was of a ruder sort than that of Greece at a corresponding stage of its literary life. Public speaking prevailed from the first in the legislative assembly, on the battle field, and on the return from a campaign, when the victorious general found eloquence a path to civil honors, as many a military man has learned since the days of Cæsar. Before the introduction of Greek literature the Romans struck out a strong vein of native oratory. Whatever they accomplished in the earlier centuries was solely by dint of practice rather than by any rules of art. Oratory was, in fact, the unwritten literature of active life, and recommended itself by its spirit to a warlike and utilitarian people. Long, therefore, before the historian was sufficiently advanced to record a speech, as Herodotus and Thucydides did for the Greeks, the forum, the senate, the battle field, and the courts had been nurseries of Roman eloquence. There is the tradition of a speech recorded even before the poetry of Nævius was written, the first poet who really deserves the name of Roman. It was delivered by Appius Claudius, the blind man of strong will, against the eloquent ambassador, Cineas, whom Pyrrhus had sent to negotiate peace. But he was no match for the blind orator, and was obliged to quit Rome in defeat. In general, however, the maturity of oratory was preceded in Rome, as at Athens, by the plays of such authors as Livius Nævius, followed by poetic comedy and tragedy, and these by epic and satire until we come to CATO, THE CENSOR, 234 B. C., a man distinguished by almost unexampled versatility and variety of talent.

With him Latin prose begins. A native of Tusculum, of ancient family, he was distinguished for courage in war and integrity in peace; a soldier first, then a lawyer, rising to the eminence of quæstor, ædile, prætor, and finally consul and censor, in which offices he manifested his talents for administration, his fearlessness, his advocacy of the oppressed, and his hatred of luxury and of vice. A lover of strife his long life was one continued combat. Loving truth he hated conventionalisms, despised rank that was not based upon merit, rejected the changes of fashion, and distrusted and condemned everything Greek in literature because he despised the degenerate Greeks with whom he came in contact. Afterward he relented in this respect like an honest man. Yet he did not love right and virtue so much as he hated wrong, and also those who opposed his prejudices. Austere, unamiable, and reserved, he gave rise to the epigram, since repeated in many forms, to the effect that he was so morose that Proserpine herself would not receive him into the infernal regions.

Some one states it mildly by saying that virtue did not present itself to Cato in an amiable form. Nevertheless Cato was morally, as well as intellectually, one of the greatest men that Rome ever produced. Self-educated and acquisitive, he was determined to excel in everything he undertook, whether war, politics, history, or oratory. Such a man must have an originality of his own, and his style will be his shadow. Cato's was rude, unpolished, and ungraceful, partly because of his hearty hatred of Greek culture and his horror of affectation. Still his statements were clear, his arguments direct, and his illustrations striking, his epithets apt, his wit keen, but never offending against gravity and never irreverent. He despised art and was too much wrapped up in his subject to be careful of his language. An imitator of no one no one was able to imitate him. Abrupt, concise, witty, his style had the rapid alternations of light and shade that are seen in nature, now rude and harsh, now pathetic and affecting. He spoke as if in a hand to hand conflict with an adversary. He was a formidable accuser and a powerful defender, pushing out with force, brevity, strong sense, and galling asperity. Such was the man and the style towards which it is a relief to turn back from the glitter and polish of the Augustan age, as men turn their eyes from the city to the mountains. Plutarch likens him to the aggressive Socrates, and Niebuhr pronounces him to be the only great man in his generation, and one of the greatest in Roman history.

There were contemporaries of Cato of no mean repute — Quintus Metellus, Cornelius Cethegus, and that SCIPIO AFRICANUS MAJOR, who, being accused, spoke till dusk the day before the anniversary of the battle of Zama, and on the day itself resuming his speech said, "I call to remembrance, Romans, that this is the very day I vanquished in bloody battle on the plains of Africa the Carthaginian Hannibal, and obtained for you an unlooked for victory and peace. Let us then leave this knave [himself] and at once offer thanksgiving to Jove, supremely good and great." The people followed him, forgetting the accusation that had been made against him, and with loud acclaim accompanied him to the Capitol.

SCIPIO AFRICANUS MINOR (Æmilianus) was a man qualified to be the link between the old and the new school of oratory. With the vigor of the old Roman soldier-like character he combined a refinement of Greek taste which did not destroy his frankness, while it humanized his rough honesty and taught him to love the beautiful as well as the good, and to see that beauty is an outgrowth of goodness.

The orator, however, who was the first to understand and apply the theoretical principles of rhetoric was SERVIUS SULPICIUS GALBA. Still his application of them was far from coldly theoretical, and he employed artifices which would hardly be effective in these days. Not content to carry away the feelings of his audience by an animated and vehement delivery he on one occasion, for example, paraded before the assembly that brought him to trial his two infant sons in order to touch the heart of his judges by his lamentations over their prospective bereavement. This external artifice succeeded in securing his acquittal of perjury in spite of the dry and antique style which was overlaid by such demonstration.

RUTILIUS RUFUS stands forth in contrast as a man who was too upright to appeal to the compassion of his judges, and Lælius is a still greater contrast. Yet though the latter was wise and gentle and smooth and learned in speech, there came a time when, after two ineffectual attempts to win a verdict, Rutilius was called in. He prepared himself by practicing in a vaulted chamber before a few intelligent slaves, and after they came out it was discovered by their bruises that he had also practiced on them in a most emphatic manner. He won the case by transferring somewhat of his energy to the court room.

But these are men of mediocrity. The great orator is the product of stirring times energizing native ability. The two conditions are inseparable. Such times were the favoring elements which brought out the natural capacity of the Gracchi and made them the founders of classical Latin oratory. For nearly four centuries a struggle had been going on between the patrician and plebeian factions, with the result of destroying the distinctions of blood and race, but only to make room for property differences. This line of demarcation had become hard and sharp, owing to the accumulation of wealth in a few hands, and the old class hostility was revived on a change of base. Added to this were the inherited traditions of the nobles, whose ancestors had held high public offices, and the claims and pretensions of new men. Both these repellent forces made the struggle for political distinction fierce between competitors for popular favor.

TIBERIUS GRACCHUS may be considered the legitimate fruit of this stirring age. He spoke from deep convictions resting upon the eternal antagonism of right and wrong, as became the grandson of that Scipio who believed himself to be the communicator to the world of divinely imparted ideas. Uniting the gift of a beautiful voice to copiousness and fluency he added to these that subdued power whose subtle influence penetrates the mind and vanquishes the judgment. Hitherto this had been an unknown force in literature, and its introduction into oratory marks the rise of that high art which Horace terms the *vis temperata*, distinguished now as an impressive calmness, becoming and effective in those to whom it is natural, but very hard to assume when it is not consonant with the disposition of the speaker. In Tiberius gentleness and kindness were the characteristics of his race. His father had won the affection of Spain by his mild administration. His mother, inheriting the genius of Scipio, had added the accomplishments of learning and social graces. And to her care in early youth the brothers Gracchi owed the development of their natural abilities and the direction of their education. Although their political principles were the same, their oratory differed as their temperaments, and the reserved and grave deliberation of Tiberius found a polar contrast in the splendid impetuosity of Caius, by nine years the younger brother. Morally inferior to the older he was his superior intellectually. He possessed the higher creative power, together with the soaring imagination which, guided aright, reaches the domain above the clouds, and sees objects from afar in their true relations and proportions. Sometimes, however, his natural vehemence would so far get the better of him that he found it convenient to have a servant stand near him with a pitch-pipe in order that he might regulate his voice when his emotion rendered his tones unmusical. The same impetuosity made him leave unfinished much that he had well begun. His language was noble, his sentiments wise and grave, but his work often lacked the last finishing touch. There were many grand beginnings which were not brought to perfection. Still he got rid of the harshness of the old school and won the reputation of being the father of Roman prose. Cicero says that he was an orator of the loftiest talent, of burning enthusiasm, of rich and exuberant diction.

Together the Gracchi mark the rise of a freer and easier mode of speaking than that of their predecessors, and together they also represent the two antithetical methods of reserved and impetuous speech, in one or the other of which the greatest orators have found their strength to lie. Between these extremes, or combining something resembling calmness and vehemence, less distinguished speakers have followed such leaders afar off, at the same time doing much to move the world in their time.

The interval between the Gracchi and Cicero boasted of many distinguished names which would have shone brighter if stars of the first magnitude had not been so near. Curio, Fimbria, Scævola, and Publius Sulpicius began to practice oratory as an art and to invest it with a polished garb. More illustrious names than these were Marcus Antonius, Licinius Crassus, and Cicero's immediate predecessor and most formidable rival, Hortensius. Antony and Crassus, according to Cicero, were the first Romans who elevated eloquence to the heights to which it had been raised by Greek genius. This remark is an indication that the leading orators had ceased to take the specimens of old Roman eloquence as their models. Both Antony and Crassus owed their eminence to Greek models, Antony attending lectures at Athens and Rhodes, and Crassus speaking Greek as if it had been his mother-tongue. It shows the unpopularity of everything Greek at Rome at this time, that the one showed open contempt for the Greeks and the other affected not to know them at all. This, however, must be taken as an indirect testimony to the element of perpetuity in Attic eloquence which survived the deterioration of Athenian character. It was Greek letters that Romans reverenced while they despised Greek manners. The modern parallel is the traditionary attitude of the English toward French literary fashions, which is unfortunately growing less pronounced.

MARK ANTONY, the orator, grandfather of the triumvir, entered public life as an advocate. Indefatigable in preparing his cases he made every point tell, and being a master of pathos he found his way to the hearts of the judges. Although not free from the prevailing fault of advocates in being somewhat unscrupulous in assertion he left expressions and passages that remained indelibly impressed on the memory of his hearers. His eloquence in the forum was such that it gave him the reputation of making Italy a rival of Greece in the persuasive art.

CRASSUS, his junior by four years, also began his career in the Roman courts. Trained in the rhetorical schools of Asia and Athens he attained an early eminence as a pleader, and established his reputation by a powerful and triumphant oration in which he espoused the cause of the senate over that of the equestrian order in the matter of the judiciary. His style is careful and yet not labored, elegant, accurate, and perspicuous. He possessed great powers of clearness in explaining, defining, and illustrating. His delivery was calm and self-possessed, his action vehement but not excessive. He took especial pains with the commencement of his speech, the first words which he uttered arresting attention and proving him worthy of it. He understood the rare art of uniting elegance with brevity. Cicero esteemed him so highly and sympathized with him so completely that he chose Crassus to be the representative of his own sentiments in his imaginary conversation in the *De Oratore*. Like Chatham he died almost in the act of supporting, by his eloquent counsel, measures of wisdom.

The last of the orators who preceded Cicero was HORTENSIUS. Scarcely eight years Cicero's senior, his contemporary and rival, he nevertheless belongs to an earlier literary period and to an age of which he himself is the last representative of the middle period of Roman oratory. Born in 114 B. C. he began his career as pleader at nineteen, with applause and success. Unfortunately his eloquence lacked the element of sobriety and therefore of lasting popularity. He was an orator pleasing to the youth of his time, but did not wear well. Brilliant and lively, he was admired for his high spirits and poetic fancy rather than for dignity and gravity. Moreover he was Asiatic in the luxuriance of his ornament and manner rather than Greek in the chastened simplicity and severity of style, and his juvenility, with a foppish and theatrical delivery, counterbalanced the finish, polish, and animation which were real excellencies in his oratory.

In the century and a quarter from Cato to Hortensius a gradual drift is observable from the ruggedness of speech illustrated by the one to the refinements exhibited by the other. More and more the influence of Greek models, sometimes in spite of outspoken protests, softened the angularity of early Latin speech, as the Norman-French tempered the Anglo-Saxon twelve centuries later, adding imported grace to native vigor. The combination of these two elements furnished an admirable foundation on which to build the crowning superstructure of Roman eloquence in the creative and critical achievements of Marcus Tullius Cicero.

VIII.

RHETORICAL SCHOOLS—CICERO, THE RHETORICIAN.

DURING the three centuries from Alexander to Augustus the fortunes of oratory were determined by the new condition of affairs in Hellenic domains. Aristotle's science of rhetoric lived on for a while in the Peripatetic school; the fashion of florid declamation prevailed in the Rhodian school of Asiatics amid mixed populations; the pure traditions of the best Greek taste had been diverted from the use of the Greek language. Hermagoras does something for the art by reviving a higher conception of it, using both the practical rhetoric of the times before Aristotle, and also the philosophical theories of this great scientist; and working the two elements into a new system, the Scholastic, as distinguished from the Practical and the Philosophical, he thus counteracted the view of Asianism, which made oratory a mere knack founded upon constant practice in speaking, instead of the severer basis of Atticism, which made eloquence the last product of the profoundest study and the most painstaking toil.

One of the greatest controversies that ever stirred the world of letters was that concerning the relative value of the Attic and the Asiatic style, the Attic being regarded as compressed and energetic, the Asiatic as florid and ambitious of splendor and striking points. This difference is supposed to have arisen from the circumstance that, when the Greek tongue spread itself among the people of Asia nearest to Greece, certain persons, aspiring to eloquence, but not having a thorough mastery of Greek, were obliged to express their thoughts in the round-about way of circumlocution. A better reason, however, is found in the respective character of the two races. The Athenians, having a polished and refined taste, could endure nothing useless and superfluous, while the Asiatics, a people vain and ostentatious by nature, were fond of a showy kind of eloquence. There was a third kind, the Rhodian, partaking of the peculiarities of each, neither so concise as the Attic nor so exuberant as the Asiatic, whose manner was the resultant of the Asian influence and the modified Athenian taste of Æschines, who carried to Rhodes in his exile the accomplishments then studied at Athens. In regard to this controversy it might be said that underneath all styles lie the laws of taste, which are not so rigid that any one style can be said to be intrinsically better than another. One may be more in accord with the mental constitution of a given people or person than another. Or again the time and the occasion may harmonize with one more than another. The degree of effectiveness is the only criterion by which the value of any mode of expression can justly be determined. With the Greeks in Demosthenes' time nothing but the purest Atticism was regarded as deserving the highest praise. It was like the beauty of the marble statue, cold but correct, without warmth and without color. And yet it is to be observed that coldness and correctness are not the only features of this sort of oratory. So great a critic as Quintilian says that "they are mistaken who think that the only orators of the Attic style are such as are simple, clear, and expressive, restricting themselves to frugality in speech and ornament and gesture. For the school of Isocrates sent forth the most eminent of the Greek orators, and he is very unlike Lysias, whom they recognize as the Attic model. Doubtless Hyperides was Attic, yet he studied agreeableness of style, and Æschines was broader and bolder and loftier than the earlier orators. And Demosthenes surpassed all those dry and cautious speakers in force, animation, sublimity, and structure of periods, delighting in figures and giving splendor to his language by metaphors, even attributing speech to inanimate objects. Let these censors judge more favorably of this distinction, and be convinced that to speak in the Attic style is to speak in the best style."

Yet in spite of Quintilian's narrowing of the terms there were, and probably always will be, some who will cultivate the plain, accurate, and moderate form of Lysias, and others the more luxuriant adornment of Gorgias; the first two representatives of tendencies which are as universal as the love of plainness and of ornament the world over. And an equally large number, perhaps larger than either, will be pleased with a mingling of understanding and imagination, of thought and fancy, the one relieving or illuminating the other. These last have on their side the analogy of nature in all its diversity and benignity—the stern mountain softened and beautified with foliage, with light and shadow; the monotonous level of the sea broken up with waves and sunlight and changing color. Such, it would appear, is the taste of our own age, whose culture is a resultant of Saxon good sense and the study of artistic work in all departments of human labor. The very plainness of the Attic style, carried into the domain of thought, produced the exuberance of the Asians, who, in the deficiency of their literature and philosophy in ideas, strove to hide this defect by external ornaments of language. At length Athens itself was not able to resist this tendency, the two schools having about an equal hold upon the Attic city in the days of Cicero. Another generation saw the supremacy of the florid style at Rome, and some time after the Asiatic taste itself was in the ascendant at Athens.

These two styles of oratory were cultivated in the schools of rhetoric which sprang up after the age of Demosthenes. Eloquence had begun to decline after the diminution of Greek freedom, and in the lack of original production men turned to the study of by-gone glories. Athens, Alexandria, Rhodes, and other centres of learning had their schools, in which teachers of greater or less repute endeavored to reproduce the achievements of the illustrious orators who had won everlasting renown. Naturally they succeeded in merely prolonging the echo through a race of imitators, who lacked both the genius and the motive which made their predecessors famous. However these schools served the good purpose of keeping alive the love of the art for two and a half centuries until its revival at Rome, when the inspiring cause of it passed out of Greece, with its liberty and works of art, to the seven-hilled city. With this transportation went Hellenists, like the poet Archias, eminent in literature and qualified to teach martial Romans, who in turn sent their youth to Athens to complete their education. The result of such intercommunication is seen at length in the reappearance of oratory in the rhetorical age of which Cicero is the best representative, which is also marked by a return to the days of Demosthenes for classic models for study and imitation. Cicero himself had Antiochus of Ascalon, Philo, the Academic, and Apollonius, the son of Molon of Rhodes, for his instructors, besides visiting the principal rhetoricians of Asia. The last of these, not understanding Latin, requested Cicero to declaim in Greek. When he had done so, Apollonius remarked, "You have my praise and admiration, Cicero, and Greece my pity and commiseration, since those arts and that eloquence which are the only glories that remain to her will now be transferred by you to Rome."

An interesting feature of this instruction in the schools of rhetoric is the immensity of the fees paid by pupils, showing the estimate that was placed upon the art in the three or four centuries before our era. When we remember that Isocrates received the equivalent of $20,000 for a single example of high oratorical art, written to be read rather than to be spoken, and that he took pupils for $250 each; that Euthalus paid Protagoras of Abdera $5,000 for teaching him the art of rhetoric; that Cicero and Hortensius bought villa after villa with the wages of their oratory; that Quintilian received a regular salary of $4,000 as late as Vespasian's reign; that Cæsar Augustus and Tiberius Cæsar attended lectures upon rhetoric assiduously—when such indications of devotion to the art appear, we can form some idea of the relative place which it held in the educational systems of the ancients, as well as in the higher occupations of their daily life. It took its position among the fine arts, entertaining the populace as music and the drama did, stirring their emotions and sympathies, raising their minds to sublime and pleasing contemplations, and elevating their moral sense to the reality, or semblance, at least, of exalted sentiments. Again it would direct their ridicule, their scorn, or their indignation toward the base and the criminal with a singleness of contagious thirst for revenge, retribution, or blood, like the fell intent of hounds in full cry for their game. Or once more it would recall the dignity and renown of a golden age of heroes, so dear to the Greek memory, and fill the soul with complacent reminiscences of an illustrious past and of the mighty dead.

After this survey of the period of decadence and transition following the age of Demosthenes it will be convenient to consider the work of Cicero as a writer upon rhetoric and oratory. That he was a voluminous writer is seen in the titles of his works alone, the whole series of which has been preserved nearly complete, consisting of the volume on Invention; The Orator; Brutus, or Concerning Illustrious Orators; of the Best Kind of Speaking; of the Oratorical Division; and Topics about the Best Class of Orators; the last a fragment on the subject of the Attic style of oratory. These works considered the art of rhetoric from different points of view, thus supporting and illustrating each other. Written for the most part in the form of dialogue they digested the principles of Aristotle and Isocrates and their followers into a complete system, selecting what was best in each, to which remarks and precepts of his own were added by Cicero himself.

The divisions under which he treats the subject of discourse are three: the Case in Hand, the Speaker, and the Speech. The Case includes considerations regarding the hearer, as well as its own character as judicial, descriptive, or deliberative. With respect to the opponent there is a fourfold division according to the fact, the nature, quality, or propriety of the case. The art of the Speaker is directed to five points: the discovery of persuasions, argumentative, moral, or emotional in character; to arrangement, diction, memory, and delivery. The Speech itself consists of six parts: introduction, statement of the case, division of the subject, proof, refutation, and conclusion.

To go somewhat more into detail he regards, with Aristotle, the invention or finding of arguments and material of discourse as the very foundation of the art. Giving a full analysis of the two forms of argument, syllogism and induction, he applied their principles to the three subject matters of rhetoric: the deliberative, the judicial, and the descriptive, dwelling principally on the judicial as affording the most ample field for discussion. We note here a return to the early and practical character of oratory in the Sicilian tribunals, instead of its later exhibitions in the popular or deliberative assembly. This treatise, *De Inventione*, was almost entirely compiled from the writings of Aristotle, Isocrates, and

RHETORICAL SCHOOLS.   111

Hermagoras, but it was a useful work and remarkable for its uniform good sense. The *Topica*, or treatise on commonplaces, is little else than a compend of Aristotle's work on the same subject, drawn up from memory at the request of a friend, on a sea voyage, soon after Cæsar's murder.

The *De Oratore*, *Brutus*, and *Orator* may be regarded as a complete system of rhetoric. The first lays down principles and rules of the art, the second illustrates them by examples from the most eminent speakers of Greece and Rome, and the third portrays the characteristics and qualities of the ideal orator.

The *De Oratore* is a dialogue between some of the most illustrious Romans, of the age preceding his own, on the subject of oratory. The principal speakers are the orators Crassus and Antonius, who are represented as unfolding the principles of their art to Sulpicius and Cotta, rising young lawyers. In the first book conversation turns on the qualifications requisite for a perfect orator. Crassus maintains the necessity of his being acquainted with the whole circle of the arts, while Antonius limits eloquence to the province of speaking well. Catulus and Cæsar join in the dialogue later, when, to Antonius' remarks on invention, Cæsar adds something on the use of humor in oratory. Antonius finishes the morning's discussion with the principles of arrangement and memory. In the afternoon Crassus explains the rules for propriety and elegance of diction, he himself being celebrated for these qualities of speech. The book concludes with a discussion of delivery and action, which were of great importance in ancient oratory.

A lofty style and tone pervade the whole work, which is almost dramatic in its allusions to the destinies for which its members were reserved.

In the *De Claris Oratoribus*, written nine years later, is given another dialogue among Brutus, Atticus, and Cicero himself. He begins with Solon, and after briefly mentioning the orators of Greece, proceeds to those of his own country, from Junius Brutus to himself. In the *Orator* he directs attention, principally, to diction and delivery, adopting a somewhat abstract and ideal conception of what the orator should be rather than of what he generally is. The perfectly eloquent man he defines as one who expresses himself with propriety on all subjects, great or small. So excellent was his opinion of this treatise that he does not hesitate to declare that he is ready to risk his reputation for judgment in oratory on its merits.

His position as a writer upon rhetoric cannot be fully understood without some reference to his philosophical, moral, and physical compositions. An enthusiastic student of philosophy, having an energy and range of intellect by which he was able to pursue a variety of objects at once, losing no spare moments in idleness, dictating his thoughts to attendants even when walking, he found time for business of state, for the courts, and for philosophical studies. His treatises were composed when he was engaged in daily disputes in questions of litigation.

In the last year of his life he composed eight of his philosophical works, besides fourteen orations against Antony. Being thus ardent in the cause of philosophy he recommended it to the notice of his countrymen, whose haughtiness had hitherto conspired with the stubbornness of the Latin tongue to keep speculative thought subordinate to practical activities. In doing this he gained honor for himself, but he also did it with the zeal of one who esteemed philosophy as the guide of life, the parent of virtue, the guardian in difficulty, and the tranquilizer in misfortune. Interesting as it was to him, however, he cultivated philosophical studies chiefly with a view to his own improvement in oratory. Accordingly he undertook the cause of the Stoic, the Epicurean, or the Platonist as an exercise of his powers of argumentation; although in his private judgment he preferred the sceptical tenets of the New Academy, which, lying midway between the other philosophies, was attacked and appealed to in turn by all. From this attitude of being liable on all sides to attack it. became as much a school of rhetoric as of philosophy, and was celebrated among the ancients for the eloquence of its masters. Cicero himself declares how much he owed to the gardens of the Academy, and Quintilian says that so wonderful a fertility of mind could not have showed itself in him if he had circumscribed his genius by the limits of the forum, and not allowed it to range through all the domains of nature. His acquaintance with Aristotle's writings amounted to a considerable proficiency in philosophy and science, while for the most of the principles laid down in his rhetorical discussions he is indebted to this great philosopher. He made no pretensions to originality in philosophy; nevertheless he was a candid and diligent inquirer after truth, and a firm believer in the great cardinal doctrines of a divine providence and a future state, and was clear and decided in his views of moral obligation, preferring right to expediency, and giving vitality to virtue, clothing it in the flesh and blood of a living example in his own life. No one more than he has emphasized the value of the ethical element in the character of an orator, and no one, not even Socrates, has more frequently drawn philosophy from above to walk among men, in attractive garb.

Cicero's rhetorical compositions were the product of theories and influences which preceded him, modified by contemporary elements and his own strong sense of what was good and right. What these influences were can be inferred from a brief retrospect of the two and a quarter centuries from Cato, the Elder, to Cicero.

The first period of Latin eloquence, represented by Carbo and the Gracchi, was learned, majestic, and harmonious in the style of its speech. The next and middle age, in which flourished Antonius, Crassus, Cotta, Sulpicius, and Hortensius, exhibited greater liveliness and variety of manner. But in the following age the art was exemplified and adorned by an assemblage of orators which, in Quintilian's opinion, could not be overmatched by Greece itself. Its most illustrious names, besides Cicero, are Cæsar, Curio, Brutus, Cælius, Calvus, and Callidus. The oratory of Cæsar, pure and forcible, was surpassed only by his military achievements. If he had devoted himself wholly to the forum, no other Roman would have approached Cicero so nearly as he. Perspicuous, energetic, and full of fire, he is said to have spoken with the same spirit with which he fought. All these qualities he adorns with a remarkable elegance of diction, of which he was particularly studious.

Cælius was a speaker of much ability and pleasant wit, especially skilled in bringing an accusation before the courts. Some ancient critics preferred Calvus to all other orators, being forcible, correct, and spirited, although he had diminished his natural energy by too severe criticism of himself and by too closely imitating the chastened style of the Attics, becoming cold, cautious, accurate, and sententious.

Brutus was gravely philosophic as a rule, although he sometimes indulged in a warmer and bolder vein; Callidus, delicate and harmonious; Curio, bold and flowing. Together they form an illustrious company, somewhat majestic and formal, like their own age, but better than the degenerate brood which succeeded them. Orators of the Republic they found opportunities for effective appeals to the emotions of their hearers in the nature of the government, while from Greek literature and philosophy they were able to draw sentiments and wise apothegms, which served to ornament their speech and delight their hearers. Their exordiums were long, their statements diffuse, divisions ample, digressions frequent, their perorations gradual and sedate. Yet so long as literature was the property of the few, and public virtue synonymous with the name of the Republic, these speaking men were the delight of the popular assembly, and the pride of an uncorrupted nation.

IX.

CICERO, THE ORATOR.

THE literary high-water mark was reached at Rome during the first century before the Christian era, and its prose representative was the orator MARCUS TULLIUS CICERO. Born in 106 B. C., at Arpinum, he was educated at Rome from his fourteenth year in grammar, philosophy, and the technical rules of verse, although the poet Archias, his teacher, could not give to the greater orator his own poetic faculty. After he was sixteen years of age Cicero frequented the forum and, by carefully exercising himself in composition, made the eloquence of the celebrated orators to whom he listened his own. At twenty-five he argued his first cause. Afterward he traveled in Greece and Asia, employing his time in the cultivation of oratory. At thirty-nine he began to distinguish himself as a deliberative orator, his speeches hitherto having been entirely of the judicial kind. At forty-three, when he attained to the consulship, the moral qualities of his character were the highest, and his genius shone forth with the greatest splendor. It was at this time that the famous oration against Catiline was delivered, and the plot which had been dignified with the title of war was broken up by the eloquence of one who wore the peaceful toga. Other triumphs of his oratorical power followed, until the year of his death, when he delivered the twelve Philippic orations—"that torrent of indignant and eloquent invective."

When the oratory of Cicero becomes a subject of analysis there are a few characteristics of it which stand forth with special prominence. His methodical laying out of his orations, according to the plan proposed in his rhetorical works, relates merely to the form in which his brilliant capacities show themselves; but it is also clear that such abilities did not spurn the so-called trammels of rule and order, for the reason that such an order has its origin and justification in the immutability of human nature. Accordingly he was careful about his introductions containing the ethical proof; the body of the speech with its statement of facts; the argument containing his inferences from those facts; and finally the peroration, addressing itself to the moral sense of the judges. And it is no disparagement that he sometimes resorts to commonplaces to conciliate the favor of the audience, or attempts to set the plane of their criticism as low as possible, rather than to allow them to expect too much of him at the start, and thus be disappointed with his effort at the close of it.

It is, however, in the part known as "the proof" that his oratorical powers begin to have their full play. He accounts for everything so naturally, makes trivial circumstances tell so happily, and so adroitly converts apparent objections into confirmations of his argument, that it becomes impossible to question the truth of his statement. Then he proceeds to heighten the effect of his proof by amplification and exaggeration. He goes round and round his subject; surveys it in every light;

examines it in all its parts; compares and contrasts it; illustrates, confirms, and enforces his views till the hearer cannot doubt a conclusion which rests on such strict and copious argumentation. Then he opens upon his opponent with polite raillery, or if the subject is a grave one, with the bitterness of irony or the vehemence of invective. At other times his peroration contains more heroic and elevated sentiments, perhaps a panegyric on patriotism and love of glory or liberty. As he himself says of all this variety of method, "Our model orator will turn the same subject about in many ways; dwell and linger on the same thought; frequently extenuate circumstances; sometimes depart from his object and direct his view another way; propound what he means to speak; define what he has effected; repeat what he has said; conclude his address with an argument; leave and neglect something occasionally; guard his case beforehand; describe the language and characters of men; introduce inanimate objects speaking; divert attention from the main point; anticipate an objection; employ examples; turn a matter into jest; decline a little from his object; speak with boldness and freedom, with indignation and invective and execration, or implore and entreat and heal an offence—in a word, put himself on terms of familiarity with his audience."

Agreeably to his own precepts Cicero does all this and more, adapting himself with felicity to every class of subjects, familiar or lofty, philosophic or forensic. And this he accomplishes more by his flexible style than by his brilliancy, plausibility, or pathos. He brought himself into harmony with the spirit and capacities of the Latin language, whose possibilities were far less than the Greek, and required fulness in order to be perspicuous. As Quintilian says, "Let him who demands from Latin writers that peculiar charm of the Attic style grant me the same sweetness of expression and equal copiousness of language. If this is denied Latins, as it is, then we must express ourselves in such words as we have, and not introduce confusion by discussing subtle arguments in a language which is too strong, if not too heavy. We can not attain the elegance of the Greeks; let us then excel them in vigor." This is the plan on which Cicero has proceeded. The first age of Roman orators had cultivated stateliness, the second had attempted strength, but Cicero made a language rather than a style, not by finding new words so much as by the combination of old and familiar ones. His great art lies, where it always lies with the true artist, in the application of materials at hand to the production of amazing results. It is his enrichments and his prunings, his systematic construction of sentences, his copiousness of diction, which constitute him the greatest master of composition, as such, that the world has ever seen. Other orators have excelled in other departments of the art, but none in the wealth and variety and adaptation of words to the purpose in view. Without the force of Demosthenes he doubtless has the other two of the qualities which an ancient critic ascribes to him, "the copiousness of Plato and the sweetness of Isocrates." Strength and simplicity cannot be claimed for him, but copiousness, fulness, and soundness of treatment no one will deny him. These are apparent everywhere—numerous verbs, nouns, and adjectives, sometimes meaning nearly the same thing, but used in order to make the roll and the swell, the fulness and the rhythm, the balance and the cadence of the sentence. The pleonastic "I implore and beseech," "stable and not changed," "brave and the spirited," remind one of the redundancy of the days when our own English was half-Saxon and half-Norman, and the mixed congregation was exhorted to "acknowledge and confess" its sins and wickedness, and not to "dissemble nor cloak" them when they "assemble and meet together," to ask those things which are "requisite and necessary." But Cicero had no such reason for the pleonastic use of words. There was but one Latin speech among an unconquered and united people. Being somewhat meagre, however, for philosophical and oratorical purposes he determined to make the most of the language and make it sonorous. He loved such far-sounding words as would suggest the long roll of the wave thundering on the shore. *Ad evertandam rempublicam, occidendum Milonem. Qui spe amplissimorum premiorum. Metu crudelissimorum.* . . . . . But while there is sound there is harmony and rhythm everywhere. The Roman loved frequent recurrence of long syllables, the Greek more of the short. Here are two illustrative examples from the English: "Soon the laurels of yonder hero will have withered; and all that active and successful talent which adorns this age will disappear; and its honored possessors, conducted in succession to their graves, will moulder amid sepulchral ashes, forgotten or remembered only by the monuments of glory they shall have during their transitory life erected." Here is a different measure: "Though he who utters this should die, yet the immortal fire shall outlast the humble organ who conveys it, and the breath of liberty, like the word of the holy man, will not die with the prophet, but survive him." The last word of one syllable would not have pleased the ear of Cicero. Three short syllables and a long was his favorite ending, like the famous *esse videatur*, or *justa repetenda silentium pollicentur*. All this better comports with the Roman character than with the English, and with Latin language than ours. Such copiousness runs into verbosity, and the sound is sometimes mightier than the sense, is too artificial and too full of display. But within proper limits the wealth of language, the brilliance, the beauty, the harmony, the graphic sketching, the lucidity, and the occasional pathos are Roman virtues of composition which are worthy of all praise and occasional imitation.

The faults that have been attributed to Cicero are that this copiousness sometimes runs into wordiness; that the sound sometimes exceeds the sense; that the style is too artificial in the whole structure, with a too bold display of the speaker's verbal power, sacrificing the subject to his vanity. The excellencies have already been enumerated—wealth and harmony of diction, solid and sententious argument, illumined with the brilliance of a poetic imagination, to which may be added the rhythmical harmony of his periods and the frequent splendor of his figures. There was argumentation for the reason, philosophical sentiments for the intellect, fervid and vehement declamation for the emotions, but most of all he would captivate his hearers, flatter their vanity, rouse their selfishness, stir their hopes and fears, and thus, by persuasion rather than by conviction, carry his points. The effect of this may not be so general or great as that of the Grecian school, but it is in all cases very different. Perhaps we may best understand the domain of both kinds by noticing those points in which the two great exponents of each can be compared and contrasted.

It must be granted that Demosthenes was the pattern by which Cicero formed himself, whom he emulated with such success as to merit what Jerome calls that beautiful eulogium in *Brutus*, "Demosthenes has snatched from thee the glory of being the first orator; thou hast deprived him of the glory of being the only one." The genius, the capacity, the style and manner of them both were much the same; their eloquence, of that great, sublime, and comprehensive kind which dignified every subject and gave it all the force and beauty of which it was capable. It was that "roundness of speaking," as the ancients call it, where there was nothing redundant or deficient, nothing to be added or retrenched. Their perfections are so transcendent and yet so similar that critics are not agreed to whom to give the preference, Quintilian, the judicious, giving it to Cicero, possibly for patriotic reasons.

If Cicero had not all the energy of Demosthenes, he excelled him in the elegance of his diction, the variety of his sentiments, and the vivacity of his wit; for, as Longinus says, whenever Demosthenes attempted pleasantries he made himself ridiculous, and, if he succeeded in raising a laugh, it was at his own expense; whereas Cicero, from a perpetual fund of wit and ridicule, had the power to please when he failed to convince, and could often save his clients from impending ruin by a well timed witticism. In common, again, with the great Greek orator he had that sublime and sonorous speech which not only instructs but also moves an audience, an eloquence born for the multitude, exciting admiration and extorting applause, on which there was never any difference of judgment between the learned and the populace. With this consent of free Rome in its best age agrees the concurrent sense of nations since, which has neglected the productions of his rivals and contemporaries, and preserved his works as perfect specimens of oratory, according him the praise of an ancient, that "Cicero is not so much the name of a man, as of eloquence itself."

Cicero and Demosthenes resembled each other, first of all, in the pains they both took to acquire the best oratorical gifts. They both sought the best masters, corrected every fault they could, and brought out every practicable excellence. They perfected, according to their respective notions, their style and manner; were alike in vehemence and profusion of action, in the carefulness of preparation, in skilful repetition, presenting again and again strong points, facts and arguments in different ways and connections. If there is any difference in the method of their seeking success in their chosen profession, it is in the singleness of Demosthenes' aim, applying all the faculties he had to make himself a master of his art without turning aside to a broader culture; while Cicero was widely educated and accomplished in other branches of learning, particularly in philosophy. This he does not hesitate to show, by the way, in a manner which the modesty of Demosthenes would hardly have allowed him to exhibit, who never spoke his own praises except when there was a necessity for it, and then in a reserved manner. Whereas Cicero's good opinion of himself was only equaled by the readiness with which he made it public. He never hesitated to proclaim the superiority of the pen over the sword, or of the tongue, either, for that matter, and his own eloquence was a favorite theme with him; while Demosthenes was accustomed to account his talent nothing more than a matter of practice, depending largely upon the good will and candor of his hearers.

The tone which prevailed throughout much of their work also differed in each. Cicero was by nature disposed to mirth and pleasantry, and was always smiling and serene. Sometimes this geniality ran him into long series of jokes, and even into indecency and scurrility, when he wished to dispose of the arguments of an opponent that were otherwise difficult to overthrow. It may be said, however, that he has never ceased to have imitators in this respect, perhaps more than in his more admirable qualities as a forensic orator. Demosthenes, on the contrary, in his oratory was without jest or embellishment, was serious and always in earnest, was temperate, thoughtful, and sincere; so much so, indeed, that his enemies called him morose and ill-mannered.

In the construction of their respective compositions Cicero has the advantage of Demosthenes in clear, methodical arrangement. He can be followed with ease from point to point, in a logical order. This is accounted for by the fact that Cicero lived at a time when rhetoric had come to be a science, deduced from the practice of many illustrious orators, a science which Demosthenes' untrammeled and unsurpassed talent had done much to create by masterly achievement. Accordingly there is more of nature in the Greek orator, and more of art in the Roman. This also was determined by the motive of each. Demosthenes had a single object and a rigid purpose; he spoke in a severe, intense state of mind, meaning to accomplish something and make men act. He aimed to convince the hearer and sweep him along in his own direction to the same goal for which he himself was making. Cicero, on the other hand, was sometimes less in earnest, more easy and sportive; pleasing, charming, and winning admiration. Consequently he makes the orator and his oratory prominent, never forgetting the importance of the speaker, while Demosthenes so links and identifies himself with the cause that he is lost in it. Therefore while the audience and the reader have unbounded admiration for the great Roman, the Greek gets his own better praise when his auditors, at the end of one of his Philippics, rise up and cry out, "Let us march against Philip!"

In the matter of style there is just as marked a difference. The Grecian is frugal in the use of figures and ornaments, rarely going abroad for them or using them for their own sake. The Roman sought after them and invented figures for their effect, and accumulated epithets from the love and relish of adornment. Therefore he was flowing and redundant, or at times verbose in his speech, where Demosthenes was concise, strong, and practical, dealing more with the idea, the substance, and the argument. There was much display of flash and fire, and beautiful clouds of smoke when Cicero was speaking, but when Demosthenes had the *bema*, heavy bolts were striking and entire throngs were swept down by the chain-shot of his close-linked speech.

There is an element in the oratory of Greece which Cicero discerned and cultivated until he was equal to the best of Greeks in his mastery of it; that is, a certain rapidity of movement, which, by the way, is never to be confounded with hurry and haste. It is rather a continuous movement right on toward the desired end and object of discourse, and when the Latin orator could refrain from lingering over and amplifying his figures or thoughts, rolling them as a sweet morsel under his tongue, he becomes strongly effective in his direct progress and rapid advance. Here is an example: " He has obtruded himself into the most hallowed rites of religion; he has broken the most solemn decrees of the senate; he has bribed the judges, driven me from my country, plundered my goods, burned my house, declared an atrocious war against Pompey, laid waste Etruria, has urged on his nefarious course till the city, Italy, provinces, kingdoms, could not hold his madness." In this sketching, amplifying, but condensing movement, Cicero abounds. He is best paralleled in recent times by Dr. Chalmers.

If it be debated as to which is to be preferred, the conciseness of the Greek or the copiousness of the Latin orator, the decision of modern taste would be for a mingling of the two. The extreme of either is faulty, as all extremes are. Copiousness, indeed, has always been condemned. It tires and leaves nothing for the reader or hearer to supply; an activity in which every attentive and thoughtful listener likes to indulge. On the other hand conciseness in eloquence has been praised so much and in such a way as to convey and give prevalence to the idea that the greater the conciseness the greater the power. There was a school holding this doctrine at Rome in the time of Cicero, imitators of the Attic method, whose disciples greatly censured the Roman orator for his verboseness. They affected a minute and fastidious correctness—pointed sentences, short and concise periods, without a syllable to spare in them; as if perfection in oratory consisted in frugality in words, and in crowding sentiments into the narrowest possible compass. O'Connell, the Irish orator, has been considered by some to be the modern representative of this style, but not to the extent that has been imagined does he fling his thoughts unclad upon the audience. There is also something of a mistake in supposing that Demosthenes always favors extreme conciseness. He illustrates its beauty and power where it is needful, but his practice does not commend an employment of it which would be fatal, unless all auditors were equally and highly endowed with the gift of ready apprehension. Copiousness is needful to the laggard understanding which is found in every assembly. Also the diversity of importance in different topics in the same discourse calls for a difference in the fulness with which they are treated. This Demosthenes knew as well as the Roman orators, and also knew better than they when to be copious and when concise. He might have said, " While the statesmen of Greece were all corrupted by Philip, nothing ever prevailed on me to betray, in the least, the interests of my country." This expresses the idea fully, clearly, and in the fewest words. But he is not satisfied with such conciseness. Instead he employs copiousness to give emphasis to the sentiment, as follows: "While the statesmen of Greece were all corrupted by Philip, neither opportunity, nor fair speeches, nor lavish promises, nor hopes, nor fears, nor favor, nor any other earthly consideration, ever prevailed over me, driving me to betray, in any one particular, what I deemed the right and interests of my country." This is copiousness worthy of Cicero, reminding us of that passage of St. Paul's, "For I am persuaded that neither life nor death, nor things present nor things to come," etc. Verbosity is another thing, unmeaning, heavy, wordy, and cold. Strong feeling may demand copiousness, but never verbosity. When we wish to prolong attention we enumerate slowly and fully, and in the order of climax, dwelling upon one thing after another in a cumulative way. But if we wish to force such a sentiment upon another, it is done concisely after such a preparation of the feeling has been made. Therefore among his full and flowing sentences the Greek orator intersperses bright and sharp ones, as sundry great English orators have done, catching his spirit.

While, then, copiousness and conciseness both have their place and value, it is to be remembered that only as they relieve and supplement each other are they greatly valuable. Either, used exclusively or generally, produces a monotony which is tiresome.

Recurring to the style of Cicero it must not be concluded that it is not good and useful in its time and place. As it pleased the great body of the Romans by its stately splendor, so it must be borne in mind that there is a Roman taste always largely prevalent, more largely perhaps than the severe Greek. The great parliamentary orators of the last century in Great Britain caught its spirit, and our own orators of the last generation followed in their steps. When the object is to soothe or please or attract or persuade, its fulness and melody are demanded. When instant and vehement action is desired, the sharp conciseness of the Greek, when he was urging an immediate deed, is equally requisite. Such is the speech for war. But in peace when the virtues of citizenship under the laws, and of learning and of morality and of religion are to be commended and cultivated, the leisurely style of the Roman orator, with its agreeable suggestion, its sound reasoning, its brilliant fancy, its mellifluous roll and cadence, its long and flowing periods, is the style which best presents peaceful truth to self-satisfied hearers.

No account of Cicero's eloquence can be complete without some mention of the ethical element which was one great factor in its power. According to his own theory, as well as that of his best predecessors, "the perfect orator is the perfect man;" and, according to his knowledge and in view of the times in which he lived, Cicero came as near his own ideal as the infirmities of a somewhat defective nature would permit. It was a character of mingled weakness and strength, tried by prosperity and adversity and praised and maligned by turns according to the bias of contemporaries or the whim of subsequent critics. His last biographer, striking a balance between the judgments of half a dozen others, says that he would have been more consistent if he had been less scrupulous. The moral instinct was too strong to allow him to resort to means of which his conscience disapproved. His standard of morality was as high as it was possible to elevate it by the mere light of nature. To fall below that standard made him feel dissatisfied with himself and ashamed. His constant aim was to do right, and his mistakes were those of his judgment rather than of his heart. The desire to please and be all things to all men was his misfortune, leading him to praise men whose characters he abhorred. His weakness showed itself again in his vanity, a harmless failing which did others less injury than it did Cicero good. One of the most forgiving of men he loved to say that his enmities were mortal, his friendships eternal. Feeling warmly he expressed himself strongly, and for this reason must have carried with his words the appearance of truth and sincerity, the first requisite in an orator, without which the graces of rhetoric may please, but are no better than curling smoke for effective conviction.

Quintilian gives, after all, as good a summary of his virtues as any when he says, "Though I acknowledge that Cicero stood at the head of eloquence. . . . yet since he did not lay claim to the praise of perfection for himself—though he had no mean opinion of his own merits—I may not unreasonably believe that the summit of excellence was not attained by him. Notwithstanding no man has made nearer approaches to it." And he ends a whole chapter on the proposition that a great orator must be a good man by saying, "I only wish to show that the definition of an orator, given by Cato, the Censor, 'a good man skilled in speaking,' is a true definition."

X.

CICERO'S SUCCESSORS, AND QUINTILIAN.

THE age following Cicero's was marked by a long list of writers inferior in vigor and boldness to their predecessors, but surpassing them all, except Cicero, in finish and artistic skill. It was an age which dwelt upon words, when the impulse to great thoughts was removed. Augustus received an adulation which amounted to worship, accompanied by a willingness to surrender all political power into his hands. As a consequence the privileges and rights of the people were gradually abridged, and the loss was made up to them by abundance of food and amusement. As a further consequence literature became enervated, having, indeed, broad sympathies and great beauty of expression, which ran naturally into poetry and poetic prose. It was an age of poets and prose writers of an imaginative turn—historians, philosophers, and moralists, who flattered Augustus and were in turn patronized by him.

Roman oratory sunk with liberty, and instead of the recent copious and flowing eloquence there succeeded a dry, guarded, sententious kind, full of labored terms and studied points, panegyrics, and servile compliments to tyrants.

This extreme refinement was not without an attempt at reaction, as is seen in the tendency toward absence of literary finish on the part of a few; but it was only a variation of affectation, forming a pleasant relief to the high-wrought refinement which generally prevailed. It was simply a protest against the surfeit of good things. Another tendency, at the other extreme, was an overdoing of elaborate writing, and a substitution of rich diction for an ornamentation which was classic already, a gilding of gold, an overlaying of Greek simplicity with Asian magnificence, painting the perfect statue. Such was the character of literature in general, faring far better than the particular branch of it under consideration. For the very conditions which gave poetry and related prose a hot-house luxuriance withered and weakened oratory, which flourishes only in the bracing atmosphere of liberty.

In the curtailment of popular rights by the emperor, and a too willing hastening of them away by an amused populace the freedom of debate upon matters of public concern first fell into neglect. For of what use was it to discuss questions of state in the forum, when a council in secret session was deciding them beyond the power of the people to alter or modify its decrees? Nothing was left to eloquence except abstract discussions upon which it was next to impossible to employ itself. Meantime growing servility to the established despotism made it perilous to utter plain truths, as a few found whose traditions of the Republic compelled them to cry out against the growth of tyranny and luxury. Oratory, therefore, in these unfavoring circumstances, narrowed its sphere to those themes which were safe to discuss, and found its chief occupation in the forensic strife of the courts. In fact it was remanded to the position it occupied in its early days in Sicily, but without possessing the nobler attitude of a growing liberty under a waning or departed despotism. Instead freedom was on the wane, and tyranny was waxing stronger every day. Much of the oratory of the Augustan age had not even the motive of a civil suit at law to inspire it. The larger part of it was mere declamation in the schools of the rhetoricians, who continued to keep up its form without its power, an empty echo of the voices which were once lifted up in the cause of freedom in two nations. Pollio, a man who might have deserved a place among the illustrious ten, was restricted to noisy declamation of what were called "suasorial" pieces, among which was the probable speech of Leonidas to his three hundred at Thermopylæ, imagined and written out to be spoken by the members of his school. Thus oratory lived on in a sort of retrospective life, reproducing the traditions of the ancients, growing more and more formal and scholastic, growing less and less real and objective, having no particular object to secure. It became a mere art without motive or purpose and therefore, artificial and empty, until at Tiberius' accession in the year fourteen of our era it had well-nigh ceased to exist, or was confined to declamation of celebrated passages out of the old orators.

Now and then, in this general dearth of eloquence, a man like Celsus would appear and carry his hearers away by a native power and dignity, in spite of faults and carelessness of speech. And sometimes personal indignation would boil over against the tyrant; but such men were likely to be regarded as semi-lunatics or self-devoting martyrs in a hopeless revolt against the established despotism, which in turn paid no attention to their stormy diatribes, or found a way to silence them most effectually. In this phase of oratory there was much that resembled a later development of it in France—full of vehemence and gesticulation, yet preserving the proper modulations of the voice without violating symmetry and decorum. The art of the rhetorical schools would regulate all that, even if it added a tinsel ornamentation belonging to an unreal age, which even so great a man as Seneca might have done something to recommend by his own manner of life and writing. For although there is much in this man of comprehensive mind and wide attainments, he was apt to dwell upon the petty and minute rather than to confine himself to the grander phases of thought.

It was not until Nerva's reign, A. D. 96–98, that anything resembling liberty of speech was restored. This emperor's policy of toleration seems to have extended to orators as well as to the political exiles of his predecessor's term of office. But eloquence could not recover its former high estate at a bound in the days when kings were made by armies and unmade by assassins. Still it had its place among the liberal pursuits and remained the highest career that an ambitious man could adopt. Even under tyrants it had served as the keenest weapon of attack and the surest means of defence, and now it promised to have a temporary revival.

PLINY THE YOUNGER, A. D. 62–116, may be taken as the best representative of this time of renewal, being far ahead of his contemporaries in accusation and defence, as well as a most telling advocate before the tribunals and the boldest orator in the revived debates in the senate. He was specially distinguished as the defender of persons who had been pillaged by rapacious governors. Only one specimen of his oratorical talent remains, the panegyric addressed to the emperor Trajan, which is replete with point and elegance, and no fuller of flattery than was essential to the governor of a province. He was also a champion of the ancient school of eloquence, as Tacitus was of the modern; two factions into which Roman oratory had split in the days of its decline.

TACITUS is commonly thought of as a historian, but according to the custom of his time an educated man must have studied many things which were then included under the name of rhetoric, as this writer had under Aper Secundus and perhaps Quintilian. Afterward he argued with such success in the courts that Pliny himself mentions it as his highest ambition to be ranked next to Tacitus. He says that there was a "peculiar solemnity in his language, which gave the greatest weight to all he uttered. His style is free and flowing, full of imitations of Cicero. After wavering long between the ancient and the modern styles he adopted the latter, which he has exalted by making it concentrated, powerful, and dramatic, the fit vehicle for portraying the sombre annals of a declining empire. The rhetorician has not become extinct in the historian, and his history becomes almost oratory." Says a French critic, "The historian rises to the sublimity of a judge. He summons the guilty to his tribunal, and in the name of the future and of posterity

CICERO'S SUCCESSORS, AND QUINTILIAN. 137

pronounces an implacable and irreversible verdict. Anger and pity in turn never cease to move him, and give to his style an expressiveness and a rich glow of sentiment of which antiquity affords no other example."

The Romans now showed all the signs of a decaying people, losing interest in everything, even in amusements; and in literature, substituting minute learning for original thought. Writing grammars and commentaries on the poets was the chief occupation of men of letters, while professional rhetoricians confined their efforts to declaiming in Greek.

The downward tendencies of the age culminated in Fronto, 90–168, who was learned enough to be chosen by Antoninus Pius to educate Marcus Aurelius. A pedant of corrupt taste and clumsy affectation he could panegyrize an emperor or compose a rhetorical exercise on the "Praise of Dust and Smoke," with equal facility. Other rhetoricians, like Antonius, Julianus, Apollinaris, and Arruntius Celsus, devoted their talents to disputations on trivial subjects, such as afterward were discussed with grave formality in the scholastic debates of the middle ages.

One writer upon rhetoric there was who so far surpassed all the rest from Cicero to Fronto that the consideration of his work has been reserved until the others were disposed of, the last of whom he antedates by some fifty years. This was MARCUS FABIUS QUINTILIANUS, who taught at Rome, A. D. 90–110.

After an age of great literary activity generally comes one of reflection upon its products and a classification of them, in the form of a science, by some analytic and inductive mind. Such a one was Aristotle, reducing the practical rhetoric of the Attic orators to a science, followed by others, of whom Cicero was chief. Another writer on oratory now appears to perform a similar office for the Latins, after the age of Cicero and his contemporaries. He was a native of Spain, the son of a rhetorician who had removed to Rome. For twenty years after the accession of Galba he was at the head of the foremost school of oratory in the imperial city. He was not without some experience of his own in the courts of law, having gained some repute as an advocate, especially in the defence of the queen, Berenice, on some charge which is not reported. Vespasian placed him in a chair of rhetoric endowed with public funds, and from that time he was somewhat grandiloquently called the "supreme controller of restless youth." In this capacity he continued until he retired in order to compose his great work on the training of an orator. Ten years later he was intrusted by the emperor Domitian with the education of the two grand-nephews who he intended should succeed him.

Quintilian's relation to the literature and culture of his time is powerful and intimate, and illustrates the change which had come over Roman taste, feeling, and society. In the days of Cicero the Greeks had kept the monopoly of rhetorical teaching. The great orator himself half apologizes for writing rhetorical works, saying that it could not be disgraceful to teach what it was not disgraceful to learn. The Greek language, too, still remained the vehicle of instruction, and contained the masterpieces of oratory in the original form. The first attempt to open a Latin rhetorical school was crushed by authority, and no teacher of rhetoric had been born to the full rights of a Roman citizen till Augustus' time. Quintilian's appointment, therefore, marks the last stage in the emancipation of rhetorical teaching from the old Roman prejudices.

Education had spread enormously in the hundred years between Cicero and Quintilian, and its climax and end was in rhetoric. All other studies were tributary to skill in speaking, which in turn was the paramount qualification for a public career. Rome and the provinces resounded with declamations and exercises which were promoted by professorships of Greek, first, and then of Latin rhetoric, endowed with public money. Mock contests of oratory excited great interest among the people. The provinces, as usual, outdid the capital in the energy with which the pursuit was carried on, and bore richer fruit in the West than in the worn-out East. Especially from Spain came teachers who dominated literature at Rome, and the voluble Gaul was not altogether silent in the second century.

Quintilian, as an orator, teacher, and author, set himself to stem the tendency of his age to decry the Ciceronian style. Political reasons had made it unsafe to admire the great orator after his death, and it was not until the age of Seneca the Elder that many dared to esteem him highly. Quintilian makes Cicero his great model, who was to him almost without the possibility of a fault. He is at war incessantly with the fashion of his day, which was to rank the great Roman with rude antiquity, to poetize prose, and to practice a thousand tricks to produce startling effects upon judges, juries, and audiences. The *Institutes of Oratory* are a long protest against the tastes of his age. He takes the child from the cradle, and omits no detail of training from infancy upward through boyhood and youth. He demands for him the widest culture, that he may extract something from every kind of knowledge, and insists upon method while pleading for nature and reality.

He also develops the technicalities of rhetoric with unequaled fulness, and illustrates his subject in so apt and dignified a way that the reader is carried along with less fatigue than in the rhetorical writings of Aristotle and Cicero. He is the Roman gentleman of culture, of wide sympathies, and generous disposition and fair judgment, justifying the opinion that ancient literary criticism reached its highest point in Quintilian. Modest, winning, and attractive in demeanor, he was full of pathos and êthos, always maintaining that ethical education should be a part of the instruction which a rhetorician was set to impart. He was courtly and a bit of a flatterer to royalty, withal, as he was obliged to be if he wished to preserve that part of himself which is most useful in literary work; but courtiers in England two generations ago showed their wisdom in a similar manner.

In the discussion of oratory he follows Aristotle, with changes to suit the different requirements of a later age and another people. There are constant references to the practice of celebrated masters of the art, with examples introduced from the poets and historians. He insists upon a wide reading in order to acquire facility of speech, and gives an entire book to the cultivation of the memory, an important factor in the oratory of the ancients, before the use of aids in the shape of notes and manuscript were introduced. Delivery was another important feature of Roman oratory, receiving the most minute and extreme care as to the smallest details of action in order to produce desired effects. Gesture was freely used and the voice trained to the fullest compass. The moral qualities were also insisted on as the basis of all worthy eloquence, the good orator, in his view, being possible only as the good man. This is one cause of his admiration for Cicero, of whom he says, "I will boldly pitch him against any of the champions of the Greeks." His integrity, honor, and uprightness are insisted upon in the twelfth book of the *Institutes.*

He says further, "If Julius Cæsar had only found leisure for the forum he would be the one we should select as the rival of Cicero. He has such force, point, and vehemence of style, that it is clear he spoke with the same mind that he warred. Yet all is covered with a wondrous elegance of expression, of which he was peculiarly studious. There was much talent in Cæcilius, and I have found those who prefer Calvus to any orator, but Cicero's style is weighty, noble, guarded, and often vehement. Servius Sulpicius has earned considerable fame, and Cassius Severus affords many points for imitation, and of my own contemporaries Domitius Afer and Julius Africanus are by far the greatest, the former in art and general style, the latter in earnestness and the sorting of words. Trachalus is often sublime, but better to hear than to read. Vibius Crispus was neat, elegant, and pleasing, and Julius Secundus, if he had lived longer, would have had a first-class renown for his open, gentle, and specious style, his perfect selection of words, his vigorous application of analogies extemporaneously suggested. My successors in rhetorical criticism will have a rich field for praising those who are now living; for there are now great talents at the bar, worthy rivals of the ancients."

Thus did Quintilian run on in his criticism of the orators of his time. He was always genial and generous and discriminating. Even of Seneca, whom he had been charged with condemning, he says that he "only desired to prevent his being placed above better men, for his style was corrupt, and pleased through its pleasant faults. If he had not broken the weight of his subject by his short, cut-up sentences, and had used his own talent, modified and corrected by another's judgment, he would be approved by the consent of the learned, rather than by the enthusiasm of boys. Yet there is much that is good in him, much to admire; only it requires picking out, a thing he himself ought to have done. One who could always achieve his object ought to have striven after the best things."

This may be taken as a fair example of his generous criticism and as a striking contrast to much that is current in our own time. How much polemic and controversial doctrinaires have had to do with keeping up a pagan spirit, worse by far than that of Cicero or Quintilian, is a question that need not now be discussed.

One or two points in the work of this writer are worth retaining before he is dismissed. He was a ripe writer before he challenged the judgment of the world. His time had been so fully occupied with lecturing as to allow no time for publishing anything until the closing years of his career. His knowledge of the subject, therefore, has that fulness which comes from long acquaintance with it and love of it. He knew by practical experience that of which he wrote, as well as by familiarity with what others had written. Even then he was modest enough to express a strong unwillingness to write, fearing to come forward as an author so late in life, or judging the ground occupied already. But his treatise is the best proof that his fears were groundless. No sooner was it produced than it assumed at once the high position that has been accorded to it ever since. His treatment of the subject of oratory is thorough, exhaustive, attractive.

Beginning with such details as the learning of the alphabet, and writing and reading and pronunciation, and committing to memory, he passes on to the advantages of public schools, touching upon grammar and words, the necessity of correctness in speaking and writing and pronouncing, upon solecisms and foreign words, authority and custom as regulators of speech, upon historical reading, and reading in general. Then follow studies preliminary to rhetoric, the utility of music to the orator, and of geometry and astronomy. The value of the actor's instruction is estimated in matters of look and gesture and pronunciation, and also the necessity of exercise with reference to bodily presence, and the laws of gesture and a manly presence learned in the camp or palæstra rather than upon the boards of a theatre. So much for the beginning of the orator's training in boyhood. In the second book he emphasizes the importance of the best teachers at the start, "because they can teach little things best." Under the head of elementary exercises he mentions the narrative or simple statement of facts, asserting that exuberance is better than poverty of imagination; that the pupils should have but little assistance; and that they should declaim passages from eminent writers rather than their own compositions.

Passing on then to rhetoric and oratory, which he defines as the art of speaking well, he discourses of nature and art, and gives the opinions of the ancients about rhetoric; also of the sorts of oratory, laudatory, judicial, and deliberative; of proofs and evidence and argumentation; of arrangement, exordium, and peroration; of style and ornament; of figures of thought and speech; of speaking with propriety; of memory and delivery; and finally of the moral qualities of an orator.

This outline has been given to show how complete were the views taken by this master of the art, and how large a place it occupied in the teaching of youth at the beginning of our era. In its comprehensive scope were included all the arts and sciences in one way or another, and even much that we now call diversion or play. It was the education and training of the whole man for the highest exercise of his mind and body; and this, if gauged by the fatigue which such activity brings, may still be regarded as the most violent exercise; or, if estimated by the effect upon men and the community and society, it is still the highest labor that the highest order of men can perform. To do this, and to do it well, involved a particularity of treatment which was exhibited at its fullest twice in the ancient world; first by the Greek Aristotle, and second by the Latin Quintilian, each in his own way and according to the spirit of his time, but by both together with such fulness and exactness that little has been added since. The modern need is of treatises adapted to the changed conditions of modern life, its haste and impatience and practicality, without loss of the vital principles which underlie the minute and comprehensive work of the ancients.

The relation, then, which Quintilian bore to the orators was that of a judicious weigher of their worth; and to his own time he was a corrector of the false taste which had arisen after the death of Cicero, who had himself done so much to create a true one. Sound judgment and fairness, generally, were Quintilian's chief qualifications. Although he had a word of appreciation for diligent mediocrity his purpose was always to direct attention to the best efforts. Knowing what eloquence is he assisted the student to attain it by rules and maxims founded upon the experience of the best. And the judgment of posterity has coincided with his as to the value of different oratorical performances, as well as in the matter of an orator's training. The difficulty in these hurried days, when other callings conflict, is to make it the thorough business of a man's life, which the circumstances and conditions of antiquity allowed and public sentiment demanded.

XI.

PATRISTIC ORATORY—GREEK.

IN THE second century of our era there was a revival of Greek literature in the Roman Empire. Dio Chrysostom, Lucian, Arrian, and Marcus Aurelius brought to life again something of Attic wit, thought, and eloquence. The Greeks, in fact, had never quite discontinued the teaching and practice of the oratorical art. When it did not flourish at home they carried it into other provinces, and under the worst emperors they found something to do in keeping up its form, regardless of its power.

Side by side with these artificialities there was, here and there, a genuine attempt to proclaim simple truths of morality and natural religion under the guise of a less exclusive philosophy than had hitherto prevailed. As it spread, however, it began to be shallow and to teach trifles with rhetorical ardor. Meantime the world, in darkness, clamored for light and guidance. Importations of wisdom from every land, resulting in a theosophy in which "one supreme being could be envisaged by the soul for a moment like a flash of lightning," did not satisfy better than the indiscriminate worship that the emperor had brought together. The time had come for a new philosophy, a better religion, and, as a consequence, a new literature and a new proclamation of truth and law. This meant a new oratory to enlighten and elevate every order and every class.

First a new faith came, and while the Teacher of it was growing up in Galilee, Horace and Ovid and Livy died, and also their royal patron, the great Augustus. It was the death of Roman creative literature. While Quintilian, the rhetorician, was gathering up its remains at Rome an apostle of the new religion was explaining it to those who were curious to hear what a parolled prisoner from a tributary province could say of its doctrines. He met in Athens about this time a mobile crowd, full of the traditions of an eloquent past and of present Epicureanism, who were as eager to hear what "this babbler" would say as their ancestors had been to listen to the Leontine Gorgias, five centuries earlier. The speaker's name was PAULUS, from that Tarsus in Cilicia where Cicero had been governor less than a hundred years before, a place, according to Strabo, more illustrious than Athens or Alexandria in all that relates to philosophy and general education, a Greek city where that language was used and its literature studiously cultivated, and its authors publicly read and taught by Hellenic teachers in the schools. It is fitting, therefore, to take this converted Hebrew and Roman citizen of Greek culture from the neighborhood where eastern, western, and southern civilizations meet, and let him hand on the religion of the East and the culture of the South to the all-conquering West. He shall be the orator of the transition from the Orient to the Occident; from Judaism to Christianity; from Greek eloquence, dying at provincial Athens for want of liberty and truth, and from its imitation at Rome, smothered by despotism, to the freer speech and the higher inspiration and the profounder philosophy which were coming with the spread of a new revelation by an invigorated oratory. But two and three-quarter centuries must elapse before all this shall be. Not until freedom of speech shall come with Constantine will eloquence return.

When the shadow of terror and of death which hung over the persecuting ages finally passed away, the lips that were unsealed gave a new character to public speech. There is a wild irregularity about it, born of sudden release from long and bitter bondage to heathen rule. It cannot get its tongue immediately, and when, it does, gratitude to the imperial deliverer and to divine providence are strangely mingled. In the mind of antiquity, it must be remembered, the distance was short between the dignity and majesty of the emperor of the Roman world and that of the Ruler of the universe. Therefore it is not surprising that titles bordering upon idolatry should be used by a thankful people for the restoration of liberty to utter the thoughts of their hearts.

To speak definitely of the eloquence of the Greek fathers it must be judged by its best representatives, those strong spirits around whom mediocrity gathered and crystalized. One such leading mind appears just at the time when the Church begins to bask in the smiles of royal favor, a dangerous season of prosperity, far more perilous than the distressing period which kept the faithful constant and true to a single belief and a single purpose. No longer obnoxious to martyrdom they were inclined to division and contention.

The storm-centre of a great strife was at Nicæa in A. D. 325. The assemblage which the emperor summoned together represented the wisdom and power of Christendom. Even heathen philosophers were attracted to the place by the prospect of conference and debate. That, however, which bears most directly on the present subject is the circumstance that, of all the assembled dignitaries, the chief speaker was a young man from Alexandria named ATHANASIUS, a name which has had an undying celebrity for the highest eloquence on the loftiest themes. His most characteristic feature is singleness of purpose. One great truth has seized upon the speaker and has become all this world and the next to him. By it the life and death of men and nations is determined. Those who adhere to it are his friends and brethren, those who deny it are enemies and outcasts. In his exordiums there is no uncertainity about the position the speaker is going to take. Cicero against Catiline is no clearer, more definite, or dead in earnest. Nor has the great Roman a keener sense of impending danger than this defender of the faith.

That which characterizes the writings of Athanasius, after the oneness of his theme, is the almost infinite variety of its presentation. Nor is this the diversity of a judicious treatment of related or coördinate topics, admitting of discursive survey of adjacent territory. He never goes so far from his subject as that would involve. It resembles rather the ceaseless variety of combination in the kaleidoscope, which allows nothing foreign to come within the field of vision, but has more changes than all outside. To the modern reader this close adherence to the subject is apt to become as tiresome as the continuous looking at the parti-colored figures; but the wonder is greater when we remember that it is a human intellect which is presenting a new and near view of one and the same theme with every sentence of transition.

To read his orations, page after page, makes one sure that there is nothing more to be said without repetition; but that is to mistake the productive and versatile power of the writer. The very nature of this characteristic, running through hundreds of pages, forbids illustration by examples cited. Nor could it interest the modern hearer as it did the ancient. Indeed sometimes we cannot see the ground for the testimony that has come down to us as to the wonderful effect these orations produced upon contemporaries. As in the case of other productions about which have hung traditions of remarkable effectiveness it must be remembered that there was a subtle, elusive element that went along with them, the personality and high character of the speaker, and possibly that which is commonly called magnetism, in the lack of a better word. We do not find it between the pages and the lines, all of it. It lives only by suggestion and memory and tradition; but once it was the nearest thing to life itself, the very speech of the soul. No typographic art can embalm it; no power of the imagination reproduce it with fidelity and fulness. But once it was among men so full and so strong that it left its wave-marks upon the age, which in turn hardened and petrified into historic record. Aside, therefore, from the internal evidence of a great intellect contained in his works contemporaneous testimony enters into the estimate of any personage removed from us by the span of centuries. It is the only fair method of judging a representative man of any age to ask what the men of his time thought of him. His literary methods may not be agreeable to us, as ours would not have been to him, but if the hearers who listened to his words were entranced and the readers who perused them afterward were delighted, the criticism of the far future can afford to concur.

Nor is much assistance to a just estimate of such an orator to be derived from fragmentary and scattered quotations from his discourse, however carefully chosen. It will readily be admitted that a few paragraphs from volumes cannot adequately represent the unity and the harmony and the completeness of Athanasius' statement of the doctrine of the divinity of Christ. As well might one pick out a bit of polished stone here and of colored glass there from the matchless mosaic of Guercino and say, "Behold the majestic Prophet of the Wilderness!" It is only when one goes over, step by step, the interlacings of word and thought, of argument and illustration, mastering the details so well that he can afford to observe the larger relations and grouping of coördinate and contrasting values, that both the unity and comprehensiveness of this great defence can be estimated; a defence to which the author consecrated every faculty of his being. Add to this the measures of intervening time and the difference of language, race, civilization, and phases of religion, and it becomes still more difficult to understand how great this man was whom his contemporaries called "Athanasius the Great."

His townsmen tried to express their sense of his services by placing him upon the archiepiscopal throne of Alexandria, within five months after his return from the council. He might as well have been made Bishop of Babel.

For into that metropolis of Egypt and market-place of the nations came men from the East and the West, with their fabrics and their wares, with their wisdom and their folly. The home mysteries of the Nile struck hands with what remained of Plato's tenets among the witty and lively Greeks. Gnosticism was making its pretensions to greater knowledge since Judaism had lived in the Chaldee provinces; disciples of Buddha and Brahma and Zoroaster brought their creeds and their philosophies to this seat of learning. Here the Old Testament Scriptures had been made known to the heathen by the Septuagint version; and here Christianity early took root and grew luxuriantly, but with many a rank weed of heresy transplanted from pagan soils. And then came divisions and sects and schisms innumerable. For fifty-six years in his cathedral at Alexandria, or in a hermit's cave in Thebais, or in some distant city of the West, Athanasius' pen and voice were always employed. Clear, forcible, persuasive, with an eloquence natural, manly, and direct, subtle and acute as any Greek in argument, but above all mere contentiousness about words, he represents the best that survived the decay of oratory in its ancient forms, renewed and reinvigorated by the spirit and power of the new faith. He is the accurate master of the divine science at a time and in a place when it needed sharp discrimination and wide separation from counterfeits. His logic and rhetoric were the buttress of many who could not of themselves give the reason of their faith; his defence of the truth was like an ancient temple, vast in extent and perfect in proportion, from whose wealth of material later builders have quarried their lesser structures in all succeeding centuries.

As Athanasius was the exponent of doctrine, so John of Antioch, surnamed CHRYSOSTOM by the generation which lived two hundred years later, was the preacher of righteousness and censor of iniquity. The descendant of a noble family, educated according to the custom of the time in rhetoric and philosophy, having a natural inclination toward oratory, he passed four years in seclusion, meditation, and in the composition of his treatises, and five years more in study at Antioch, to fit himself for a work from which hastily prepared preachers would shrink in these impatient days. Three times a week, and sometimes seven days successively, he set forth the meaning of the sacred text, now a paragraph and then a whole book, as the manner was at that time. Not to empty pews nor to regular church-goers alone, for Jews and pagans and the motley throng as well as the learned and the cultivated came streaming from every street to hear the latest message he had to deliver. Of profound erudition, large and grand in apprehension, keen in perception of what to say and when to say it, and, what is harder, when to keep silence, he was at the flood-tide of success and popularity at the very start. A prevailing characteristic of his speech is a pointed directness, combined with a dignified familiarity that went straight to the understanding and conscience of his hearers. He spoke as if his pulpit were in every pew and not at the conventional distance from all the pews. With an ardent temperament, an irascible manner, a forcible expression, and a genuine hatred of shams he lacked somewhat the geniality, the tact, and the suave manner which would have helped the less agreeable virtues. His acidity was undiluted.

Accordingly when he fulminated against immorality in a city which was oriental, and moderately Christian, his maledictions seemed intolerable. He attacked avarice and luxury until it was complained that he was stirring up the poor against the rich. He execrated the theatre and the circus, the cheap consolations for thraldom to a despot, and the multitude execrated him in turn. He descended to trifles, sometimes, and seemed to confound little things with great. The ear-rings, the gold bits for horses, the rich carpets, the marble and ivory walls, the silver couches, the gold utensils, in all these luxuries he saw nothing but their price for distribution to the poor. He advised the dandies of the city to wear their magnificent boots on their heads. He rebuked the ladies for their silk robes and gold embroideries, and drew vivid pictures of the prevailing gluttony and frivolity. At the same time he gave vent to unsparing invective on the lax attendance at church, which led to improvement, indeed, but enthusiasm evaporated in applause of his preaching or crocodile tears of repentance.

Still Chrysostom was not so wholly absorbed by the work of reformation among his people that he could not have an eye to the larger affairs of the Christian world. He obtained fresh decrees from the emperor for the suppression of paganism, and sent forth missionaries into various lands, above all among the Goths, in whom his prophetic vision saw the future conquerors of the Roman empire. He was equally free from the ambition for worldly dominance; otherwise he might have been the most powerful person in the capital and have controlled the destinies of the Eastern Empire through his strength of character, weakened though it was in its influence by the austerity of his demeanor and the violence of his speech, qualities which had accompanied him from the desert cave to corrupt cities. For though men revered the monastic life they shrunk from much share in its strictness; and when reformation went on too fast in high ecclesiastical places, and the empress herself became alienated from her former favorite, the ultimate fate of the uncompromising apostle of righteousness was sealed. It was then a series of banishments from one remote place of exile to another. Nicæa first, then the black valley of Cucusus; and when his friends found him there he was hurried on between two soldiers toward the shores of the inhospitable Euxine, until he fell by the way and was buried in a martyr's grave.

There were others belonging to this group who deserve mention: Basil of Cæsarea, Gregory of Nazianzum, Diodorus of Tarsus, and Gregory of Nyssa. First in order is BASIL of Cæsarea. A defender of the advantages of pagan learning, a scholar of elegant attainments he became an orator prominent among the orators of his time, and a philosopher among philosophers. His education was Greek, Latin being then regarded as barbarian. Homer, Hesiod, and the tragedians were not withheld from the young theologian, nor Herodotus, Thucydides, and Demosthenes. His oration on the study of classical literature is full of interest, as showing how possible it is to draw from the pages of the classics lessons of virtue and practical religion. He, too, was in no haste to become a preacher, giving thirty years of study in preparation for a work which lasted twenty years.

The eloquence of Basil is conceded to be in many respects worthy of comparison with that of the best Greek orators. He had their earnestness and sincerity, with the new inspiration. It is the oriental fire of Isaiah, chastened with Greek culture. He has the power of impressing a central thought upon the hearer, compelling him to dwell upon it without monotony by contemplating it from different points, in shifting light and shade. His personal and practical teachings might have an interest at the present day, showing as they do that all ages resemble one another in the things of every-day life. For instance in those days certain would-be scientists declared that they were descended from the shell-fish of a remote geologic age. Basil's reply is that very likely this is true, judging from the products of their brains and the results of progressive evolution, as it is now termed. Again he hits off the usurer with no money to lend until a high rate of interest is mentioned; is sharp on the corn speculators, who hold back the grain and keep up the price until there is a famine. He animadverts upon houses with troops of servants, and shining with marbles, mosaics, and gold. Nor does he spare the multitude and their half-pagan doings, their heathenish talk, their religion mixed with astrology and belief in charms and the black art. The feminine part of his congregation gave him much annoyance, as was the case with Chrysostom. On one occasion he says, " Light-headed women shook off the yoke of decency, shook out their hair, trailed their tunics with tripping feet, and with glancing eyes and peals of laughter danced like Bacchanals, and inviting the attention of the young men arranged their dances in the very church. How can I keep silence about such things? I deal sharply with my best friends, if they act contrary to what is right, and do not win followers by introducing the manners of the bar and the theatre into the sanctuary." It is not difficult to see that Basil's preaching was not calculated to win popularity.

Of GREGORY NAZIANZEN as much might be said as of the others, but the best testimony to the character and value of his oratory is his own estimate of it when he declares, "I have retained nothing for myself except eloquence, nor do I regret any of the labor and risks I ran on sea and land in search of it. I would desire this gift in perfection for myself and all my friends. After the duties of religion and hopes of things invisible it is the possession I have most cherished and to which I cling the most. I retain no art save that of language; it is my choice, and I would not willingly forsake it; for I take more delight in it than if I added thereto all that forms the delight of most men. Eloquence shall be the companion of my life, my faithful counselor and depository of all my confidence, my helper in battle and my guide on my heavenward path. Since I have despised all earthly pleasures my heart has the more turned toward eloquence, for it leads insensibly to God, and teaches us to know Him more dearly and preserves and strengthens that knowledge in us."

Of all this time it is just to say that it was full of unrest. The storm of persecution which had raged for three and a quarter centuries was over, indeed, but the tumult had not subsided, the troubled sea still cast up mire and dirt. The heathen had ceased to rage with fire and sword, but the people still gathered together in factions and imagined vain things and quarreled over trifles. Therefore the disciples of the new faith, no longer required to bear witness by martyrdom, were compelled to defend it by appeal to the reason and conscience of men. Especially were they called upon to distinguish it from other gospels that were being diligently taught, and to discriminate between its code of morals and those of the various philosophies and religions which prevailed in that century of disintegration.

To be a formative and reconstructive power in such a time required elements of mind and soul stronger than in any preceding crisis in history. The issues at stake were greater than those involved in any panhellenic union against oriental despotism which had inspired Athenian orators, or those bound up with the republicanism which was defended and supported by Roman eloquence, or blended with the ruin of a declining empire. A greater foe than Philip was invading a larger kingdom than Greece, and the freedom that was to be established was for an empire greater than Cæsar's. Therefore the cause to be maintained was more sacred, and the demand for able advocates more imperative. Measured by the standards of high art the orators of the fourth century after Christ may not conform to the standards of the Attic age, more than a Christian church conforms to the pagan temple in ideal architecture; but we all are ready to admit that the motive and purpose and value of the cathedral outweigh those of the heathen temple a hundredfold, as expressions of the religious sentiment of the human family. So also is it with the oratory of the Greek fathers as compared with that of the Greek statesmen in earlier ages. The ruling ideas are what give inspiration to each. Great and noble as is the love of a native land, and laudable as may be the ambition for a city's preëminence, and deeply as these things may stir the heart of man, there are profounder depths in his soul, and higher ambitions for the life that is endless. These interests and ambitions, being so much more real and great and strong, may so possess the whole man that the expression of them shall be somewhat untamed and irregular, wild and uncouth at times, it may be; but they will, like all voices of nature, speak to the natural man with a directness and a force which he cannot resist.

It was in this way that Athanasius spoke at Nicæa, and Basil at Cæsarea, and Gregory at the Second General Council, and Chrysostom at Antioch and Constantinople. And we compare their eloquence with that of Pericles and Isæus, Isocrates and Demosthenes, as we compare the Asian splendor of the church of Holy Wisdom, in the Christian city of Constantine, with the severe perfection of the Parthenon in that Greek city where it was harder to find a man than a god. Some there are who will prefer one of these styles to the other, and many will desire a due mingling of both, but none will deny that the inspiring motive of the later eloquence is above that of the elder, and that it elevated the oratory of the Greek fathers above that of their predecessors in all that belongs to the highest interests of mankind. Still one cannot help imagining what a legacy the old Athenian orators might have left to Christendom if the higher truth had come to them in the days of their glory; if to perfection of form had been added the inspiration of a larger revelation. Nor should it be forgotten how much they indirectly contributed, by their achievements in the narrow domain of Hellas, to the extension of the greater kingdom that was to come four centuries later.

XII.

PATRISTIC ORATORY—LATIN.

FOR the first three centuries the Christian religion was mainly Greek in its outward form. Its gospels had been recorded in Greek, and its truths proclaimed in the same tongue. The cities where its churches were built were Greek cities, in which the results of the great Alexander's conquests were more apparent than effects of a later Roman domination, while Greek philosophy, tinged with orientalism, prevailed in all the intellectual centres of the Empire. By their political or commercial prominence certain cities like Alexandria, Antioch, Ephesus, and Constantinople gathered in strong minds and controlling spirits and placed them in positions of influence and authority. But when paganism became extinct Greek Christianity appears to have accomplished its mission. Greek language and thought had done the work which needed to be done in proclaiming the new message to the nations, and in differentiating it from the former religions and philosophies that were trying to prolong their effete existence by affiliation with its immortal life. And having done its work so well that it needed not to be done again Greek Christianity handed over its trophies to the Latin church, which in turn was to accomplish results that the West was better fitted to secure than the East.

TERTULLIAN, of Carthage, was the first western orator

and writer who commanded public attention. From the first Latin had been the language of African theology, and of the five or six greatest names among the earlier western fathers three, Tertullian, Cyprian, and Augustine, were from the North African coast. Out of a region famous for its constancy to the truth it is natural to look for such a man as Tertullian, a prophet lifting up his voice in the silence which prevailed in the dreadful reigns of Commodus and Septimius Severus. The son of a Roman centurion, educated liberally in Greek language and literature, familiar with its poetry and mythology, and having some acquaintance with its philosophy, he became an aggressive Christian as he had been a violent pagan. Somewhat gloomy and not wholly free from superstition about demons, dreams, and visions he plunges into controversy with the training of a lawyer and the inherited zeal of a soldier. The whole world appears to him like a battlefield between the Christian host and demons. John Bunyan had not more vivid revelations in Bedford jail, nor Martin Luther in his study, nor Dunstan more lurid visions at his forge.

A turbulent spirit in a violent age he exults in strife. Pagans and Christians alike are treated with audacious and unsparing severity when there is occasion. Magistrates and the public are addressed in terms which belong to a man who must have believed that he held a charmed life. He taunts the heathen with gross injustice and flings back their counter-charges upon themselves and their gods, telling them that Tartarus itself is peopled with wretches who most resemble their own deities. He denounces their idol worships as senseless; he pours forth his maledictions upon their bloodthirsty games and then, after declaring the innocence of their victims, he exclaims, "Now, O wretched Gentiles, I will grapple with you about your gods!" He does not do this by halves. Elijah's mockeries of Baal are flatteries beside Tertullian's scoffing jeers. Why the descendants of the old worshippers of the Sidonian god did not rebuild the image-furnace and toss him into its fiery arms can be explained only upon the belief that the same providence that kept the three children saved this bold spirit to be the scourge of paganism. To some who had blamed a soldier for refusing a laurel crown from heathen hands Tertullian says, "The only gospel precept they care to remember in persecution is to pack up their baggage and flee from one city to another." In the longest and most elaborate of his writings he attacks Marcion, first by characterizing the country where he was born as a sunless, misty, wintry region of savages; and then adds, "But nothing there is so gloomy as this man, more grim than a Scythian, more ruthless than a Massagete, darker than a cloud, chillier than winter, more brittle than ice, more treacherous than the river, more intolerable than the wild beasts." This would not now be accepted as a model of controversial style, and even then it deserved some of the criticism it received; but if a good hater ever deserved approbation it was Tertullian.

There was plenty to stir a strong, fearless man. Unmixed paganism and a mixed and African Christianity together furnished social and intellectual obliquities enough to craze a vehement soul upon which truth and righteousness had taken fast hold. When Scapula, going beyond Trajan's decree of death by the sword, ordered Christians to be burnt, Tertullian says, "We do not fear or dread you in the least. We shudder at your future destiny. We worship one God; you worship demons. Numerous as we are, almost the larger half of the citizens, we obey all lawful authority, and sacrifice for the emperor, but with prayers and not bloodoffering in which demons revel. We grieve at the calamities you will bring upon yourselves. Scant harvests, cataclysms of rain, fiery visions over the walls of Carthage, are meant to warn you. Think of the misfortunes which have fallen on you personally since you condemned Mavilus of Adramentum to the wild beasts! I warn you not to fight against God." It is the last of the recorded language of the great Latin soldier of the cross. Narrow, intense, unorthodox in his later years, by reason of his extreme views, he was nevertheless strong in righteousness in an age of mingled good and evil. He was eloquent with the power of undaunted sincerity, rough in speech, but unmistakable in his meaning. He was not all bitterness, however, as his panegyric on the family and his beautiful tribute to Divine Goodness abundantly show. All in all he was the most powerful speaker and writer who had appeared since the impetuous St. Peter. The creator of a Latin Christian literature he is rich in thought and learning, though careless of form. Too fervid in his nature to be restrained by rules he suffers from mistakes which rules would have prevented. But in spite of this marring and wasting his fierce and turbulent eloquence has left its volcanic monument on the north African shore.

PATRISTIC ORATORY—LATIN. 165

By the middle of the fourth century all the broad West and the far-off islands have begun to hear of the coming of a new empire, no longer in the lowliness and distress of its beginnings, but with something of power and majesty. Kings and nobles are in its train, peace and war are at its bidding. And now that it is safe and honorable to be its citizens there will be need of wisdom to guide and speech to control the populations in a tumultuous time when the northern tribes are coming to feast in the South. Who, then, is to be the foremost man to defend the faith in the age when each human interest must fight for its place or go down in the general struggle?

AMBROSE of Milan was the son of a governor of Gaul. As a youth he had every advantage that wealth and station could offer. He was educated for the highest civil offices, to which he was easily in the line of promotion. After gaining great reputation as a rhetorician and distinguishing himself in the profession of the law he was elected President of Upper Italy, and at length Bishop of Milan. The motive of his oratory can be traced to his zeal in refuting the great error in the West which Athanasius was combating in the East. In this contest he was approved not only by the half of his fellow citizens, but also by the Empress Justina herself. We might expect, therefore, that his words would be chosen with such care and constructive significance as his legal and rhetorical training would lead him to adopt, having an eye to imperial favor as well as to the truth, as he held it. By no means. He spoke as a king on his own cathedral throne to the emperor and empress, whom he regarded as in the church but not over it; spoke with boldness, dignity, and consistency. He did not meddle in imperial affairs, nor did he permit royalty to interfere with his own. His preaching was almost continuous, every Sunday, and sometimes for days together in the great Basilica. His voice was feeble, but the nobleness of his thoughts, the perspicuity of his ideas, the variety of his learning, and the elegance of his language drew crowds of attentive and admiring hearers. From the far East and from remote Africa came back the echo of his reputation, while at home the complaint sprang up that his eloquence was winning the members of noble families, especially the daughters, to the seclusion of the cloister. He used to reply to such censures by asking if they could mention a single instance of a young man looking for a wife who had the least difficulty in finding one. One of the greatest of his oratorical triumphs was his reply to the noblest and most eloquent advocate of a decaying heathenism, the prefect Symmachus, when he appeared before the emperor to plead for the restoration of the Altar of Victory in the senate house. It was the last conflict in words between a dying but venerable "pagan creed outworn" and the growing faith. The refutation of his adversary's arguments was easy, and a return to idolatry was prevented.

In an encounter with the empress the populace rose on all sides in his favor. For days there was a riotous disturbance, quelled at last only by the discourse of Ambrose upon "Patience," which the soldiers who had been sent to surround the church were so eager to hear that they joined themselves to the people and listened attentively. His oratory, however, could be tender as well as severe. His eulogy upon the youthful Valentinian, who had been assassinated on the banks of the Rhone, and for Gratian, is like the lament of David for Saul and Jonathan. " Oh, my Gratian, my Valentinian, beautiful and most dear, how brief your term of life, how near together your sepulchres! Inseparable in life, not separated in death! Woe is me, what pledges have I lost! How are the mighty fallen and the weapons of war perished!" With such words he opened the funeral oration for emperors who regarded him as their sole, effective guardian. With similar words he pronounced the eulogy over the great and good Theodosius, of which it has been justly said that if it was less magnificent than that of Massillon over Louis Fourteenth it was at least more sincere and far better deserved.

It need not be affirmed that Ambrose was the greatest of Latin orators. The secret of his eloquence cannot all be found in the words that have been recorded. Contemporary testimony is afforded in the saying of a general whose march he stopped by persuasive speech, "Ambrose came into my camp, spoke words, and I gave up my hostile purpose; I know not why." The second time he would not see him for fear of a power which he could neither resist nor explain. The outward sign of it was the straightforwardness and sincerity of his speech; the inward power is too subtle for analysis. Ambrose writes like a man of large knowledge of human nature, as became a jurist and a magistrate, and as one who was familiar with the Greek classics and with such science as was then known, though always modest in the domain of theology, because he had come to its study so late. But in the sphere of morals and of practical, direct instruction he is unsurpassed. His sermons, abounding in allusions to the trials and vicissitudes of that uncertain time, told with thrilling effect upon the congregations of Milan. In the dark misery of the time, with its deep chasm between boundless wealth and poverty most abject, its grinding burdens of an insolent army and luxurious court, with no redress to be hoped for from an isolated emperor, with cities growing in size and distress, and a countryside at the mercy of famine-breeding speculators, the voice of Ambrose was raised against the oppressive greed of the wealthy on one side, and on the other against the lying imposture of mendicants. He denounced the vices of drunkenness and reveling, rebuked the perfumed youths, the women with their silver couches and jeweled cups, and the men who cared more for their horses and hounds than their fellow Christians. Half-pagan superstitions had veiled themselves under a thin disguise of Christianity, and these he did not fail to inveigh against.

Considered in its widening influence the greatest triumph of his oratory was the conversion of Augustine, who had come to Milan as a professor of rhetoric. At the earliest opportunity he went to hear the great preacher, not for the truth he taught, but because he was eloquent and attractive. Almost unconsciously the matter of the discourse began to interest the critical listener, and from that moment onward the story is that of a man asking for light. It belongs to another great orator, and may serve as the introduction to the character of his eloquence.

AURELIUS AUGUSTINUS, the greatest of the Latin fathers, was born A. D. 296, in an obscure town in Africa, and grew up under the influence of a heathen father, whose chief ambition for his son was that he should become a rhetorician and lawyer. Oratory became his chief study, as it was of most young men in the ancient world, with such other studies as would most contribute to success in public speech. Of the advantages offered at Carthage he made sufficient use to gain the applause of his teachers and rose to a high position in the school of oratory. He was early established as a teacher of rhetoric in the city and was soon making his own way in the world. His chief desire was to have good pupils "to whom without wiliness he might teach wiles; not that they might injure the innocent, but sometimes defend the guilty." His desire was gratified in the main at Carthage; but there was a gang of turbulent youths called the "Upsetters," who, protected by a bad custom, were allowed to burst into the classes of any professor whom they chose to disturb and break up the lecture. Quitting the city in disgust he went to Rome, where such incursions were forbidden by law; but then the cheating of professors out of their fees was not forbidden. Accordingly when a body of students had learned as much as they desired of one professor, they passed into another lecture room and left term-bills unpaid. This is what Augustine got for teaching what he called in later years "a most wretched and most furious loquacity."

One more deliverance came in his election to a professorship at Milan, where his success opened to him a new career, and where a fixed salary placed him beyond the uncertainties of academic finance. It would be of interest to speak of his pupils, afterward men of eminence, and of his methods of instruction. Suffice it to say that in Augustine's time it was largely a matter of declamation from the old orators, and of the pupil's own compositions on light themes, together with oral discussions which were taken down by a shorthand reporter in a remorseless way for future examination. There were lively disputes then, as now, over what should be allowed to stand uncorrected; and some of these boyish faults have been preserved in the amber of the teacher's writings to this day. A Greek in acuteness, a Roman in wisdom, and eloquent as a preacher he was clear, noble, and devout in the writings which he composed through a period of fifty-four years. They abound in passages of fervid emotion and undying beauty, written from the fulness of his mind and heart. Everywhere, however, the metaphysical and speculative bent is seen, although he makes faith to go before discovery, as great discoverers have always done in every department of knowledge. It is as true of Augustine's *Summum Bonum* and his *Enchiridion* as of a western continent and of the planet Neptune. How far Augustine's eloquence contributed to his undying influence is not easy to say. If men were first attracted by his spoken discourse, the written treatise has also been helped by the same qualities of style which are found in the oratory of this great Latin father. Author of mediæval scholasticism and mysticism through a dialectic mind and a devout spirit he is also in sympathy with what is now called protestantism, and was a forerunner of the Reformation. A man of his own time he also is a prophet of a transition age, standing between the old civilization, passing away before a barbaric invasion, and a new order which was to succeed the pagan.

The closing period of patristic oratory is best represented by LEO the Great, the man who combined the practical imperialism of old Rome with the faith so long apologetic, but at last triumphant. Moreover in the general disintegration of a rotten society and in the alarm excited by the approach of northern barbarians Leo had stood between the devoted city and the wrath of Attila. Encamped where the Mincius flows into Lake Benacus, his cavalry trampling the ground which once was the farms of Catullus and Virgil, the Goth awaited a solemn and suppliant embassy, sent by the emperor, senate, and people of Rome to deprecate his vengeance against the Eternal City. At the head of the ambassadors was Leo, the Bishop, in the robes of his office, majestic in mien, persuasive and urgent in his eloquence. The barbarian monarch was moved to veneration for the spiritual father of the Christians, and listened with respectful and favorable attention, consenting to evacuate Italy on conditions which his speedy death made it unnecessary to fulfil. But Leo was credited with saving Rome from the most terrible of barbarian conquerors by his urgent and commanding eloquence. Again, years afterward, when the Vandals were clamoring at the very gates of Rome, Leo once more mitigated the fierceness of the invader by the same eloquence, full of authority and intrepidity. His name stands forth in that time as the only great one in Christendom, in state or church.

A Roman by birth and sentiment he was the embodiment of the ambition, the unyielding perseverance, the dignity, the self-confidence, the belief in title to dominion, the respect for law and custom, which belonged to the noblest of the ancient race. Surveying a world chaotic in the breaking up of old beliefs and full of the errors which were cast up like scum in the conflict of superstitions brought from every quarter of the earth he sees with the eye of a prophet an ultimate reorganization, and seizes with the grasp of a leader the opportunity to reconstruct and to reanimate.

The pulpit is where he will stand to move the world in the direction he has marked out. He knows that the rostrum is still the guiding power which the people obey, when the genuine orator appears and when they are free to follow his counsels. He enters the pulpit, therefore, as a man with a mission to his own age and people, with the high confidence of a commanding mind. Sure of his own strength he feels able to cope with the popular uncertainty and unrest. His sermons, accordingly, are not Greek in subtlety of discrimination, in profundity of erudition, in picturequeness of imagery. They are brief, direct, and plain. They are also as effective as the Roman short-sword in the hand of a Roman. There was no foil-play of the fencer. Through complexities of controversy intricate as chain-armor, through defences of error cunning as scales triply plated the word of Leo pierced, dividing asunder the soul and body of opposing faction; condemning the vices of the people, dictating the decalogue anew, and announcing with authority a neglected gospel. Nor was he less plain in his practical preaching, especially in his reprehension of the pagan craze for the amphitheatre. "I am ashamed to speak, but I ought not to keep silence. Demons are of more account to you than apostles, and insane exhibitions get a better attendance than the martyr commemorations."

To emperors, also, he is equally plain in speech, and while showing the traditional respect for royalty, such as an Englishman has at this day, he addresses earthly sovereigns as an equal, or, more often, as their master, in the consciousness that to assume the noblest responsibility of preserving Rome and Christendom itself from threatened barbarism he was supporting the majesty of religion. Such assumption could not have been sustained by simple assertion. If he had stood up in the Basilica and said, "I am Leo, successor of Peter, and am going to establish the spiritual and temporal dominion of Rome," it is probable that, as at Athens four hundred years before, some would have mocked, and others would have said, "We will hear thee again of this matter." The measure of his oratorical power must, therefore, be found in the accomplishment of his designs. He did not, indeed, avert the final catastrophe, when the wealth and pride of the Imperial City were transported to Carthage in ships of Genseric; but on the ruins of paganism he founded a spiritual and ecclesiastical empire, which became the refuge of Europe until the times of regeneration came after a thousand years. He could not have done this except by an eloquence which stirred and led a people from whom the traditions of ancient oratory had by no means departed. Or if they had been lost, the illustrations of a fresh and powerful eloquence were not beyond their hearing in the pulpits of Milan and Treves and Rome itself. The pulpit alone was the guide and leader of opinion and the instructor of the people. It had the entire field to itself, with no competitors.

Furthermore oratory was the chief study of the ancients; their schools were schools of rhetoric, their teachers rhetoricians. It is not strange, then, that in the early Christian centuries the apt pupils of these schools should find their way into the pulpit, some of them having been teachers of the rhetorical science and art, like Ambrose and Augustine and Basil.

Among the Latin fathers Leo was the practical preacher rather than the cultivated orator, like Chrysostom, or the refined theologian, like Athanasius. He resembled more nearly the rugged Antiphon of the early Greek period, or, still more, the elder Cato, lawyer, soldier, and orator of republican Rome. His style is earnest, forcible, and full of thought; and if sometimes heavy, turgid, and obscure it is because it is loaded with the multitude of things he has to say, which to him are apparently of more consequence than the manner in which they are said. Once more it must be believed that the tremendous personality of the man lay back of his speech, giving to his words a piercing power like arrows from a bow which Ulysses alone could bend. It is the shadowy image only of the great Leo that we discern behind the printed page, after fourteen hundred years.

It was a hundred and thirty years before another such appeared. If two renaissance-centuries after Chaucer were needed in order to produce a Shakespeare, it is not strange that, in declining ages, four generations should pass away before a GREGORY should come to the chair of Leo, and like him, obtain from contemporaries and from posterity the agnomen of "the Great." Still his greatness was not, like Leo's, in the gift of speech. Each of the rude tribes of Europe had now a dialect of its own, and oratory must be a thing of local power and provincial character. Bernard will be great at Clairvaux, Peter the Hermit at Liege, Philip of Neri at Rome, and Savonarola at Florence. One and all will turn back for their model and oratorical inspiration to Ambrose and Augustine, to Hilary and Leo, as these in turn must have received their impetus in no small degree from the Greek fathers before them, Athanasius and Basil, the two Gregories and Chrysostom, and these again from the old Athenian orators.

Taken all together this period was one of oratorical power to which there has been but one parallel—in that fourth century, B. C., when Antiphon, Gorgias, and Lysias, Isæus, Isocrates and Demosthenes made Attica a synonym for eloquence. But there was a difference between the two periods in their respective motive and purpose which is symbolized by the legend of the Cypriote king who carved for himself a statue of marvelous perfection, but valuable, chiefly, as a wondrous interpretation of the laws of form. It was when he prayed that the ivory might become animate that there came into the matchless harmony of proportion movement and understanding and trust and faith and love and devotion. So into the chaste eloquence of the Hellenic age was breathed the spirit of a new and higher life, in an age of sacred oratory, moving men to a loftier understanding, a profounder faith, a sincerer trust, a nobler devotion, and a surer hope of immortality.

XIII.

MEDIÆVAL PREACHERS.

THE age of patristic eloquence ends with the death of Leo the Great, A. D. 461. The fourscore years between him and Gregory, A. D. 540, are noted for writers rather than for orators. Vincent of Lerins, Prosper of Aquitaine, Boëthius, and Cassiodorus compose treatises on the Scriptures, canon law, philosophy, and traditions of the saints. A century later Isidore becomes a chronicler, and Ildefonse writes of illustrious men in the West, while John of Damascus concentrates the expiring energies of Greek theology in the East, about A. D. 700. Monasticism absorbs the great body of ecclesiastics, and the ritual of the service receives more attention than preaching. What there is of this becomes theatrical and finally falls into neglect, and therefore into disrepute.

The Middle Ages begin at the middle of the eighth century with the rise and growth of a new Roman empire in the West, Franco-German, in alliance with the papacy, which now exalts its claims to universal obedience and enters into contests with princes. The great men of the time for a hundred years are compilers and chroniclers, jotting down records of councils, papal appointments, and wars. Under Charlemagne schools begin to be established teaching the famous *Trivium* and

Quadrivium—grammar, dialectics, rhetoric; music, arithmetic, geometry, and astronomy, A. D. 750. Rabanus, poet-laureate, writes a commentary; Ratramn, *Concerning Predestination;* also Hincmar and John Scotus; while Alfred the Great translates the *Psalms* and Gregory's *Pastoral* into Saxon, A. D. 880.

When oratory is sought for in these ages of oppression and superstition it will be found in the pulpit if at all. Early in the seventh century the voice of one Paulinus was heard in the wilderness above the mumbling controversies about image worship and scholastic subtleties. The chroniclers of the time declare that there were few such preachers as this archbishop of York, who could convert a whole township by a single sermon. Tall of stature, of reverend and majestic mien, with the look of a scholar, he was chosen to expound the doctrines of Christianity before the king and the chief of the Druid priests. He did this so effectively that the Druid called for a spear and a horse, and charged at the door of a temple where his idols were, and commanded his followers to finish the work of destruction which he had begun. This brief chronicle, coming out of the darkness of Northumbrian paganism before the year 650, shows that the power of the spoken Word was still prevailing here and there.

A clearer record comes to us in the literary remains of the VENERABLE BEDE, monk of Wearmouth and Jarrow on the Tyne, A. D. 672. He is the historian of England down to the eighth century, a man of varied attainments, pursuing a life of study in the monasteries, which were the colleges of that time. Such a man would not, of course, be a Chrysostom or an Ambrose, dealing with sinners in corrupt cities. His was rather the oratory which corresponds to that of an Oxford or Cambridge university-preacher, dealing with theological themes for the defence and confirmation of the faith. Forty-seven of his sermons are on the course of the ecclesiastical year, setting forth objective truths in the order of the calendar, in a scholarly and practical way. Twenty-two belong to the Lenten season, and forty-eight were delivered on days commemorating the saintly characters who have been eminent enough to be canonized in the good opinion of succeeding ages. Twenty more of a different character are manifestly intended for country congregations. It was in the darkest period of letters that this man became the embodiment of what learning survived the decay of Roman literature. And if as an orator he cannot be ranked with the great preachers of the fourth century, he certainly kept alive the spark of eloquence until better conditions for it appeared.

It is a remarkable fact that in the general dearth of mental activity in the East, Britain, in the remotest West, should become the home of learning, such as it was. Grammar, philosophy, and theology were cultivated in England, and particularly in Ireland, when much of the continent of Europe was in the shadow of an intellectual eclipse. The great religious houses did an inestimable service to learning in the multiplication of manuscripts, not only of the Scriptures but also of the classic authors of antiquity. And this at a time when the destruction of that great treasure-house of antiquity, the Alexandrian library, had made scarce and costly the works of the ancients. So great, indeed, had become the literary activity of the British Isles that a Saxon school was founded at Rome, and learning and religion were carried together to the provinces of the Rhine. Moreover Theodore of Tarsus came to Canterbury out of that Athens of Asia Minor where St. Paul grew up, bringing an inheritance of Greek culture which he diffused in England. Of it the Venerable Bede is the chief representative.

That eloquence was possible in this time of general ignorance and that this Greek importation, together with the treasures of Latin literature held in the religious houses of Northumbria, did something for oratory in a rude age may be seen from the following extract from Bede's sermon on the glories of the celestial country: "Wherefore there is no night there, no darkness, no gathering clouds, no asperity of cold or heat. . . . But above all things is the association with angels and archangels, thrones and dominations, principalities and powers, and to behold the squadrons of the saints adorned with stars, the patriarchs glittering with faith, the prophets rejoicing in hope, the apostles who, in the twelve tribes of Israel, shall judge the world. But of the King, who is in the midst, no words are able to speak. That beauty, that virtue, that glory, that magnificence, that majesty surpasses every expression and every sense of the human mind. For it is greater than the glory of all the saints to attain to that ineffable sight and to be made radiant with the splendor of His countenance. . . . Is it not, then, well worth while to endure earthly sorrows, that we may be partakers of such good and such glory?"

The man who could write such sentences as these must have communed with what is best among the ancients.

Frequent journeys were made to Rome, and from its treasures works of literature and art were brought continually. Along with relics of a saint or a volume of Basil, Jerome, or Augustine, would come a copy of Aristotle, Plato, Homer, or Virgil, to be read slowly and carefully and reflectively by the Saxon scholars at Hexham and Jarrow and Lindisfarne. And thus the wisdom of the ancients was treasured and transmitted until the universities took the place of the monasteries, the doctor of letters succeeded to the diligent recluse of the cloister, and the college professor to the scholastic monk. Familiarity with the classics is seen also in Bede's poetic compositions, where traces of acquaintance with Lucretius, Virgil, Horace, Sedulius, and the early hymnists appear.

His oratory, as has already been remarked, is of the quiet order, adapted to the tastes of the simple-hearted scholars and recluses who kept to the security of the houses of religion and learning, in stormy times when nothing else was respected by lawless barons. There is little show of deep thought in his discourse and no attempt at originality; but the address is direct and the language plain, varied by a persuasiveness which sometimes comes very near the most effective eloquence. That Bede was a recognized master of this kind of composition may be inferred from the fact that among his voluminous works there is a treatise on tropes and figures, in which he brings to the notice of his readers many forms of figurative language utterly overlooked in modern systems of rhetoric, naming them and marking them by their distinctive characters and definitions. In general he must be regarded as the scholar who in an age of silence added to his literary pursuits the frequent exercise of address on the homely duties, expounding the Scriptures to those who were associated with him, but limited in his influence by choice and the necessity of his monastic life. It was an age of wars and desolations, and it is remarkable that there was any learning or study or speech. They were not desired in kings' courts; they were possible only in the sanctuaries to which religion and letters had fled for refuge.

Another Briton of this age was the famous WINFRID or BONIFACE, A. D. 683, who earned the appellation of the "Apostle of Germany." The examples of his oratory which have come down to us are chiefly valuable as showing how so great a missionary preached to a rude people. Besides, it is more than probable that they are inadequate reports of what he actually said. In any case they are plain and practical homilies on the first principles of religion. If they had been more than this they would have been of less value to the hearers he had to address. Here is a passage which may stand for many: "Observe the Sunday and hasten to church. There pray, and diligently guard against idle stories and much talking, and do not gossip uselessly. Give alms according to your power. Be hospitable one to another, because the Lord will say in the judgment, 'I was a stranger and ye took me in.' Whence also some have received angels unawares. Take in strangers, and remember that ye yourselves are strangers in this world. Give tithes to the church, because the Lord commands to render unto Cæsar the things that are Cæsar's, taxes and tribute, and unto God the things that are God's, tithes, first-fruits, and all your vows. Love justice. Consent not to the persuasions of the devil. Humble and lowly, we have enumerated these things to you that no one may excuse himself, saying, 'I cannot distinguish between right and wrong; I know not what to leave alone and what to do!' Therefore, now, depart from evil and do good, which, if ye shall do, the Lord will increase you in understanding and virtue and give you the eternal and heavenly kingdom."

There is no pulpit eloquence here, as it came to be reckoned in later times; but it may be questioned whether if, in its plainness, directness, simplicity, and familiarity with the Scriptures, an occasional sermon by Boniface or Bede might not come with refreshing power, even in our own intellectual times, to heads weary with six days' thinking and planning and hearts distracted with anxieties and cares, with ambitious schemes and vain hopes. On the other hand it may be asked what effect would have been produced upon the half-civilized tribes of Germany if a modern sermon had been preached to them, with its high ratiocination and higher theology. But to every age belongs its own speech, and the most praise to that which best meets the demands of its own time.

Boniface stands upon the dividing line between the great patristic orators and those minor ones who should succeed them for the next seven and a half centuries. For the most part they are plain speakers, on simple subjects, to ignorant and superstitious people. A passage from a ninth-century sermon of Rabanus, in the days of Louis the Debonnaire and Alfred the Great, will illustrate the capacity of the hearers and the style of oratory that met their needs:

"You must know, beloved brethren, that our holy fathers ordained and commanded all Christians to rest and abstain from worldly labors on the festivals of the saints, but more especially on Sunday, so as to more easily be able to understand the word of God. It appears also in Holy Scripture that the day is holy; it was the first day of all; in it were formed the elements of the world; in it were angels created; in it also Christ rose from the dead; in it the Holy Ghost came down upon the Apostles; in it manna was first given from heaven in the desert. From such proofs as these Sunday comes before us as an illustrious day; and the holy doctors of the church ordained us to transfer all the glory of the Jewish Sabbath to it. Let us observe, therefore, brethren, the Sunday and see that our rest be not in vain; but from the evening of Saturday to the evening of Sunday have nothing to do with any country work, or any other business, and give yourself up to God's worship only. Let every one, therefore, who can, come to vespers and to nocturns, and there pray in the congregation of the church, confessing his sins. And he who cannot, let him pray in his own house. And on the day itself let no man occupy himself in hunting, nor engage in the devil's work, nor roam about the fields and woods, shouting and laughing."

Then he hints very plainly at worse doings inside or outside the church, law business, dice, games, and even fighting. Then turning his attention within the walls he adds,

"Do not give your attention to vain talk; for there are many, principally women, who so chatter in church, who so keep on talking, that they neither hear the lessons themselves nor allow others to hear them."

Then follows a cut at the men who want the minister to shorten the service so that they may go hunting the earlier. Of course this is not eloquence as we reckon it; that would have been out of place and useless with that kind of people.

Here is a sermon which shows that, in some things at least, the world has moved forward since Ethelwulf of England brought a crown of gold to Pope Benedict III, in 853. It bears the title, "Against those who raise an outcry during an eclipse of the moon," and begins, "It is a great joy to me to see you frequent the churches, seek baptism, and study the worship of the true God; but it grieves me exceedingly that I see many of you implicated in certain follies, mixing among the truths of religion certain false things which in no wise should be done." Then he describes the shouting, blowing of horns, casting of javelins and arrows against the moon, much after the fashion of our own aborigines. This was in Germany.

"What madness is this, brethren! What insanity! . . . How can ye bring help to the heaven and stars who are not able to protect yourselves on the earth? I praise you not, since, being deceived by the devil, ye are devoted in no small degree to pagan errors. And whence is this except from the pagans, whose company ye love and whose customs ye imitate? I have often forbidden you to consort with them, or to take part in their abominable feasts; but avarice hinders you from obeying me. Ye love money and are not afraid of hell. . . . 'For this cause many are weak and sickly among you and many sleep.'"

The plainness of this discourse is a revelation of the state of mingled religion and superstition which prevailed in the half-barbarian empire of the Franks in the ninth century. Rabanus' sermons have one quality which would commend them to this hurried and impatient age—they are short. But a contemporary, Otto, of Verceil, surpasses him in this respect. His sermons occupy ten or twelve minutes in delivery, but not satisfied with such brevity he sometimes appends a shorter form and adds, "the last sermon abbreviated, lest the common people should be disgusted."

Another prevailing feature of the preaching of that age is illustrated by Peter Damiani, Cardinal of Ostia. It is the stringing together of texts of Scripture with scarcely a connecting word, and yet making a connected discourse. In one page of a sermon on the Epiphany can be counted twenty-seven different quotations, with only four connecting clauses, all other words of conjunction being particles. This might be called easy composition if it did not imply such a familiarity with every part of the Bible as could be obtained only through constant study. It was a time of few theological works and fewer still of any other kind, and the Bible was the basis of all religious discourse and the principal possession of the clergy.

Another characteristic which had come down from remote times was the scriptural symbolism, which these mystical preachers drew out in a marvelous manner. Thus Damiani finds in the two cherubim above the mercy-seat a type of the two Testaments, the old and the new, and in the cross the concord of the two; and in the same paragraph he finds twenty-five other things of which it is the type, of which the key to open paradise may stand as an example. His apostrophe to it borders upon that worship of the sign for the thing signified, which was growing up at this time, and came near to idolatry in after centuries.

The oratorical style of Damiani in his perorations rises above that of his predecessors, as was possible in the passionate appeal to even an uncultivated audience. Some of his discourses on the Evangelists are marked by force and energy, combined with gentleness and sweetness, equaled by no mediæval preacher until we come to Bernard.

The *Sæculum Obscurum* has settled down upon the nations, the Dark Age of crime and ignorance gathers like a cloud around the thousandth year. The schools of Charlemagne have died out; there are no writers worth mentioning. Doctrine is received by rote and tradition, and the clergy know little but the routine of the church service.

It is only a lone watch-fire burning here and there in this universal night, like Rabanus and Damiani, that prevents the extinction of hope. The fact that such a discourse as the one on the Glory of the Heavenly Jerusalem, by Damiani, could be composed in that age must be attributed to the special divine illumination, or to disgust with the kingdom of heaven on earth as it then appeared. It is too long to quote, short as the homily is; but it has the strain and the spirit of the old Latin hymns, Jérusalem the Golden, the *Vexilla Regis*, and the Hymn of Adam of St. Victor.

XIV.

PREACHERS OF THE CRUSADES.

THE general expectation of the end of the world after a thousand years, and seemingly at hand by reason of the general corruption of the times, had not been met. The day of doom had not fallen on a disordered world, with its stagnation in learning and in life. As the eleventh century begins there are signs of revival. In Greek and Mohammedan cities learning is cultivated by such men as Avicenna and Avicebron, by Gerbert at Rheims and Lanfranc at Canterbury, while theology takes on a new form in scholasticism, reducing traditional dogmas to scientific unity by the aid of revived dialectics, combining Aristotelian metaphysics and logic with the traditions of the church and decrees of councils.

Its realism is not that of the New Testament, however, and its nominalism is transient. Before the end of this century the great battle will have begun between the papacy of Hildebrand and the spirit of feudalism and the rights of church and state in England, France, Germany, and Italy. England will not yield to the pope, France will remain independent, Germany will be humbled but will triumph over the pope, who in turn will never ask an imperial sanction to his election again. It is time to be looking for some intellectual activity in these stirring years. But the human mind had sunk so far that it was equal only to a brief revival of Greek literature under the Comneni in the East, and to Latin translations of Euclid with mystery plays and the songs of romancers and troubadours in the West. History becomes a monkish chronicle. The hope of the century is in the rise of the university, with its colleges of theology, philosophy, and law. Meantime crusades engage the rank and file of humanity, and an orator steps forth suited to the fanaticism of the times.

PETER of Amiens, in Picardy, A. D. 1050, had already served under the counts of Boulogne when he betook himself to the austerities of a hermitage. Emaciated in body and inflamed in fancy, he soon came to have dreams and visions of wonderful reality and vividness. From a pilgrimage to Jerusalem to visit the Holy Sepulchre he returned to rouse the martial nations of Europe for the rescue of the holy place from infidel possession. It seemed, no doubt, a wild boast for a small man of contemptible appearance to make, but the pope applauded his design and gave him letters of authority. William of Tyre, chronicler, has a note about him, which runs thus: "He is little and contemptible in person, but of lively wit, and has a clear-seeing eye and pleasing, and a free-flowing speech is not wanting to him." This is a moderate commendation of a great natural orator, whose literary outfit was as meagre as his wardrobe was scanty. However he compensated for his ignorance and lack of rhetorical methods by passionate appeals and loud ejaculations, calling upon Christ and Mary and the saints and angels in paradise, with whom he professed to have conversed. He had seen visions, he said, and a letter had fallen from heaven addressed to him. The Lord had appeared to him in person, charging him to rouse the western nations for the deliverance of the Holy Land from Moslem domination. Accordingly he set forth, preaching to high and low, in churches and on highways, until words and breath failed him. Then he took to weeping and groaning, beating his breast and pointing to the great crucifix which he always carried. The multitude listened with rapture. They showered gifts upon him which he flung to the poor. His greatest difficulty began to be, not to persuade the throng to enlist in a crusade, but to keep them from starting at once for Palestine. As it was, the impatient multitude urged him to set out and lead them on five months before the appointed day. In consequence he had to cross the Rhine at Cologne at the head of the motley host bound for the East by way of Constantinople. Five hundred thousand perished in the first wave of fanatic zeal that rolled toward Jerusalem. The story of those that followed is too familiar to be recounted. It is the record of a religious war, of Christianity against Islam, the movement of Europe against Asia.

The man who set Europe in motion, ignorant and fanatic though he was, had the satisfaction of beholding results of which the most consummate orator of Greece would not have dared to dream. He had pushed the western nations to the East. The most of them went to their destruction, to be sure, but Jerusalem was delivered out of the hands of the infidel, and the Holy Sepulchre reclaimed. It was the grand achievement of the eleventh century; and

Peter the Hermit, after proving his sincerity, as Demosthenes did, by fighting for the cause he had proclaimed, retired from the conquest of Jerusalem to the seclusion of a monastery of his own founding near Liege, where he remained until his death fifteen years later. The secret of his power lay somewhat in the temper of his age, no doubt, as is the case with every great orator; but it was more largely due to the fact that an idea which was in the very air of the time had taken complete possession of a man of the time, who believed himself sent on a mission to his generation. His oratory, rude and uncouth, was like the age; but it had in it the ring of all genuine eloquence, sincerity, and directness, and, moreover, what that century permitted, a wild abandon to the impulsive utterance of conviction, without art and without restraint. It cannot be weighed by our present standards. Its only criterion is its measure of success, the final test of all true eloquence in whatever age it occurs.

There were other orators in this dark century less eloquent than Peter of Picardy, but more learned than he. ANSELM was such a one, the acutest thinker and the profoundest theologian of an age which ran to metaphysical subtleties. A piquant and interesting preacher, according to the standard established in great monastic houses, he would be called in these days an expositor, giving running comments on biblical books and chapters and verses. Scriptural quotations he intersperses with his discourse with a marvelous facility, showing that his familiarity with the text was beyond that of many modern preachers.

ABELARD, IVO of Chartres, and BRUNO of Aste were

representatives of their age and their order, the last of whom has a curious piece of mystical interpretation in a sermon on Zacchæus in the sycamore tree. "This tree," he says, "is faith to which many come, who, climbing into it, though of little stature themselves, having made small progress in knowledge, have thereby been able to behold the Lord." This generation of preachers was apt to see fanciful significances in everything, a habit which Bruno himself criticizes when he remarks that there are those "who, understanding too subtilely things which are plain, render them difficult."

Other orators who made their mark in their time, like Hildebert of Tours and Guarric of Igniac, Ældred and Adam Scotus, had each some excellence of his own; one for strength of thought, another for sympathetic power, another for earnestness, another still for an occasional burst of genuine eloquence.

The Hermit of Amiens excepted none came so near to stirring all Europe as BERNARD of Clairvaux, a would-be recluse in the Valley of Wormwood, the haunt of robbers. This retiring man was constantly summoned by the great powers of the earth to reconcile disputes and arbitrate between popes and princes. No man of the age had such influence, and no man his kind of eloquence. Henry of Sens and Stephen of Paris were supported by the commanding voice of Bernard in their appeal to the pope from the king. Its tones were heard in the stormy debates about the Knights Templars. In the great contest between Innocent II. and Peter of Leon for the popedom, in which the sovereigns of Europe were involved, Bernard espoused the cause of the former and won the kings of England and France and the emperor of Germany by his persuasive oratory.

Had he lived five hundred years later he might have been just as eloquent in the cause which Luther espoused in Germany and Cranmer in England. There must have been something behind his eloquence more and greater than the gaunt and bowed figure which was more conspicuous than pope or prince in the famous procession through Liege. His renown had preceded him as the man who bent kings and nobles to his purpose. But that purpose was always good for the times in which he lived. It was his joy to reconcile hereditary foes. Cities were not too great for his efforts. Genoa and Pisa, whose jealousy of each other was obstinate and deep-rooted, were made friends by his preaching. Turbulent Milan was charmed into submission by his eloquence and claimed him as their bishop; but he preferred to dictate the faith from a convent rather than the cathedral chair.

Twice more he was called out, once to meet a rebel baron, whom he literally floored with an argument which would be less effectual in these indifferent days, by lifting the consecrated wafer and saying, "You have despised and mocked me; now comes to you the Son of Mary; now stands here thy judge, the judge of all the earth." The haughty count fell like a dead man at the feet of the prophet; at least so says Peter of Cluny.

His next triumph was a victory over King Roger of Sicily, who had taken Rome and the Holy See. The unity of the church and the right of majorities were the arguments that, in the mouth of Bernard, sent him home.

Another man might not have made them convincing, as we have seen in our times. Then came the conflict with Abelard and the Council of Sens, from whose sentence of heresy Abelard appealed to the pope and died on the way to Rome.

Bernard lived on for still greater achievements. He lived to see himself of more consequence than the pope, and in this way: the Christian kingdom in Palestine, which had been established by the first crusade, was rent by intestine feuds and menaced by the gathering forces of the Saracens returning to claim their lost territory. A call for aid was sent to the West from the East. Bernard took up the mission of Peter the Hermit. Through France and Germany he hastened, stirring up the high and low, calling saints and sinners to join in a holy war. He made the rich pour out their treasures; to the poor he promised spoils, to the profligate he offered pardon. The power of his eloquence had been equaled but once before. His success was immediate and marvelous. Time and again his robe was torn in pieces to make crosses for volunteers. Cities and castles were deserted. Like Peter he had to check the torrent of enthusiasm which his preaching had roused. Two great expeditions set out in the same year, 1147. The usual confusion and disaster attended them, but no less on this account was Bernard's oratory the inspiring power. He had deprecated the evils and protested against the blunders of the campaign; but when the ill-starred expedition was over he was cursed for its fatal result. In vain afterward did leaders try to engage him in the preaching of another crusade. Instead he turned his efforts to a warfare with heresy in Languedoc, like a second Athanasius. Soon after his public life was finished, and his days were ended in comparative retirement at Clairvaux. The public voice demanded his immediate canonization, and few men have better deserved this mediæval token of distinction for goodness and greatness. The grandeur of his eloquence is of chief interest here among his manifold attainments and virtues. His marvelous powers of oratory won all who heard him. Wives kept their husbands away from the spell of his eloquence, and mothers the sons whom they did not wish to be swept into the crusading host by his irresistible persuasion. Kings, councillors, and the pope himself were alike subject to its universal sway. It was not the wild harangue of a fanatic, accompanied by dramatic contortions and convulsions, but the earnest, clear, sincere expression of profound conviction. The impressiveness of his discourse, the magnetism of his presence, the winning tones of his voice, the power of his personal character are all matters of tradition, but history gives the best testimony to his eloquence in its records of the results he accomplished.

Of other lights in an age of comparative darkness there are but few who are worth mentioning. No doubt that many of them had a local and temporary fame, but for only two or three can be claimed a lasting renown. ANTHONY of Padua was an effective and popular preacher at the beginning of the thirteenth century, but his circuit was limited to the north and centre of Italy. Churches were thronged from daybreak whenever he was going to preach. Often he had to come out and address multitudes that could not find room within. Shops were closed and places of business deserted. Thirty thousand was an ordinary attendance. Nor were the effects of his preaching less remarkable. Enemies were reconciled, lives reformed, treasure poured out. It cannot be seen why, from the meagre transcript of his discourses that has been preserved. Ultra-mystical, crammed with Scripture quotations, quaint and distorted in illustration, the hearer, to understand them, must have been almost equal to the preacher in his invention. It is probable that his wondrous facility of homely comparison entertained simple-minded hearers, and not them only; for if this faculty is the highest, according to Bacon and Sir William Hamilton, there were men of strong minds who would appreciate this power of his to make mysteries clear by the things that are seen. He makes most singular comparisons, however, drawing out the likeness between virtues and a ship's rigging, between saints and eagles, hypocrites and hyenas, penitents and elephants, apostles and ichneumons, merciful men and cranes, sinners and hedgehogs. "Note," he says, "that the hedgehog is full of prickles, and if anyone tries to take it, it rolls itself up and becomes a ball in the hands of the holder. So a sinner, if you try to convince him of sin, he immediately rolls himself up and hides by excusing his fault." It is not by such discourse alone that he could gain eminence. It is by something more than sensationalism in any age that preëminence is attained. It is rather the same secret over again, of a living, intense personality. He threw himself into his discourse.

Bonaventura, his contemporary, did the same, and

Albertus Magnus and Thomas à Kempis; and in a more eminent degree the later preachers, one of whom is full of illustrative anecdote, with a fondness for mystical interpretation which was a fashion of his age. Once he was preaching in a most scandalously demoralized city on the seashore, and being disgusted with the inhabitants he preached a sermon to the fishes in the water close by, from the text, "Ye are the salt of the earth." He begins by saying that they have at least two good qualities, they can hear and cannot speak; also they were created first of all living creatures, and cannot be tamed or domesticated, and none of them trust man but all avoid him. They fared best in the flood, and though they eat one another it is no worse than the men of this city. The bully-fish he upbraids, and the flying-fish he despises for setting up to be a bird. "He that can swim and desires to fly, the time will come when he can neither fly nor swim.

"With this last remark, I bid you farewell, my brethren and fishes. As you are not capable of grace or glory, so your sermon ends neither with grace nor with glory."

The same may be said, in general, of the oratory of this period.

XV.

ECCENTRIC ELOQUENCE.

BY THE close of the fourteenth century oratory had become sadly debased, though a few great preachers still kept up the traditions of brighter ages. Among these Savonarola at Florence, Philip of Narni at Rome, and Louis of Granada in Spain, shone as beacon lights. But for the most part there was affectation and vanity, not to say profanity and buffoonery. All natural eloquence was stifled and distorted. Free action was cramped by artificialities. Sermons had marginal directions such as, "cough here, sit down, stand up, mop your face here, now shriek like a devil." An aged doctor of divinity tells a young preacher to "bang the pulpit, roll his eyes toward the crucifix, and say nothing to the purpose," if he will be a great preacher. In all this century sermons are hammered out in this way; sixty-eight sermons on the one text "Come up into the mount." Having given out his text the preacher pronounced a long exordium, containing, perhaps, an allegory or an anecdote from the classics, or a supposed fact from the science of the day. Then he would return to the text and begin to discuss a question in theology, and one in civil law remotely connected. Division and subdivision would each be illustrated by a classic saying or a pointless story, sometimes doubtful in tone. A peasant who had heard the praises of Apollo from the pulpit bequeathed his old cart-horse to M. Pollo, of whom such fine things had been said by the curé. A bishop preaching on Christmas day compares the Holy Child to Bellerophon, who, "mounted on the Pegasus of his humanity, has overcome the world. He is our Horatius, overcoming the three Curatii of ambition, greed, and vice; he is our Hercules who has beaten down the triple-throated Cerberus." Sometimes they dropped into burlesque in order to attract the attention that their thought or style could not command. Preaching friars, "hedge priests" they were called, were the sensational preachers of the time, with methods not unknown in our day. Speaking in the popular dialect, with a display of their smattering of knowledge, they ran through the titles of such books as they had read or heard of, to the admiration of the assembled rustics—the sibylline books, the Iliad, Æneid, and such other classics as could be recalled.

Their logic was of the same order. Michael Menot reasons thus concerning the ways of the evil one: "1. The dance is a circular way; 2. the way of the devil is circular; 3. therefore the dance is the devil's way." He illustrates his views as to the value of magistrates by the fable of the cat, the mice, and the cheese. His description of the prodigal son, wasting his goods, is a mixture of bad Latin and worse French; but it is graphic, to say the least; too graphic to edify a modern congregation. *Pueri qui semper dormierunt in atrio vel gremio matris suae nunquam sciverunt aliquid, et nunquam erunt in nisi asini et insulsi, et ne seront jamais que nices et béjaunes. Bref qui ne fréquente pays nihil videt.*

It is doubtful if this clerical jester ever preached this sermon; and again, all preachers of this age were not jesters. On the contrary they were, many of them, grave and dignified. Their sermons were simple in construction, and full of wisdom and fervor.

GABRIEL BIEL was such an orator. A scholastic divine, a careful reader of patristic lore, and a professor in the University of Tubingen he was a man of gravity and learning, preaching sermons that were popular by reason of their simplicity and intrinsic excellence. He did not try to amuse his hearers, as was the custom of his contemporaries, nor to puzzle them with scholastic quibbles, but gave them good, practical advice in plain, homely words. "His simple earnestness is his charm; but his simplicity is that of a well-read and thoughtful man, full of wisdom expressed in a straightforward manner and applied in short and nervous sentences; many thoughts in a few words."

JOHN RAULIN represents another type, too frequently met with in the fifteenth century, playing and trifling with the highest themes, making them a series of Sunday puzzles, enlivened by stories more pointed than classic. To parents whose children are perfection in their eyes he tells the story of a toad who wished to send a message to his son in church by a hare that was going that way. "How shall I know him?" asked the hare. "Nothing more easy; there's not so good looking a fellow in the crowd." "Oh, I know him—the swan." "Swan! that fellow with splay feet and a crooked neck!" "The bird of paradise then." "You insult me by thinking that cracked-voiced thing my son. Look, you," and he puffed himself up, "he is remarkably handsome—ahem, the very image of me; has goggle eyes, a blotched back, and a great white neck." The fable would not fail to reach many fond parents, but it would not do in a modern pulpit.

In an Easter sermon he asks why the news of the resurrection was announced to women? and replies that they have such tongues that they would spread the news quickest. He enlarges on this topic and explains the mystery of their loquacity in this manner, "Man was made of clay, woman of bone. Now if you move a sack of clay it makes no noise, but only touch a bag of bones, and rattle, rattle, rattle is what you hear."

All fifteenth century discourse had not descended to this level, but that such effusions were common and popular shows what sort of cultivation and taste prevailed among the masses. The supply is generally according to the demand in oratory as in other things, and some of these pulpit wags had carefully measured the capacities and requirements of their congregations, and gave them what they most appreciated. In nothing, perhaps, is the advance of civilization shown more than in the style of pulpit oratory now, as compared with that of the fifteenth century preachers.

Even the dignified, earnest, and learned, like MATTHIAS FABER, are not over-nice about their anecdotes and similes. This divine, whose sermons contain much thought, does not scruple to illustrate backsliding by the habits of frogs who crawl out of the swamp a little way, but at the least alarm, he says, "flop into their slough again." Servants' obedience to their masters he compares and commends by the obedience of a man to the barber who is shaving him, turning his head this way and that, putting his chin up or down at the slightest sign. He illustrates the value of vigilance by the story of a farmer who was presented with a sealed box which he was to take daily to his kitchen, his garden, his storehouse, his cellar, his stable, and his field. He found provisions wasting in the kitchen, vats leaking in the cellar, laborers idling in the field, and opening the casket at the end of the year he found nothing but a slip of paper on which was written, "If you wish to make every day full of success, fulfil your own task every day." It was telling, of course, in a New Year's sermon.

But it must not be concluded that there was no sober and useful preaching in those degenerate days. Instead there was equal plainness of speech when it came to a matter of rebuke, instruction, or exhortation. A profound depth also of knowledge and understanding, and a sincere emotion in the presence of the greater facts of human life were equally present in the greater orators, like PHILIP VON HARTUNG and JOSEPH DE BARZIA. The first of these had his mind stored with material; so full indeed that the elaboration of it is sometimes neglected, and the rough ore is thrown at the hearer rather than the minted coin; but there is vigor and beauty and considerable originality. The remarkable realism of the topics he treats of shows how fearless was his handling of the plainest truths of the Bible. In one Advent he preaches to a rural congregation on the appearance of the sign of the Son of Man, on the trumpet call waking the dead, on the questioning of the risen ones, and on the final doom of the good and bad; all most striking sermons.

Those of De Barzia are like those of the modern mission preachers, and of the better class of revivalists. Interesting, pointed, full of illustration and appropriate anecdote, they are eminently qualified to arrest attention and arouse the conscience. His strong point was in never allowing the attention of his audience to flag. To this end he did not wear out his subject, but left some things to be suggested; and before he had exhausted one topic he started another, thus keeping the minds of his hearers alert and refreshed by change. The divine judgments were the themes which he developed with the greatest power, as the divine love was the burden of his contemporary, MARCHANT, the great preacher in the Low Countries at the beginning of the seventeenth century. He is the opposite of John Raulin; never trifling with sacred matters, full of reverence for the Scriptures, and with little care for pagan learning, which was beginning to be revived by the men of his day. It is in this century that the character of the sermon is changed from the expository form it had maintained throughout the patristic and mediæval centuries.

JOHN OSORIUS is an innovator, developing a single topic instead of running on from verse to verse by way of exposition. He seldom relates anecdotes, and omits those stories which his predecessors delighted to introduce. Instead he uses the brief simile, sometimes too frequently; fifteen in one sermon being abundant, to say the least. But their fitness and beauty compensate for their frequency. Here is one that is curious. He says that as he lies in bed he hears the stroke, stroke, of his heart; and it sounds to him as though within two wood-cutters were engaged day and night in hewing down a tree. "Nor am I wrong in thinking so," he continues, "for Flux and Reflux are engaged every hour in laying their axes to the root of the tree of life." In another sermon he speaks of men fretting over the loss of worldly goods and neglecting their eternal inheritance as resembling "a little boy who has built a mud castle, and cries when a passer-by overthrows it with his foot, though he cares nothing that a lawsuit is going on at the time by which a large inheritance is being wrested from him."

To show in what repute a great preacher was held the case of MAXMILIAN DEZA may be cited. A man of apostolic zeal he was nevertheless fond of exhibiting his classic learning; but that it was acceptable to the age may be inferred from the fact that he was in request in many cities, at Turin, Milan, Genoa, Venice, and Rome. His sermons, sometimes two hours in delivery, had to be enlivened by devices not known to our Puritan forefathers, who used to preach quite as long. Accordingly he works one point up to a climax that must have made his hearers hold their breath, and then drops the topic and gives them time to relax their attention till he deems it fit to produce another effect, thus avoiding anything like monotony. But he is careful to avoid dulness in these lighter portions which insensibly, but really, lead up to the next topic of his discourse. For example in the midst of a sermon on "dust to dust" he suddenly points to the hour glass and exclaims, "Look! this hour is stealing away in grains of dust, warning you to remember what you, too, ere long will become." Working this out with great solemnity he suddenly breaks off with a description of glass and its manufacture. He says it is made of sand and ashes, fused by heat and formed by breath blown into it. "Is not that like man, made of dust, kindled by the breath of life?" Then he goes on to show in six particulars how man is more perishable than brittle glass, and having amused and rested his hearers he begins another earnest appeal to them, and explains that the immortal in man cannot perish, however fragile his mortality may be. Then he rests his hearers again by playing with a description of dust agitated by the wind—the driving dust-cloud, spinning above the tree-tops, falling again, obscuring the landscape, blinding eyes and parching throats, returning to itself again, dust to dust. "Is not this a picture of man," he asks, "carried up and hurried about by the winds of his light fancies and ambitions, and then dropped a helpless atom into his native soil?" And so through the whole sermon, a point of interest and then a climax of eloquence, which is worthy of the best days of pulpit oratory in any age. Quoting Solomon's words, that the life of man is as a "ship that passeth over the waves," he adds, "and leaves no trace; no trace but the foam-bubbles, to be brushed away by the next wave, and this sweeping resistlessly to the rock on which it will be shivered with a roar; a roar like the life of man, loud and fierce for a moment, and then carried off on the wind; the wind, like the life of man, sinking into a lull and lost." For vehemence and word-picturing, combined with rhythm and cadence of sentence and paragraph, his equal would be hard to find in all the round of oratory.

In the main there has been great improvement by reason of increased learning and light. The Reformation is drawing on, and although the preachers here mentioned were not Protestants, in the modern sense, they did nevertheless protest most vehemently against the grosser errors of the time which they helped to reform. Permeated with scriptural knowledge and spirit and knowing the nature of the human heart and the experiences of human life these single-hearted men spoke the truth with directness and fulness and sincerity. They sometimes mixed celestial things with terrestrial in a unique, if not grotesque, manner; but their purpose was single and clear. The man who should do as some of them did would now be called a jester and mountebank. The man who should set forth the great facts of life and death as others of them did would be called a revivalist, a ranter, perhaps a fanatic; but he would also have, sooner or later, a following that would overwhelm him. Now and then an evangelist appears who can draw crowds as they did; but how to secure lasting results and to organize and direct the crusade that has been eloquently preached belongs to but one or two in a century. For models of sincerity and reality in morals and doctrine the present age can learn much from the best of these preachers.

XVI.

SAVONAROLA.

BEFORE leaving the fifteenth century and the preachers who represent all the oratory that is worth mentioning it will be proper to notice one who surpassed them all. For this reason SAVONAROLA is considered apart from his contemporaries. Born in 1452 at Ferrara, the son of a court physician, his youth was passed amidst the dazzling splendor of a careless and corrupt age. Traditions of paganism were revived, and the inhabitants of Italy were absorbed in wanton and thoughtless enjoyment. In the midst of all this feasting and dancing and occasional bloodshed this young man lived a sad and lonely life. He knew that far below the music and the revelry in the palace immured victims were groaning and clanking their chains. He could find no refuge from a dissolute age but in a religious house, and accordingly he became a monk, to find the peace within cloister walls which he could not find in a turbulent world. Even there his reflections on the state of the church roused him to fury at its debasement. Rulers were elected by purchased votes; treasures got by grasping avarice melted away; cities were bought for favorites, and nepotism made archbishops of knaves. Cardinals rivaled dukes in lavish expenditures. Men mourned long-lost liberty, but more the loss of administrative vigor in the tyrants that ruled over them. Ambition had given place to cunning, and valor to treason. Luxury had rotted society, and then out of corruption sprung conspiracy and rebellion against feeble tyranny. Desperate men hatched plots against despots; priests carried assassins' daggers, backed by archbishops and popes.

It was amid such surroundings that the mind of Savonarola took shape. By his superiors he was advanced from instructor to preacher. He gave up his intention of keeping silence, and yielded to the demand from within and without to become a prophet to an evil generation.

His first preaching resembled the quiet instruction of his lectures in the monastery, based upon the Aristotelian principles of discourse which still held authority. He soon drew away from these to evangelistic methods, inspired by biblical study. He was sent to Ferrara, his native town. Its inhabitants cared as little for his preaching as townsmen proverbially do for a prophet in his own country. Alarms of war caused him to be transferred to Florence. Here he found a city under the rule of supreme indifferentism to everything sacred while given up to festivities, dances, and tournaments. Culture of classical learning was kept up in a way, and literature was cultivated in the form of learned essays and imitations of Virgil, Cicero, Homer, and Pindar. The old pagan philosophies were welcomed and revived, and fortunes were spent in collecting manuscripts and art treasures from Greece. It was an age of scepticism and flippancy, precursor of the revival of learning in which a later Italy was to lead the world and become the civilizer and teacher of Europe; now it was mere scholasticism. With this Savonarola had little sympathy, though he had given years to the study of philosophy. He was still farther apart from the Florentines in an irreconcilable diversity of temperament. They affected refinement of style and expression, in imitation of the ancient classics of similar character. He was rough in speech and manner, harsh in accent, homely in diction; but what he spoke came from the generous and sincere impulse of an honest heart. Sincerity and honesty, however, were counted as indifferent virtues in the reign of Lorenzo the Magnificent. Furthermore Savonarola was unsparing in his denunciation of the vices of the time, and of the scanty faith of clergy and laity alike. He had little commendation for poets and philosophers, condemned the craze for ancient authors, and quoted only from the Bible. This book the Florentines did not read for fear of corrupting their style, having discovered that its Latin was not classically correct.

Beginning to preach to a coldly critical public which delighted only in pagan quotations and elegant turns of speech he soon succeeded in emptying his church. Checked and disheartened at this cold reception he began to ask himself how he could move such hearers toward faith and virtue, and furthermore how could he get any hearers to move. The orator who best represented the taste of that age was one Mariano, whose preaching is thus described by a contemporary: "And now, behold, he begins to speak! I am all ears to the musical voice, the chosen words, the grand sentences. Then I note the clauses, recognize the periods, and am swayed by their harmonious cadence." It was such a speaker, then famous, but now obscure, who overshadowed Savonarola. Even his faithful friends said to him, "Father, one cannot deny that your doctrine is true, but your manner of delivering it lacks grace, especially when you are compared with Mariano." To which he replied, "These verbal elegancies and ornaments will have to give way to sound doctrine, simply preached." But that was still in the future. Meantime the city ran after polished niceties from the Platonic Academy of Ficino, while the irritated prophet questioned himself and nursed his faith in the future. He recalled the prophets of Israel and their fightings against a nation's ingratitude, and his wrath grew hot and resolution grew strong to attack the scandals of the age. He waited in fasting and contemplation for a revelation from on high. He began to see visions and to hear voices urging him to persist and not be cast down by the indifference of the people. Then came a turn in the tide of public sentiment. Pope Sixtus had been no better than his age, but his successor was such a man as made his contemporaries look back with longing for the days of Sixtus. All hope and faith in the future were lost, and a corrupt people were revolted by the conduct of a court more corrupt. This year, 1484, Savonarola was Lenten preacher in a town among the Sienese hills, where he could raise his voice freely and utter words that had long been burning in his soul. "The Church will be scourged; it will be regenerated; all will quickly come to pass," was the burden of his prophecy.

He discovered that similar presentiments were lurking in the hearts of his hearers, and that his own thoughts had found an echo in theirs. At last he was beginning to find his place. In Brescia his words were fervent and his tone commanding as he reproved the people and denounced all Italy. His voice seemed to them to come from another world as he predicted the calamities which should befall the city. Then he went to Genoa, to be recalled to Florence by the prince, who did not know that he had sent for the destroyer of the power of the Medici. The people soon demanded to hear him preach. After a time he consented, and on a Sunday in August, 1489, the church of St. Mark was thronged with people to hear the preacher who had become so famous in upper Italy. Expounding the Apocalypse of St. John he raised his audience to the highest pitch of enthusiasm as he pronounced the three predictions already mentioned. But such prophecies of judgment and immediate purification were not so pleasing as his intellectual prowess and wonderful eloquence; some were therefore quick to say that there was more elocution than logic and truth in his oratory. Still the people flocked to hear him, until St. Mark's could no longer contain the multitude. His imagery enchanted them; his predictions of coming calamity were the voicings of their own fears; but his condemnation of the scepticism and indifference of the literary class was the beginning of disaffection. He told them that there was no office in the church that was not bought and sold; that the city was a den of thieves and murderers. In spite of this he is invited to preach at the palace on Easter-day. He says he does not feel at home as in his own pulpit; nevertheless he preaches a fearless sermon to the prince and his court. It increases his popularity with the people, and he is elected prior of St. Mark's. In this position of increased independence he is visited and courted and beneficed by the prince, who in return gets only exhortations to repent and rebuffs for his patronage. The former chief preacher of the city is then enlisted against him, but overdoes the matter and miserably fails, vowing vengeance in consequence.

Up to this time there are only rough notes of his sermons; their character is known chiefly by the effect they produced. The earliest of them do not exhibit the highest order of his eloquence. A heterogeneous mass of raw material is gathered around a text; but now and then he touches on a point of vital interest, and all at once the great and powerful orator appears. His mind throws off original thoughts, his imagination pictures vivid scenes, voice and gesture emphasize living truths. Ignorant of the rules and principles of oratory it was only when a subject took full possession of him that his natural gifts supplied the place of art, and that he could attain to real eloquence. It is when we view the performance of born orators that we most prize the value of oratorical science; for few men and few ages are possessed of overpowering motives for irresistible eloquence, such as Savonarola, Bernard, and Peter the Hermit had. Even they would have been able to produce a more uniform excellence in their efforts if they had understood a few more of the laws of thought and its expression.

The simple eloquence of the fourteenth century had

passed away. The contemporaries of Savonarola were fanciful rhetoricians or scholastic disputers, darkening the truth with subtleties, if they did not indulge in fantastic buffoonery worthy of the comic stage. This new preacher's success was based on his sincerity and ardor, directed by a large sympathy with the people, which they in turn reciprocated. He used language which they could understand, and addressed them in familiar tones. Although it was easier for him to write in Latin he was careful to speak to the people in their own tongue, rather than in the language of the learned class throughout all Europe at that time. His topics also came home to their hearts. Since the Christian fathers and doctors passed away, only at rare intervals had such a voice been heard, or such an uncompromising message. He was restoring pulpit eloquence to its old post of honor with renewed life, and was making for himself the place of the first orator of his times, in the year that Columbus discovered a western continent.

This year of 1492 was an evil one for Italy. Lorenzo the Magnificent died, refusing to grant liberty to Florence. His son did not raise the hopes of a despairing city when he came to the succession. Infamies reached their climax in the house of Borgia, and Italy was filled with dismay. Savonarola saw the visions of a drawn sword above the city, and of the black cross spanning a stormy sky, and the golden cross to which all nations flocked. He preached of morals, of the state, of the church, inveighing against princes and clergy, likening himself to the hail which pelts every one who is in the open air. He discoursed of a second flood in a series of sermons. And when the day came when he should take for his text, "I will bring a flood of waters upon the whole earth," the vast church was filled with a crowd that had been waiting since the early morning. The next greatest preacher of the time said that a cold shiver ran through him and his hair stood on end as this voice resounded through the church like a peal of thunder, and Savonarola declared that he himself was no less agitated than his hearers.

His prophecies were being fulfilled with literalness. A prince and a pope had died, and now armies were pouring over the Alps to the conquest of Italy. The terrified inhabitants saw the vision of the drawn sword of the wrath of God. But the Friar of St. Mark's had declared all these things before. Therefore all Italy rang with his name, and all eyes were turned toward him. The full effect of his preaching cannot be apprehended. Men and women of every age and condition, workmen, poets and philosophers, made the church reëcho with their lamentations. A reporter writes, "At this point I was overcome and could not go on." But the imperfect report furnishes no basis for the estimate of such eloquence, nor justifies the effect that it produced upon the Florentine public. It is the old story of personality over again, with its power that vanishes. The chief point of all his utterances is a belief that a great regeneration was near at hand through conflict and chastisement. Yet in the absence of complete records there is abundant testimony as to the effect of his words, and this is perhaps the truest test of their fitness to the people whom he addressed. In no other way can a just estimate of their real power be made.

He had changed the whole aspect of the city from gay to grave, from evil ways to sober behaviour. Women threw aside their finery, riotous young men became religious, usurers restored ill-gotten gains. All men were amazed at this almost miraculous change. It was the day of Savonarola's triumph, and he might have died content. With a greater victory won than that of the Hermit or of Bernard, because harder to accomplish, he might have rested from his labors. But an evil fate awaited him in prolonged persecutions by the papacy and the civil authorities under the pope's direction. Mock trials, torture, and martyrdom end his days at the age of forty-five.

For eight years he had preached almost uninterruptedly in Florence for the moral and material benefit of those who at last condemned him to a temporary, and then to a perpetual, silence. The time came when they saw his prophecies fulfilled and his wisdom justified. Then they worshiped his garments, cherished his relics, wrote and rewrote his biography, composed services in his honor, and invoked his aid as a prophet and martyr.

It was his mission "to dare to believe amid general doubt, and to uphold against the scandal and scepticism of the time the derided rights of Christianity, of liberty, and reason." It was his to proclaim to his contemporaries that without virtue, self-sacrifice, and moral grandeur both mankind and society must fall to ruin. It is the manner of this proclamation that places him in the upper rank of the world's great orators, among the exalted few who have known how to stir the hearts and direct the wills of their fellowmen. It has not always been in precisely the same way, as the Greeks and the Italians, two thousand years apart, were not similar people. On the other hand the same principles of our common nature were wrought upon, the same hopes, fears, ambitions; but in a different degree and with larger scope and higher aim as new centuries revealed new and wider fields of truth and achievement.

XVII.

ORATORY OF THE REFORMATION.

WHILE Savonarola was preaching repentance and the doom of the Medici at Florence, mediæval philosophy and religion and oratory were drawing to a close. The Reformation was about to usher in the beginning of modern history with the year 1500. Around that year is grouped a company of names which were to be identified with a revolution in ecclesiasticism that should make a new order of the ages and give a new inspiration to human thought and activity. The ancient church had been under the patronage of the state for four centuries; the mediæval church had subjected the state to itself; the modern church was to keep pace with the nations in their civil and social development, and to follow the course of maritime discovery with its enlightening and elevating influence. The men who initiate this movement on the continent are Luther, Zwingli, Melancthon, Calvin; all born between 1483 and 1509.

Contemporary with these continental reformers is a group in England of equal zeal and greater wisdom and greater eloquence, who will be noticed later.

Preëminent in this company of continental leaders is MARTIN LUTHER, who, as early as his sixteenth year, manifested, according to Melancthon, a "keen power of intellect, and was, above all, gifted for eloquence."

The habit of monasticism was still upon the times, and the place of such a man would naturally be in the religious house where his eloquence would be confined to the limited circle of the brethren, or at most in the University of Wittenburg where he lectured on philosophy. It was while there that he became an assistant to the city preacher, and preached with great vigor and earnestness. Especially when Tetzel began the sale of indulgences not far from the city did Luther warn the people against their purchase, in words that had no uncertain significance.

In all the controversy that followed he speaks as a man with irrepressible convictions, freely and fearlessly. He is fertile in words and full of illustration, with a wonderful freshness and vigor of expression, coupled with a dauntless boldness and a rude vehemence that was invincible. His language is pungent, simple, and clear, equally free from exuberance of fancy and dialectic subtlety. He did much in the way of learned treatises in the Latin tongue to forward the Reformation in the literary world; but it was his public preaching that carried it beyond university walls to the popular assembly and among men of all trades and professions, who knew little or nothing of the language employed by scholars. He preached several times in a day and his eloquence called out crowds to hear him. It was a rare sight in those times, when all interest in spiritual things had centered in ceremonial. There was no Basil or Gregory, no Augustine or Bernard. The great Florentine prophet was beyond the mountains. Geiler of Kaisersberg had gathered great concourses of people along the Rhine by his rude and captivating eloquence, but he cannot be reckoned among the memorable orators. To Luther alone must be accorded the tribute of an oratory which produced abiding results, and the praise of being not only the most celebrated reformer, but actually the greatest pulpit orator of his time. In an age of sacerdotalism and ritual he revived the primitive spirit of Christianity, which demanded that all ceremonial should be subordinated to the preaching of the Word. He was a man fitted to illustrate by his own eloquence the claims of the pulpit, which had been neglected for an altar which itself had not been too well served. His stalwart form, piercing eye, penetrating voice, and natural manner, full of freedom and force, were all favorable to eloquence.

His mental furnishings were equally favorable. His intellect was powerful and acute; shedding a flood of light upon a subject or penetrating through the subtleties which scholastic refinements had woven around a truth it brought to view the central and essential meaning. Strong in logical faculty and disciplined by study he was stronger still with the common people in his plain and practical sense, which brought him into sympathy with all men of sound mind in every rank and order. This learning and logic and common sense were illumined by a poetic temperament which made his oratory glow with the light which comes from whatever is beautiful and significant in nature and art. More than all he was earnest and sincere in his speech, valuing it as a means to an end, and not as an art to be exemplified, or even elevated, for its own sake. He had the higher purpose of changing the drift of his age from formalism to reality, from glosses on the truth to the truth itself, from a dead ceremonial and a perverted doctrine to that of personal responsibility and a living faith. It was this oratory, characterized by self-possession, vivacity, wit, and rare knowledge of human nature, and an unequaled command of the people's language, that made him to be universally acknowledged as the prince of orators in his age.

He had a singular opinion of his own performances. "My style," he said, "rude and unskilful, vomits forth a deluge, a chaos of words, boisterous and impetuous as a wrestler contending with a thousand successive monsters. I feel, however, that in these times there is need of the hard against the hard, of the rough against the rough. To clear the air the thunder-storm is still required. I would rather sin in disseminating truth with hard words than shamefully retain it captive. If great lords are hurt by them they can go about their own business without thinking of mine, or my doctrines."

Thus did Martin Luther wrestle with papal despotism and the evil one alternately, and sometimes the two antagonists merged themselves into one and the same without much distinction in his eyes. But by his uncompromising speech he won spiritual liberty for himself and his people in spite of papal anathemas and imperial legions. He represented the early enthusiasm of the German Reformation and the ardor of its beginning.

A calmer period was to follow, requiring steadiness and patience and a more intellectual and sustained effort. The pen was to preserve what the tongue had uttered, and give system and order and permanance to the outpourings of liberty and truth. Therefore we do not find another such orator, but scholars and theologians instead. Erasmus the erudite, Melancthon the gentle, Zwingli the intrepid were great and useful each in his own way, but it was not Luther's way in all that relates to eloquence.

BUCER, perhaps, came nearest to it by his direct and moving appeals to his countrymen. As preacher for twenty-five years in the Church of St. Aurelian and as lecturer on theology in the University of Cambridge in England he earned for himself the epithet of "the eloquent." Invited to this professorship by Cranmer, the counterpart of Luther in England, Bucer brought into the labors of the Anglican reformers elements which were not exactly in accord with their spirit; but this is aside from the present purpose of tracing a slender thread of oratory which ran through these controversial years without making much show in the midst of a great amount of written material, which has survived the ephemeral but effective utterances of the pulpit.

John Calvin, even, cannot be enrolled among the orators of the Reformation, for the less conspicuous Farel and Viret surpassed him in the pulpits of Geneva. His controversies were waged with the pen, backed by the faggot in one instance. Both methods were then in vogue. His intellect was greater than his heart; and a man of no sympathies can never move and seldom convince the multitude.

The names of Martin Luther and his continental associates are so commonly connected with the Reformation in Germany that it is too often forgotten that a corresponding work was going on in England, under the direction of such worthies as Latimer and Cranmer and Ridley; the main difference in results being that on the continent the work was destructive of the mediæval system, root and branch, while in England whatever was good in the living tree was saved, the dead wood being cut away remorselessly. Some doubtful branches, also, were allowed to remain, to live or die, as the temper of future times should determine. Three centuries have sufficed to cleanse and revivify the whole organic structure, without destroying its integrity and continuity from the days of Athanasius and Chrysostom and Ambrose and Augustine.

Among the preachers of the English Reformation HUGH LATIMER must be counted preëminent. If not the most effective speaker of his age he was certainly the most pungent and indefatigable. He was also a departure from the conventional preacher of his time, an original thinker, expressing his thoughts in an original manner. A man well stocked with the learning of the day he made very little show of it, preaching as if a sermon had never been preached before, without much order or plan in what he said, discursive commentaries on the condition of the church or nation, the news of the day, the state of the public mind, the abounding temptations; in short, free talks on all sorts of subjects that could be forced into the region of Christian truths or motives. At one moment he is stern and vehement in rebuke, towering in his indignation like a Hebrew prophet, again drawing upon an inexhaustible fund of wit and drollery, passing from the gravest themes to the gayest with the remark, "And here, by the way, I will tell you a merry toy," but from it deriving some illustration that helps him get a firmer grasp upon the mixed multitude before him. He was not particular where he preached; cathedral, village church, or open street served his turn equally well. His most powerful sermons were delivered in a public garden of the palace "where," he says, "there was constant walking up and down and such a buzzing and huzzing in the preacher's ear that it maketh him often forget his matter." But he remembered enough to impress his hearers with truths they did not easily forget. He spared none of them, not even King Henry the Eighth. It is a wonder that the great beheader did not send Latimer to the block. Instead he gave him the bishopric of Worcester. Later the king's countenance toward the bold preacher changed and he was sent to the Tower.

His doom was averted by the death of the king. Edward set him at liberty and made him his preacher. Twice each Sunday during this reign Latimer delivered eloquent and forceful sermons in the chapel royal. They are full of information on the condition of society, the state of opinion, and the prevalent degree of culture. On most topics they display keen insight and profound practical wisdom. With a loving heart, a merry wit, and a subtile spirit, dauntless and incorruptible, he is always publishing the truth which has been released from a long bondage of corruption. Here is a sample of a discourse which he delivered at Paul's Cross, London, January 18, 1549. It is on the Parable of the Sower. "Honorable audience," he says, "ye may not be offended when I compare the preacher to a ploughman. It hath been said of me, 'O Latimer, I will never believe him while I live, nor never trust him.' . . But it was as I said, according to that which Peter saw and said, there should come fellows by whom the way of truth should be ill spoken of. . . . Ye must not be offended when I liken a prelate to a ploughman." He then proceeds to draw out the similitude at length. But by and by he says, "Ever since prelates were made lords and nobles the plough standeth; there is no work done, and the people starve. They are so troubled with lordly living, they be so placed in palaces, couched in courts, rustling in their rents, dancing in their dominions, pampering of their paunches like a monk that maketh his jubilee, moiling in their gay manors and mansions, and loitering in their lordships, that they cannot attend to ploughing and sowing the seed. Some are in the king's matters, some are ambassadors, some at court, some in parliament, some presidents, and some comptrollers of the mint; and money is worse than it used to be since they have been ministers. In this behalf I must speak to England. Hear, my country, England, that Paul was no sitting bishop, but a walking and preaching bishop. Wo worth thee, O devil, wo worth thee, that thou hast prevailed so far and so long that thou hast made England to worship false gods. Yea, holy water yet at this day remaineth in England to drive away devils, and for a remedy against spirits, and I would this were the worst; but good hope there is that here in England we shall have all things well, for the king's majesty is so brought up in knowledge, virtue, and godliness." These are sentences taken at intervals from the discourse to show its tone and spirit. The language is free and familiar and unsparing; the speaker is holding a colloquy with the people standing around the pulpit, as the custom then was. It is an outdoor address, and has all the freedom of the every-day talk of the time, and all the unsparing truthfulness of a man who knew that he might hang for his words, but who did not stop for that.

All this free speech was ended when Mary came to the throne, and Latimer, at the age of eighty, was kept in the Tower for sixteen months before he was sent to the stake. His words there partake of the nature of his prophecy. "Be of good courage, Master Ridley, and play the man; we shall this day light such a candle, by God's grace, in England, as I trust shall never be put out." This is the best remembered and oftenest quoted of all his sayings, and of all that was said in that reign of blood and fire.

In Scotland the leader of the Reformation was JOHN KNOX, a headlong sort of a man of vehement energy, who was tossed about from "one kingdom to another people," but who could keep silence nowhere. Politics and religion were alike the theme of his oratory; and when his tongue was tied he could write such tracts as that entitled, "The First Blast of the Trumpet Against the Monstrous Regiment (rule) of Women;" Mary of Guise being Regent of Scotland and Mary Tudor queen of England. His preaching in the Cathedral of St. Andrew's united magistrates and citizens in a crusade against monasteries and churches, while his bold and bitter discussions in the presence of Mary, Queen of Scots, drove her to tears. For three days he disputes with Abbot Kenedy, and though stricken with partial paralysis he utters such tirades from the pulpits of Edinburgh that he is compelled to flee the city. His last speech was more worthily employed in denunciation of the atrocities of the St. Bartholomew massacre.

XVIII.

THREE FRENCH ORATORS IN THE REIGN OF LOUIS XIV.

AFTER the Reformation there was no immediate revival of eloquence in England. It does not share the triumphs of dramatic literature, of science, and the arts in Elizabeth's reign. The next outburst of it occurs in France, where certain conditions favorable to oratory existed. First a long and almost uninterrupted line of literature had been accumulating since the eleventh century. Troubadours had sung their lyric songs, the trouvères had celebrated heroic deeds of kings and knights and nobles. Romances of Alexander and Arthur and Charlemagne were succeeded by the beginnings of history in the chronicles of Villehardouin, 1207, culminating in Froissart in the fourteenth century. The biographies of Comines, the writings of Rabelais and Montaigne led up to the philosophic theology of John Calvin's Institutes. At last, after five centuries, French prose had grown strong enough to become the medium of eloquence. Malherbe, the corrector of poetry and "tyrant of words and syllables," with the French Academy establishing rules for the language, made it capable of expressing the high philosophical thought of Descartes; while in the vehement eloquence of Pascal's Provincial Letters a standard of French prose was established for that century. All this growth found its fruitage in the splendid literary period which is styled the Age of Louis XIV., 1638–1715, in which a group of illustrious minds applied themselves to the elaboration of every branch of literature. It was in this age and under these favoring conditions that pulpit oratory was made conspicuous once more by such men as Bossuet, Bourdaloue, and Massillon.

Of these BOSSUET was first in the order of time and of excellence. Born in 1627 he was educated after the manner of his age in a Jesuit college, where he spent ten years in diligent study of the prescribed curriculum of the order. At sixteen his eloquence attracted the notice of literary people, paving the way for preferment to ecclesiastical offices. He became the most admired and popular preacher in Paris. Churches were filled to overflowing when he was expected to preach, and illustrious persons were eager to become his auditors.

His success was the talk of society and led to his introduction to the great world of Paris and the brilliant assemblies of the court. An account of his precocity has been preserved in the story of a patron who boasted that if the youthful improviser were given a subject and a few moments for recollection, he could pronounce a creditable discourse upon any topic selected. Accordingly the boy was sent for near midnight to preach before a numerous throng of literary fashionables. Taking his theme aside for a few moments he re-appeared much sooner than was expected and took the critical circle by storm. Summoned by a bishop to repeat the experiment in a graver assembly he received, instead of fulsome flattery, kindly advice and a warning against the danger of premature success. However there were admirers enough to keep before him his vocation as an orator, if he had not himself been mindful of it. Consequently he used every effort to cultivate his powers, even attending the theatre when Corneille was king of the drama, to catch what hints he might from the actors.

His more sober studies were in St. Chrysostom, whom he regarded as the greatest preacher of antiquity, in Origen and Augustine. In this study of sacred themes no toil was too great. He had indeed drawn largely from classic sources. Homer, Tacitus, and Thucydides furnished strength and vigor to his style, and the prophets of the Old Testament inspired him with sublimity and pathos. Such wide range of study gave him comprehensive views on every subject.

His career as a pulpit orator is divided into three periods; the first showing progress toward his highest attainment, the second that of his meridian splendor, the third that of his decline. In manner and matter the first is distinguished by the length at which the subject is treated; the second by rapidity, strength, and pathos; the third by order, finish, and symmetry, with somewhat of diminished energy and force. In all there was a vast fund of biblical and patristic lore, upon which he drew for impassioned speech of the most brilliant and learned character. Careless in his style in early years he came at length to correct, alter, abbreviate, and condense, often entirely changing his original sentences, and except under the pressure of a most imperious necessity he would never preach without a sketch of his main points and the prominent lessons he wished to teach.

Living in the palmiest days of monarchy it should be said to his credit that he never truckled to royalty. In the words which he addressed to Anne of Austria, "It is too cruel a flattery to tell the great that they are faultless. Their very eminence makes no fault of theirs trifling." To the humble, on the other hand, he did not lower himself, but tried the rather to raise them to a higher plane by the clearness and simplicity of his thoughts and expressions, thundering against deadly sins, or again speaking words of the sweetest mysticism to an assembly of the faithful. He strove to strip his oratory of whatever should please rather than edify. Of him Pére de Neuville says, "He is the unique master of the sublime and the energetic and the pathetic. Born an orator there is as much folly in attempting to imitate him as of madness in hoping to do so." Yet there were imitators. Admitted to the highest literary society that France or the world could boast his entrance was signalized by the statement that he had won the applause of France by his far-famed preaching and the éclat with which he had filled the pulpit. Such was his introduction to the Academy. "Eloquence in him," it was said, "is not the result of study; everything is natural and superior to art. Those noble forms, those grand lights, those bold, living expressions which nothing can resist." Vigorous, manly eloquence is joined to full, solid learning; and to sweet helpfulness of the meek and lowly is united stern and uncompromising denunciation of vice in a wayward king and a corrupt court.

Lamartine best discriminates as to the character of his eloquence. He speaks of the "strong vein of sound sense, consistency, and tempered discipline which ran through all his eloquence, as timbers underlie the magnificence and ornament of the building they support. His style rises to an equality with the majesty of the themes—simple as the oracle which disdains to please, unpremeditated as the word uttered in the rapidity of thought, slow as meditation, rapid as the inspiration which fears to escape from itself, collected and reflective as the temple, sometimes as unpolished as the people, always guided by nature to the idea it wishes to express, poetic and yet logical, losing sight of the audience and the chain of reasoning to give vent to emotion and direct address, which suggests the inspired eloquence of the ancient prophets."

Unfortunately we are obliged to depend more upon the testimony of contemporaries than upon the sermons of Bossuet for an estimate of his oratory. Notes and rough sketches are the only inheritance left us. But from these can be gained some idea of the impression which the entire discourse must have made upon his auditors. His elocution was not inferior to his composition. A deep-toned voice, controlled by the soul of the speaker more than by rules of art, a lofty stature and imposing presence elevated the man above the professional preacher, whose torrents of eloquence overwhelmed the audience and left them not so much in admiration as in agitation.

His best productions were the celebrated funeral discourses which he pronounced over the great dignitaries of his time, such as Condé, Henrietta, the widowed queen of England, and Anne of Austria. Some remarkable discourses were also pronounced when certain followers of Louis XIV. renounced the gayeties of his court and took upon themselves the vows of religious seclusion, in those days the next thing to a living entombment. It was such eloquence which secured to him ecclesiastical promotion.

When he abandoned the pulpit for the episcopal chair another orator took possession whose name will always be associated with Bossuet's. This orator was BOURDALOUE. Comparisons were often made between these two rivals in eloquence. The number of each one's admirers was not far from equal. Indeed Bourdaloue's argumentative discourse was better understood by the average auditory than Bossuet's impassioned eloquence; for logic, going on foot, can be more easily followed than the poetic flight of genius. Still there is much to be said in commendation of Bourdaloue's peculiar method. Voltaire said that Bourdaloue was the first who made men hear from the pulpit reasonings that were always eloquent; and a writer calling himself Alexander Vinet observes that it would have been better to say, "Eloquence always reasonable." Bossuet, always eloquent, was not always reasonable, while Bourdaloue, if not always eloquent, never trangresses the severe exactions of good sense and sound reasoning. His language is just what the subject requires, no more and no less. It is sententious without the appearance of trying to be terse, concise without being cramped for room. Sparing of images and figures he fills his discourse with thoughts, using an enormous number. It might be expected that he would exhaust his store before he reaches the second quarter of his sermon; but the old law of the free-giver is true here, and of the fountain which yields the more plentifully as it is drawn upon. His economy is not that of ideas, fearing that he will run out and be impoverished; it is rather of words and imagery.

He says of himself to his hearers, "You have been touched with sympathy a hundred times; now I wish to instruct you. Your hearts have been moved with fruitless compassion or transient remorse; my design is to convince your reason as a foundation for all the feelings of piety which this mystery must inspire." It has been remarked that Bourdaloue was popular from the abundance of that which generally is most destructive of popularity, the logical element in discourse; but the more he reasoned the more he was admired. He made his hearers use their own reasoning faculties, and they were flattered and pleased. He did not go much beyond this ratiocination to touch the fancy and the heart. He addressed the understanding and was satisfied. Such a speaker would find hearers in a time when there was danger of being surfeited with the graces of an imaginative style. There are reactions in a poetic age which call men away from its usual forms to sturdier expression, and in the reign of Louis XIV. the logic of Bourdaloue was a grateful contrast to the imagery of Bossuet.'

A glimpse of the preaching of the time is afforded in an account of Bourdaloue's sermon before the king, as depicted by the author of *Bourdaloue and Louis XIV.* The preacher had in mind, as everybody present had, the separation of the king from one of his favorites. The place was the chapel royal at Versailles; the time the commemoration of the Crucifixion. "Never," says the writer, "was an assembly more devout in appearance, or less so in reality. The sermon had commenced. Who had said that it would not be an ordinary one and that the king would go as he came?" It should be remarked here that the preacher had prepared two perorations, one flattering the king and another denouncing his evil course. "As the sermon went on he was constantly tempted to use the one with smooth words of adulation, and as he drew near the moment when he would be forced to decide, the more terrified he became as to which side to take. Twenty times he was on the point of losing the thread of his discourse. He felt this, and gave the more vehemence to his utterance. He draws near the close, and does not yet know what he shall do. Another page and hesitation will no longer be possible. One phrase only is left; he dashes on and lets go the first words that come into his mouth. All is lost! It is the wrong—the flattering conclusion. It is as if the devil had whispered in his ear. Suddenly he stops, and sees in a remote corner his mentor, the man who had charged him to strike and spare not. Humiliated he bows his head and clasps his hands. But he recalls himself. Now it is your turn, Louis the Great! 'Ah, my brethren, what was I about to say? Is it at this hour that I can have the courage to praise? Does it not cry out that all men are sinners? And shall I dare to make one exception? No, sire, no! I will not set even you apart. Woe to the king who shall imagine that there are two roads to heaven, one for himself and one for his people.' And then he went on to mention the illusions under which a king labors as to the extent of his crimes. Happily the king cast down his eyes, which somewhat relieved the agonies of those present. If he had but frowned they would have wished the earth to swallow them. He did not move, except to bend down his head. Bourdaloue saw nothing, heard nothing. There was no longer the slightest trace of indecision or terror. He dashed headlong into passages which he had most dreaded beforehand, pronounced with vigorous assurance those words which he had trembled at in reading. Twenty minutes after the service was over, in an anteroom the king said to a courtier, ' Is Father Bourdaloue there?' 'Yes, sire.' ' Bring him to me.' 'Well, my father, you ought to be satisfied. The person you have in mind is at Clagny!' 'Yes, sire, but God would be better satisfied if Clagny were seventy miles from Versailles.' 'What! you distrust me still? But I thank you for your sermon. It was your duty, you have fulfilled it. You must give me the peroration. I wish to read it again.' "

This sketch pictures as well as anything can the difficulties and dangers that beset a little company of great preachers who, because they were eminent, were in demand at the court of the royal rake Louis XIV., where the best of everything was demanded. Nobles and princes could display their loyalty by the most servile adulation, but the preachers of righteousness had much to render the course difficult between fidelity to the king and the King of kings. To their praise, be it said, that the pomp and glory of the visible did not blind their eyes to the things unseen. The ephemeral nature of worldly grandeur appears to have been forced upon them by frequent instances of mortality, and into the midst of all the splendor of regal life death was continually intruding. At such times the great pulpit orators of that magnificent age asserted the preëminence of the eternal over the temporal, of the infinite over the finite.

This was especially true of MASSILLON, the third great orator of this illustrious group. He succeeded to Bourdaloue, as Bourdaloue had succeeded to Bossuet. As the career of each had ended another took his place. But each differed from the other in many respects. They are alike only in the power each one possessed, in his own way, to sway the multitude by his eloquence. The individuality of Massillon consisted in the introduction of pathos into discourse, and a slight softening of the divine message without detracting from its truth and authority.

"Does it not seem to you," said those who had heard him, some years afterward, "does it not seem to you that you see him still in the pulpit, with that artless look, that modest bearing, those eyes meekly dropped, that careless gesture, that affectionate tone, that appearance of a man deeply moved, illuminating the minds of his hearers and stirring their hearts with the tenderest emotions?" He did not thunder in the pulpit, nor frighten his hearers by the violence of his outbursts and the explosion of his voice, but by sweet persuasion he poured into them the sentiments which melt the heart. There were no far-fetched flowers of speech, there were few gestures even, only a rare raising of the eye; but when he did it was the finest of gestures, for it was an eloquent eye.

He was particularly happy in his exordiums, securing an attention which he was able to keep to the end. Simple in arrangement of his plan he excelled in the development and amplification of it, justifying the maxim of Cicero, that the "height and perfection of eloquence is to amplify a subject by adorning and decorating it;" or as Quintilian puts it, "A certain assembling of thoughts and expressions which conspire to produce the same impression." Thoughts and phrases spring out of each other in natural sequence in his discourse, moving along like a harmonious group to the melody of rhythmical expression. Graceful and easy in diction his long and flowing periods carry with them the weight and volume of the rolling billow. Elegant in simplicity, rich in culture, sober in ornament, with a certain repose in movement, he appealed to those who have the instinct for harmonious and well-regulated speech, and are removed in their taste from feverish thirst for the sensational, and from idle, listless acceptance of mere commonplaces. Such is the summary of impressions which contemporary testimony leaves. Add to this the tradition of a voice possessing all the tones which a soul needs to express its manifold emotions, accompanied by temperate action, and a combination is produced of which a great actor said, "There is an orator! we are but comedians." A better praise was given by the king himself, who said to Massillon one day on going out after one of his sermons, "My father, I have heard several great orators, and I have been very much pleased with them; as for you, every time that I have heard you I have been very much displeased with myself."

It is one of the distinctions of Massillon that it fell to him to pronounce the funeral oration at the obsequies of the king, in whose life-time this remarkable display of sacred eloquence occurred. The exordium of the oration will be longest remembered. Silently running his eye over the magnificent funeral trappings of the king, whom men had called Louis Le Grand, he said, "My brethren, God alone is great."

One of the passages, in which he observes the old maxim, "to speak no evil of the dead," is as follows: "From that fund of wisdom proceeded the majesty displayed in his whole person; in his most private life he never forgot the gravity of royal dignity; never did a king sustain better than he the majestic character of sovereignty. . . . . Meanwhile, as you know, that majesty had no fierceness, but a charming address, when it was willing to be approached; an art of timing its favors, which touched men more than the favors themselves; politeness of speech which knew always how to say that which men most loved to hear."

As this brief and inadequate extract may indicate, Massillon was preëminently the orator of emotion. Bossuet had spoken as one inspired and with authority; Bourdaloue had poured out the treasures of a mind full of thought; and to these Massillon succeeded with a heart full of sympathy for his fellowmen. In this development of eloquence may be discerned a progress similar to that which marks the growth of literature from the poetic to the intellectual, and finally to the emotional. Imagination is succeeded by the understanding and the understanding by the emotions. Massillon addresses the heart in the plain language which best describes what passes in the heart and life of man, awakening joyful and painful sentiments by turns, but always with propriety and moderation. Like Demosthenes, with whom Theremin compares him, he takes a few simple thoughts as the ground-work of his discourse and uses them in a great variety of ways to accomplish his purpose. Like Chrysostom he presses upon the wavering hearer with immediate address arguments drawn from a profound knowledge of the human heart and of human life. As Bossuet had spoken from the bishop's throne and Bourdaloue as from scholastic surroundings, so Massillon spoke to men and women of the world in the cultivated language of society upon themes which most vitally concerned them.

Who is greatest in this kingdom of eloquence in a kingly age it is not possible to pronounce with authority beyond personal preference. As one admires brilliance, profundity, or sensibility, will be his verdict. Each orator has had his following in his own day and since. Covering the last half of the seventeenth century, an age rich in highly gifted men and marking a splendid epoch in literature, an age not lacking in piety but burdened with worldliness and a corrupt court, this coterie of orators may be regarded as the fruit of their time, ripened by the sunshine above and the decay beneath them. After them literature declined, and with it eloquence and morality and liberty, until human rights were reasserted in the most inhuman fashion of the French Revolution, toward the end of the succeeding century. Another sort of oratory then sprung up which was as wild and erratic as the movement which it accompanied.

XIX.

ORATORY OF THE FRENCH REVOLUTION. NAPOLEON.

IN ESTIMATING the eloquence of the French Revolution it should be remembered that the best oratory cannot be reduced to the measure of any arbitrary standard. As there was one criterion of excellence for Athens and another for Ephesus and another still for Rome, and each in a different age and under a different civilization, so it must not be thought abnormal if a singular irregularity in public speech occurred under the conditions which prevailed in France near the close of the last century. It must be borne in mind that the easy-going times when the cultured few basked in the smiles of royal patronage were over. Tyranny was reaping as it had sown. A down-trodden people were springing up with tremendous energy. Surprised at their unexpected success they were wild with the first flush of triumph, yet so uncertain of ultimate victory and so undetermined among themselves as to a permanent course to pursue, that there was abundant need of counsel and leadership. This was met at first by the orators of the nation.

The task before them at first was to destroy any lingering reverence for kingly authority. No half-measures appeared to be consistent with the emancipation of France. Heroic and even violent treatment was the only remedy for evils that had been increasing for centuries. It must be the power of the people, utter and complete in its rule, or royalty would lift up its head to their destruction. In such a case and with such a people nothing but the most radical counsels would be listened to, and the man who should go farthest would be likely to have the greatest following. At the outset this man was MIRABEAU.

A glance at his portrait shows what might be expected of him. It is the personification of impudent defiance. Born into the world with a pair of grinders, tongue-tied, and one foot twisted, it is said he grew up "as ugly as the nephew of Satan," "a monster, physically and intellectually," as his father averred. But his father was another monster in his treatment of him, and it is a wonder that the boy did not turn out a reprobate. As it was, after a most eventful youth, and an early manhood passed in the army, in prison, and in Bohemian wanderings he came to Paris in 1785, where he found himself a penniless writer of political pamphlets, one of which was ordered to be burned by the common executioner. Elected to the assembly of deputies by the third estate for the city of Aix he became the mouthpiece of the revolution. It should be remarked, however, that he represents the transition period, and was not at first hostile to royalty. He would secure liberty to the people while sparing the throne. Regarding mobs and riots with disfavor he was ready to restore the king's legitimate authority as the only means of saving France, as he thought.

This was the period of his immense activity. To his

absorbing duties as deputy were added those of a journalist of the convention. To meet the exigencies of his manifold duties he resorted to assistance which is novel in the work of the orator, though not so in that of the journalist. He called around him coadjutors such as Dumont, Duroveray, Reibaz, and others who might claim a large share in the composition of some of his best speeches. They furnished what he regarded simply as materials into which his genius infused new life, as Shakespeare did into the old plays which he recast and revivified; so that it has been said that between a speech written for him by Dumont and Duroveray and as delivered by himself there was as much difference as between the dead and the living, vested as it was with the life and splendor which came from himself alone. It was the reverse of the speech-writing of the ancients, which lost by the unprofessional citizen's delivery. He would receive notes as he ascended the tribune and weave them without apparent reflection into the texture of his discourse. He would give the plan of a speech, and after it had been written out by another, retouch it with his practiced judgment and strengthen it with his vigorous thought. Most of his discourses, however, were premeditated. The famous speeches on the Constitution, Royal Veto, and National Education were written out with great care and elaboration. Strong, energetic, natural, and without ornament, he is eloquent in the simplicity of his diction. Clear in the statement of facts, positive in the statement of questions, ample and sonorous in phraseology, he unrolls the fabric of his discourse with measured solemnity. Seeking not so much the harmony of words as the connection of thoughts he secures a sequence of effects which is irresistible in cumulative power. His order of advance is impenetrable, his method of attack irresistible, and escape from his conclusions impossible. Here is an example of his manner in the speech on National Bankruptcy, equivalent to enumeration:

"Two centuries of depredation and robbery have excavated the abyss wherein the kingdom is on the verge of being engulfed. This frightful gulf it is indispensable to fill up. Well, here is a list of property-holders. Choose from among the richest so as to sacrifice the smallest number of citizens. But choose, for is it not expedient that a small number perish to save the mass of the people? Restore order to our finances, peace and prosperity to our kingdom. Do you imagine that because you refuse to pay you cease to owe? Vote then this subsidy, and may it prove sufficient. Vote it because the class most interested is you yourselves. Vote it because the public exigencies allow of no evasion and no delay. Beware of asking time; misfortune never grants it. To-day bankruptcy, hideous bankruptcy is before you. It threatens to consume you, your country, your property, your honor. And do you deliberate?"

Admirable as Mirabeau was in his premeditated discourse, his extemporaneous utterance was full of vehemence and fire. He roared, he stamped, he shook his shock of hair, and trod the tribune with the imperial air of a king. His habitual grave and solemn tones were gone, and in their place rang out accents of thunder and heart-rending pathos, and all without losing his self-control. But these improvised efforts were short and wisely ended when the blow was struck. He was not subject to the common infirmity of extemporaneous speakers, not knowing when to stop and how.

Nothing of Mirabeau can better show the greatness of the man and the orator than his independent attitude toward both the populace and royalty alike. To those who contended that the Assembly ought not to have the initiative in the impeachment of the King's ministers he replied, "You forget that the people to whom you oppose the limitation of the three powers is the source of all the powers, and that it alone can delegate them. You forget that it is to the sovereign you would deny the control of his own administrators." And to ambassadors going to the king to request a dismission of the troops he said, "Say to the king—say to him that hordes of foreigners by whom we are invested have received the visits of the princes and their presents. Say to him that the whole night these foreign satellites, gorged with gold and wine, have been predicting the enslavement of France and invoking the destruction of the National Assembly. Say to him that in his very palace the courtiers have led their dances to the sound of this barbarous music, and that such was the prelude to St. Bartholomew."

No brief extract can give an idea of the impetuous onset of Mirabeau's eloquence. It must be read by the page to measure its power, and even then it must have been heard to feel its tremendous force.

To understand the progress of eloquence in the

French Revolution the great struggle between the Girondists and Jacobins should be recalled. The first of these factions embraced in their number some of the finest orators France ever produced. Idealists, with a fond looking backward toward the glories of Greek and Roman republics, they dreamed of reviving ancient liberty in their own time and nation. Meanwhile the Jacobins were declaiming of aristocracy and privileged orders in Paris and arousing the hatred of the populace against them. The time itself was inspiring. The fall of a throne, the sudden rise of a republic in its place, the removal of restraints that had fettered thought stirred men's minds to intense activity. All the great interests of life were merged in the conflict, and life itself was the price that the principal actors had to pay for their part in the overthrow of the ancient order.

Add to this the collision between the two parties who were trying to guide the storm, each in its own way, and a new inspiration is contributed. On the one side a band of noble and eloquent men; on the other dark, intriguing, desperate characters. The collision between these two groups produced examples of oratory unlike those of any previous or subsequent time; not the highest, or the most deserving of imitation, but unique and unsurpassed in the direction of impassioned speech. A paragraph from VERGNIAUD indicates the spirit that was riding upon the whirlwind. It was on the occasion of the failure of the first conspiracy of the Jacobins against the Girondists, of which party the speaker himself was a member. "We march from crimes to amnesties, and from amnesties to crimes. The great body of citizens are so blinded by their frequent occurrence that they confound these seditious disturbances with the grand national movement in favor of freedom; regard the violence of brigands as the efforts of energetic minds, and consider robbery itself as indispensable to public safety. 'You are free,' say they, 'but unless you think like us we will denounce you to the people, we will abandon you to their fury unless you join us in persecuting those whose probity or talents we dread.' Citizens, there is too much room to fear that the Revolution, like Saturn, will devour all its progeny, and finally leave only despotism with all the calamities it produces." His prophecy proved true, and he was among the first to be devoured by the guillotine; perhaps because he had been the chief orator in the Reign of Terror.

Others there were who, in a less turbulent age and with fewer contemporaries in eloquence, would have made themselves illustrious examples of persuasive or coercive speech; men like Roland and Lanjuinais, Louvet and Barbaroux, Desmoulins and Varennes, Marat and Robespierre. In this tempestuous time DANTON may stand for the whirlwind as Mirabeau had stood for the gathering storm.

As the clouds began to pass over and the Revolution to retrograde there was but little display of eloquence. When Bonaparte came into power he preferred to do most of the speaking himself. At last censorship over tongue and press was established, and oratory became the echo of his sentiments concerning the glory of France. Wild dreams of republicanism had their fulfilment in boundless enthusiasm for a military leader who knew how to appeal to men in many ways, not the least effective of which was by means of the greatest military oratory the world has known. The great captains of a remote antiquity addressed their soldiers, so far as we know, mostly in the language of Herodotus and Thucydides, Livy and Tacitus, or in the terms which these historians think they ought to have employed. Napoleon spoke in the words of his own choosing. Cæsar most resembled him on the battlefield, encourageing his troops with inspiring words; and there is the possibility that the elegant and accomplished Cæsar rewrote his military harangues in the seclusion of his tent or of his house at Rome. But Bonaparte is near enough to our own times to be judged correctly in respect to his eloquence, for the record of it has been preserved with remarkable fidelity.

The main feature of it is its adaptation to the needs of the hour. Knowing men as few leaders of men ever have known their followers his words to them are such as they needed to hear. The same unfailing perception which told him what to do in every emergency directed him in what was best to say. Coupled with this rare intuition went an authority in speech, surpassed only by his commanding presence. One remarks of him that he speaks "as if he stood on a mountain, and was himself a hundred cubits high." To be sure, the highly wrought language he uses would be overdrawn at the present day, but in his own the general imagination was at the highest pitch of excitement, for the groundswell of the Revolution had not wholly subsided. Besides he was addressing an army, and not an accomplished audience. Plain words spoken to the heart rather than the head, appealing to the emotions rather than the reason, was the only form of harangue that he chiefly employed.

"Friends," said he to the army of Italy, at the outset of his career, "Friends, I promise you that glorious conquest; but be liberators of peoples, be not their scourges." His addresses are strong in their commendation of what his soldiers have achieved. It might be called flattery if it were not truth. "Soldiers, in fifteen days you have gained six victories, taken twenty-one stands of colors, fifty pieces of cannon, and made fifteen hundred prisoners. You are the equals of the conquerors of Holland and of the Rhine. Destitute of everything you have supplied yourselves with everything. You have won battles without cannon, crossed rivers without bridges, made forced marches without shoes, bivouacked without spirituous liquor, and often without bread. Thanks to you, soldiers. Your country has a right to expect great things of you. You still have battles to fight, cities to take, rivers to pass. Is there one among you whose courage flags? No, there is not one among the victors of Montenotte, of Millesineo, of Diego, and of Mondovi." After this he marched from triumph to triumph.

Entering Milan he encouraged them in this way: "Soldiers, you have rushed like a torrent from the Appennines. Milan is yours. You have crossed the bulwarks of Italy. Your friends rejoice at your triumphs. Let us on. We have yet forced marches to perform, enemies to subdue, laurels to gather, wrongs to avenge.

To reinstate the Capitol, to awake the Roman people from the lethargy of ages of enslavement—this is what remains for us to accomplish."

French soldiers had not been accustomed to such language. They were infatuated with their leader, and they would have followed him to the ends of the earth, whither, in his inmost soul, he intended to go. Accordingly when starting for Egypt he says, " Frenchmen," (they were well at sea before he disclosed his plans), " Frenchmen, you have great destinies to fulfil, battles to fight, fatigues to surmount. Europe has her eyes upon you. The first city you are to enter was founded by Alexander the Great." At the pyramids he tells them that forty centuries are looking down upon them.

Sometimes he takes another course and, as on the morning of Austerlitz, throws himself in their keeping, saying, " I will keep away from the firing, if with your wonted bravery you carry disorder and confusion into the enemy's ranks. But if the victory should be for a moment doubtful you will see me rush to fall in the front of the conflict."

And after the battle he thus addresses them: "Soldiers, I am pleased with you; you have decorated your eagles with immortal glory. When the French people placed upon my head the imperial crown I relied upon you to maintain it ever in that eminence of glory which alone could give it value in my eyes. I will soon lead you back to France where you will be the object of my tenderest solicitude." Sometimes his ardor gives wings to his words, as in the expedition to Naples : " Soldiers, march; hurl into the waves the impotent battalions of those tyrants of the seas. Let me hear quickly that the sanctity of treaties is avenged, and that the manes of my brave soldiers are appeased."

And then in his farewell are found the same identification of himself with his troops as in the days of his glory: "Soldiers, I bid you farewell. For the twenty years we have been together your conduct has left me nothing to desire. I have always found you on the road to glory. All the powers of Europe have combined against me. France herself has desired other destinies. Be faithful to your new king, and desert not our beloved country. Do not lament my lot. I shall be happy when I know that you are. Adieu, my children; the best wishes of my heart shall be always with you."

There will always be differences of opinion concerning the motives which underlay Napoleon's activities. He will be regarded as the great military genius, or the great pretender of history; but as an orator his words and his personal magnetism were sufficiently powerful to draw all France after him into whatever quarter of the earth his ambition might lead him. As it is only the man as a speaker and persuader that is now contemplated he must be accorded the first place among military orators. His words are simple, his sentences are short, but they went directly to the hearts of plain men and brought devotion back to him who uttered them.

XX.

ORATORS OF THE RESTORATION.

AS HAS been remarked Napoleon chose to be the sole orator of his time. Nor was it until the Bellerophon was bearing him away toward St. Helena that unrestrained liberty of speech was restored.

DE SERRE was the first orator of the Restoration in point of time, an orator who crushed a civil war, saved the monarchy, and defended liberty. His oratorical career was brief but full of success. Energetic, forcible, versatile, he was equally strong in the consideration of the subject, in the deduction of proofs, and in refutation of his opponents. Clear in the division of his subject, firm in his treatment, and sustained in his reasoning, he shows the strength of his discourse on every page. He was a man to strike out epigrammatic sentences that have become famous. But his triumphs were soon ended by the misfortune that befalls a man who occupies a moderate position where factions rage. Considered too liberal by the royalists and too royalist by the liberals he was sent into the exile of an embassy to meditate upon his past achievements. His masterly description of the freedom of the press in England and the United States shows him at his best, and more like an orator in either of these countries than in his own.

To him succeeded GENERAL FOY, mounting the tribune with the characteristic sentence, "France has still an echo for the words honor and country;" a sentiment which caused tears to flow from the eyes of all the old warriors of the empire. It seemed to them like the war-cry of Napoleon. The speeches of this man were marked by three cardinal excellencies, good sense, rare intelligence, and the knowledge of contemporary needs. They addressed the people in the language of the day and of the hour. The speaker was at one with his time. Besides he had the advantage of being a military orator, a character which always commends itself to Frenchmen. The fact that he was in unison with his time gives, however, an unfavorable complexion to his oratory as compared with the great efforts of the greatest orators. The age itself was narrow, and his oratory was no broader than the observed constitutionalism which he supported. Judged from the present view-point his splendor was somewhat glittering and sensational. He would suddenly leave his seat, scale the tribune as if he were taking a rampart, launch forth words of command, and dazzle the multitude. Frenchmen admired all this display and applauded accordingly.

A contemporary writer says, "It has been observed that a man over forty years of age does not learn extemporization any more than swimming, horsemanship, or music. To supply this defect in his education it is interesting to observe the methods of this orator of military training. He was accustomed to formulate and distribute in his memory the whole plan and proportion of his speech, disposing his exordiums, classing his facts, and sketching his perorations. Then he ascended the tribune and gave himself up to the current of his thought. He knows what he is going to say, but not how he is going to say it. He has the end and purpose of his speaking in view, but not the road by which he is to reach it. It is a mixed process of writer and impersonator, drawing material from the premeditated and the unforeseen alike, from nature and from art. Memory and invention, originality and taste, the ease of the gentleman and the erudition of the scholar, all combined to make the second orator of the Restoration."

The third was BENJAMIN CONSTANT. Without the power of De Serre or the brilliancy of Foy he was more intellectual and prolific than either. With something between a lisp and a stammer in his speech he would rest his hands on the front of the tribune and roll forth a flood of words. The graces which nature had denied him he supplied by force of intellect and labor. For fifteen years he wrote and spoke, and spoke and wrote by turns. Whom he could not reach by tongue he touched in print, and had thousands of readers where he had hundreds of listeners. It was the age of transfer of power from the rostrum to the press, or, more exactly, of division of attention. Most exactly, it was the perpetuation and wide distribution of oratory through the pamphlet and newspaper.

It is the orator, however, that concerns the present subject rather than the editor. Such an orator was he that Frenchmen to-day read his longest speeches without fatigue. Animation, imagery, illustration, art in reasoning, variety in topic characterize his eloquence. It was sometimes too highly finished for the multitude, and better understood in reading than by the hearing. As one of his critics says, " Orators are like those statues placed in elevated niches which must be chiseled somewhat roughly to produce an effect from a distance. Fine antitheses and knotted reasonings fatigue the attention. Repetitions even are preferable to fine drawn distinctions and elaborate arguments."

His command of language, his wit, his presence of mind, his ready adaptation to the fickle tempers of his audience made him always master of the situation. His brilliant denunciation of the lottery system is an example of his oratory, which is not out of time if it be out of place in these days. " If there existed, gentlemen, in your public squares or in some obscure den a species of game which brought infallible ruin upon the players; if the director of this illicit and deceitful concern were to avow that he played with an absolute certainty of winning; that to insure the success of his dishonest speculation he lays his snare for the class most easily deceived and corrupted; that he surrounds the poor with allurements and drives the innocent to most culpable deeds; that his lies and impostures are hawked in open day in every street in the city; what would be your sentiments?"

The eloquence of Constant was not, however, of the overwhelming sort which sweeps all before it. It was rather of the entangling, delusive kind, more adroit than vehement, more persuasive than convincing, more artful than strong. He never forgot that he was an editor, and his speeches show niceties of style that belong to the press rather than to the platform.

ROYER COLLARD was the first of parliamentary writers

in this period, and no mean orator. Elaborate in the artifices of language, erudite and magnificent in speech, he reminded his hearers of Mirabeau. Single truths in his hands expanded into multitudinous forms, like a tree beautiful in form and vigorous with shoots. He speaks as follows of the two parties of the day: "There is a faction born of the Revolution, of its bad doctrines and bad actions, whose aim is usurpation. There is a faction born of privilege, which detests equality and seeks to destroy it at any cost. I know not what these factions do, but I know what they mean and I understand what they say. I recognize the one by its hatred of all legitimate authority, political, moral, religious; the other by its instinctive contempt for all rights, public and private, by the arrogant cupidity which leads it to covet all the advantages of public office and of social consideration. These factions, reduced to their proper force, are weak in numbers; they are odious to the nation, and will never strike deep root in the soil; but they are also ardent, and while we are divided they march toward their object. If they should come into collision once more, I declare to the victorious faction that I shall detest its victory; I ask from this day to be inscribed on its list of proscriptions."

His discourse abounds with beautiful sentiments, somewhat French in their expression, as they must be, but still beautiful. For example, "Representative government is justice organized, reason animated, morality armed; but like the laborer they live by the sweat of their brow." "Constitutions are not tents erected for sleep." "There are all sorts of republics—the aristocratic republic, that of England; the bourgeois republic of France; the democratic republic of the United States." "Human societies are born, live, and die upon the earth; but they do not contain the entire man. There remains to him the noblest part of himself, those lofty faculties by which he soars to a future life and the invisible world. These are the true grandeur of man, the consolation of misfortune, and the inviolable refuge against the tyrannies of this world."

MANUEL represents a new phase, unlike the vehement style which had prevailed in the stormy Revolution, or even among the more restrained and guarded conditions of the empire. A man of lofty reason, master of himself, he was one in whom the people believed and in whom they could confide in the disordered times that followed the abdication of Napoleon. He had the patience to disentangle difficulties rather than to cut them. He explored and explained and unfolded in easy and intelligible language, to the delight of the common understanding. Coming to the Chamber of Representatives with a colossal reputation he was one of the few whom the trumpetings of fame did not injure by raising too high the general expectation. He did not disappoint it. Without large views, profundity, or fine style his speeches exhibit remarkable subtlety of dialectics and abundance of amplification. In his improvisations he was prolix, diffuse, and sometimes inclined to repetition, as all extemporaneous speakers are apt to be; but he had a singular faculty of rapid appropriation and fresh reproduction of ideas. He was the forerunner of what may be called the blocking opposition, a man to twist and turn, delay and extend a question by pretended investigation and amendment and sub-amendment. He would have been of incalculable value in our own Congress to the party that wishes to temporize until the hour of adjournment arrives.

The two French maladies of imagination and enthusiasm did not mislead or confuse him. He did not lose his head when the other side shrugged its shoulders, turned its back, murmured, groaned, and finally flung taunts, sarcasms, and epithets at him. Impassive and serene, he waited till silence was restored by the power of his unruffled patience and admirable temper, and then proceeded like a skilful general, now advancing and now retiring, defending every position until his victory was assured and complete. Some of his sayings show what a judicious spirit he had and how he fathomed the real character of the French people. Having republican sentiments rather than republican opinions he preferred Napoleon II. to a republic, saying, "The republicans are men not ripened by experience;" and again that the republic might have charms for men of elevated soul, but that it was unsuited to a great people in the actual state of our society; and lastly "The throne is the guarantee of liberty."

The name that comes next links the past with the present. It is as if after a long journey we suddenly should catch a glimpse of a familiar spire, and find ourselves nearing home. LAFAYETTE was not of the class of orators which belongs to the Revolution, full of lightning and thunder. He was rather the serious talker, whose ideal speech is that of elevated conversation without figures or imagery, but commending itself to the hearer by its moderation and sobriety. It was an address to the understanding and the common sense of his auditors. Once, however, when he denounced the dastardly abandonment of the Greeks and Poles, his indignation knew no bounds, and his language, ordinarily cheerful, was charged with the fire of righteous wrath. Generally he conforms to the description which one of his biographers gives of him, "A mixture of French grace, American indifference, and Roman placidity." The friend of Washington every one knew that he must be a republican. He defended republican principles with a speech full of the feeling which comes from conviction, replete with systematic reasoning, expressed by proper words in fitting places. His American experience gave a reality to his words which the speculations of Frenchmen concerning liberty, equality, and fraternity could never give.

Other orators of various types belong to this uneasy age. ODILLON BAROT was imposing and staid rather than brilliant and impetuous, like most of his countrymen. Philosophic and reflective also, he viewed things in their general aspect rather than in their practical bearings, a theorizer and dogmatizer, and yet an honest man with a political reputation untarnished and high. He was an orator to calm a turbulent opposition rather than to fire his own party with enthusiasm.

Near to him is DUPIN, the versatile advocate, lively, sarcastic, and rough, blunt and impetuous and desultory. An attorney general of the gravest court of France he kept it in laughter over his anecdotes and witticisms. Yet his sense is strong, his judgment sure, and his arguments models of perspicuity, precision, and logic. With the eloquence of strong common sense he combined a fiery delivery which electrified an assembly. Solid, cogent, concise, and luminous, he is to be reckoned among the most rational of dialecticians and vehement of orators.

LAMARTINE is another name to bring us upon familiar ground, Lamartine the poet, orator, and historian of the Girondists. As an orator he carries into his efforts the imagination of the poet, with a distinct and vivid perception of each subject, illumined by a gorgeous coloring and adorned with abundance of imagery. One who prefers logic to imagination and the language of business to poetry would choose a more vigorous discourse rather than so much melody and color; but these again are natural to the poet-orator and in no wise the ornamental affectations of a prosy man turned poetical for the occasion. One of his French admirers says, " I like his balanced and rhythmical phraseology, though it be more fit to deliver the oracles of Apollo than to express the passions of the forum. I like it because it rolls along like a river, with sweet and plaintive lamentings like the scattered limbs of Orpheus. I like it because if it is not the prose of oratory, it is at least the prose of poetry."

Still another familiar name is GUIZOT, whose books have been our instructors. When he quit the elaborate artificiality of his pen and mounted the tribune, it is said that his thoughts flowed freely and clearly, colored without being surcharged with ornament, grounded upon facts and examples, and adapted to the ordinary understanding. The reason for this modification of style that has been given may apply with truth to all men in their writing and in their speaking. In writing the writer is alone, or attended by the imaginary audience with whom he is only remotely in contact; but when he comes to speak his audience is before him, and he must be governed more or less by their living presence. This will also account for the observed difference between a written and a truly extemporaneous speech. Two excellencies Guizot had worthy of imitation, lucidity of thought and a corresponding clearness of expression which goes directly to the point, saying only what is needful, and saying it well. Accordingly he is one of the few extemporaneous speakers whose reported discourses read well. Still, men did not call him eloquent. He was too cautious and guarded in manner, without that animated, imaginative, and emotional style which occasionally carries one out of himself and takes his auditory with him.

The highest eloquence he ever reached is said to be his famous words about the Constitutionalists of 1789: "I cannot doubt that, in their unknown abode, these noble spirits who have labored so much and so honestly for the weal of humanity must glow with a profound delight in beholding us steer clear to-day of those shoals upon which so many of their own benignant and beautiful hopes have been wrecked." With this may be compared Demosthenes' recall of the warriors who fell at Marathon, Cicero's arraignment of Verres, Bossuet's description of the terrible night that brought the tidings of

Henrietta's death, Mirabeau's apostrophe of the bayonets and the Tarpeian rock, the triple "audacity" of Mirabeau, Vergniaud's "Saturn-like republic, devouring its own children," and O'Connell's re-echoing voice of liberty.

THIERS, best known as historian, was an orator of another kind; vivid, brilliant, airy, voluble, lively, a Frenchman of the French. A flood of words, dexterously handled, full of sudden turns and surprises, and labyrinthine crossings and recrossings, illumined by ingenious reasonings, amazed and half-confounded his auditors. He was seldom unprepared upon any subject, prompt in defence, in attack, in reply and retort. Disorderly in arrangement, precipitate in manner, he twists facts and figures to meet his purposes. A natural free-and-easy discourser he conversed rather than declaimed. He amused his audience while he convinced, interested while he moved them. He was enough of an actor to please his countrymen, and could play his part to perfection in the parliamentary drama of his day. Around the questions of his time he turns, gets up and down, hides, reappears with the agility and cunning of a monkey, and attitudinizes with the vanity and versatility of a tropical bird. With an afternoon's preparation it is said he could make a three-hour speech upon any subject under the sun—architecture, law, poetry, military affairs, chemistry, astronomy, commerce, journalism. As is the case with great talkers, he might have omitted with advantage some things he said. An uninterrupted and continuous flow of wisdom is too much to expect from such volubility. Still he was a man of wonderful mind, fertile in expedients, clear, keen, and versatile, and natural in an artificial age and nation.

There were other orators of the Restoration, but these are chief. From a constitutional monarchy France had passed into a free republic, thence into a wild anarchy of revolution, thence into a glorious empire, and now was falling back to the Bourbon. Every phase was represented in the parliament of the people, royalists, red republicans, and soldiers of Napoleon. Such discordant elements brought to the surface corresponding styles of opinion and of oratory, as diverse as if they belonged to different ages of the world. No one phrase can characterize it unless it be said that it was French, and therefore varied, versatile, vivacious, and uncertain; full of wild theories and wilder impulses; restless, unsatisfied; having lofty visions of human rights and liberty, but evermore lacking the restraint and the wisdom and the steadfastness to make its high hopes a fortunate reality.

XXI.

PARLIAMENTARY ORATORY—CHATHAM.

IN accounting for the remarkable exhibition of eloquence which occurred in England during the last half of the eighteenth century it is hardly sufficient to call attention to an observed appearance of men of genius in groups, inspiring one another and attracting within their orbit such affinities as may be in the field of their influence. The reign of Elizabeth had seen such a constellation circling around a great dramatist, and other reigns, at home and abroad, had been signalized by other literary groups of varied distinction. The same is true of every period of eloquence that has been reviewed, in which a coterie of orators have discoursed upon related themes, inspired by kindred interests. Causes, however, which were more than fortuitous have preceded such occasional developments. In this instance the intellectual revival which had followed the fall of the Stuarts undoubtedly contributed something to the ability of the common people to appreciate the best oratory, more than to the education of the orators themselves. Few will add to these influences the inspiration of royal example and court patronage in the reigns of the Georges of Hanover. Nevertheless there were causes for so conspicuous results.

The third George ascended the throne of England

with greater advantages than had belonged to the accession of any British sovereign previously. He was the first of his house to be born in England, and the prejudice against his family ceased. Party spirit had become almost extinct. Members of the administration, led by the surpassing ability of the elder Pitt, were in harmony with one another. Wonderful success had crowned British arms, and it seemed in the power of the king to extend his conquests still further, or to give peace to the world on his own terms. In the East and West new lands were coming under the dominion of Great Britain. It was the era of England's colonial extension and of her supremacy among the nations. Her traditional enemy across the channel had been worsted in India and America. In the latter the strife for possession of a new continent gave it to England and opened a new world to British enterprise. There seemed to be no limit to a dominion which was extending its boundaries eastward and westward.

Such ages of military success and vast acquisition demand corresponding statesmanship to guide counsels, to restrain ambitions, and to check follies. The time of prosperity to nations, as to persons, is fraught with more dangers than the day of adversity. Giddiness may get into a nation's head. Pride, arrogance, and self-sufficiency are as fatal to a kingdom as to any of its subjects. Therefore at such a time there is great need of wisdom near the throne and at the head of national affairs. Fortunately for England there was enough of this indispensable quality to carry the nation through imminent dangers, but not without mortification and loss. Of this, however, it is not within the province of this subject to speak, except as this and kindred matters affected the character of the oratory which now began to appear.

As might be expected there is a largeness and majesty about it which belongs to the peers of a realm which had, as our own great statesman declared, "dotted over the surface of the whole globe with her possessions and military posts; whose morning drum-beat, following the sun and keeping company with the hours, circles the earth with one continuous and unbroken strain of the martial airs of England."

In the reign of George the Third this was truer than when this beautiful reflection struck the imagination of Webster standing on the ramparts of Quebec. The belt of England's domination did not then reach the Pacific by way of Canada alone, as now. The broad zone of her possessions, running from the seaboard into an unexplored wilderness, typified the sense which Englishmen had of their right of way in the world. If another nation, like the French, attempted a barricade, colonists joined with Britons in sweeping it away, thus contributing to the glory and the eloquence of the home government; and later, Americans themselves furnished topics for parliament to discuss. To be sure, British eloquence was not occupied with American affairs exclusively, but it was in the days of England's colonial power, and the height of it and the transitions of it, that her orators made the age more famous than it otherwise would have been.

There were orators in England before the House of Hanover came to the throne. In the reign of Charles I.

the great commoner, Sir John Eliot, advocating the second charter of English liberty, the Petition of Right, in 1628, is a prophecy of what eloquence is to be. In 1641 the Earl of Strafford made his memorable defence before the House of Lords against the impeachment for high treason. In 1706 Lord Belhaven, in a burst of patriotic feeling, poured out his protest against the disastrous union of England and Scotland. Twenty-five years later Sir Robert Walpole exemplified the practical discussion of the time, with its keen encounter of wit and its doubtful presentation of facts, in the free and colloquial manner which is still in vogue with the businesslike legislators of Great Britain. Chesterfield, associated most often with graceful letter-writing, was counted by Walpole as the chief speaker of his time; but his power lay in keenness of wit and sharpness of tongue, although he had considerable force of intellect and great play of fancy.

Near the middle of the last century the first of the oratorical giants appears, taking his seat in Parliament at the age of twenty-six. This was WILLIAM PITT, first Earl of Chatham. He had devoted himself to rhetorical studies at Trinity College, Oxford, chiefly in the perusal and repeated translation of Demosthenes, varied by reading the voluminous writings of Dr. Barrow, and Bailey's dictionary, which he conned word by word. Continental travel enriched his mind with what Stanhope called a "vast amount of premature knowledge." He had uses for it all before his career was over. Macaulay describes him as he first appeared in parliament: "His figure was strikingly graceful and commanding, his features high and noble, his eyes full of fire. His voice, even when it sunk into a whisper, was heard to the remotest benches; when he strained it to its full extent the sound rose like the swell of an organ in a great cathedral, shook the house with its peal, and was heard through lobbies and down staircases. He cultivated all these natural gifts with the greatest care. His action was equal to Garrick's, the actor. His play of countenance was wonderful; he frequently disconcerted a hostile orator by a single glance of indignation or scorn. Every tone was at his command."

It is not necessary to trace at length his political life. A leader of the opposition, hated by Walpole and the king he filled the few early offices he held with an integrity that refused the customary perquisites upon which other incumbents had grown rich. The people triumphed over royal disfavor and made him prime minister. Disaster to British arms immediately changed to victory and conquest in the East and West. In India and America the old enemy, France, was repeatedly worsted. "The king was conciliated, the commons acknowledged his leadership, the people adored, and all Europe admired him." He was the first citizen of the first nation in the world, raised to this primacy by his abilities. "The great commoner could look down on coronets and garters." Then he was created a noble earl; but the gout, which had tormented him from childhood, put an end to his public career. At intervals he appeared in the House of Lords to speak on questions of great importance; the last time on the second of April, 1778, when he opposed a motion for the acknowledging of American independence. At the end of his speech he fell, and was borne home to die in a few weeks.

Of Lord Chatham as an orator it has been said that the general consent of critics places him among the most powerful, some say the chief, of modern orators. Others may have excelled him in some particular, but no one has combined so well the various elements that make for oratorical primacy. Nature had fitted him for this high eminence. To natural powers he added careful cultivation of action, in the oratorical sense of the word, and compass of tones with vehemence and grace of gesture. Back of these advantages of nature and education lay the sublime personal character of the man, that ethical element which every hearer recognizes whenever it is contrasted with mere wordiness and fluency. His broad views, generous and comprehensive policy, his sense of national honor as superior to temporary expedients ally him to the great Demosthenes in his devotion to what was honorable. An intense spirit of liberty pervaded every act and every speech, and found its response from all liberty-loving people. To the end of his days he stood forth as the defender of popular rights. Not for popular votes or favor, but because freedom was the animating principle of his life, with a spirit of uncompromising truth and integrity that was higher than his eloquence, exalted as that was. Franklin, with his usual discriminating judgment, said, "I have sometimes seen eloquence without wisdom, and often wisdom without eloquence; but in him I have seen them united in the highest possible degree."

Every resource of the orator was at his command,

conciliation and winning persuasiveness when he chose to ingratiate himself by plausible speech; force, severity, ridicule, contempt, and irony when he chose to overwhelm an antagonist. Wide in the range of his thought, comprehensive, acute, and vigorous in his grasp of situations he went straight to conclusions with intuitive decision where most men labored along with slow logical steps. Simple, direct, and plain in his treatment of great themes he made them luminous in the glow of an intense emotion and unclouded with secondary and subordinate considerations. Proof went with the manner of his statement and illustration with the light of a clear understanding. The genuine feeling that accompanied his intellectual efforts gave the force of conviction to all that he uttered, while a vigorous imagination lent the crowning charm to his eloquence. If examined word by word and sentence by sentence his speeches are full of instruction. The style is natural, easy, and varied, with short clauses expressing vivid ideas—the style of a man pressing right onward to the end he has in view, diverted by no by-play and checked by no inferior purpose. He had faults belonging to a self-confident and somewhat arrogant disposition, but they were faults of taste and not of motive. Counterbalancing and overwhelming all these minor defects was an impetuous earnestness, based upon deep conviction, which could not be expressed without the stamp of absolute sincerity. It was this quality that could not be hid by the wealth of poetic utterance nor obscured by the emotion which sometimes accompanied it. With versatile temper he would pass from grave themes to gay, from severity to pathetic appeal. His thorough belief in himself gave others a similar confidence in his capacity to do what was best for them and the nation. His speech was powerful, not because of its beauty, or even its strength, but because it was in harmony with principles of truth and righteousness which he knew, and made others feel, are eternal, and therefore to be followed. Yet there was no lack of beauty, nor strength, nor range of expression, nor intense emotion, nor winning persuasiveness, nor, above all, of an authority in his words and manner which could command the wills of freemen.

The most celebrated of his speeches are those relating to the policy of the British government toward the colonies in America, and of these his greatest effort was that of November 18, 1777, on the motion for an address to the Throne suggesting the arming of hostile Indian tribes to coöperate with British troops in the war upon the colonies. As one editor of his speeches remarks, "It would be difficult to find in the whole range of parliamentary history a more splendid blaze of genius, at once rapid, vigorous, and sublime." Furthermore, it is a speech which probably was revised by himself, an unusual circumstance even in that day of imperfect reporting. A few extracts may indicate the general tone of the speech, but nothing more: "I arise, my Lords, to declare my sentiments on this most solemn and serious subject. . . . It is a perilous and tremendous moment. . . . It is not a time for adulation. The smoothness of flattery cannot now save us in this rugged and awful crisis. It is now necessary to instruct the Throne in the language of truth. We must dispel the illusion and darkness which envelop it, and display in its full danger and true colors the ruin that is brought to our doors. . . . . Who is the minister, where is the minister that has dared to suggest to the Throne the unconstitutional language this day delivered from it? . . . . The Crown from itself and by itself declares an unalterable determination to pursue measures; and what measures, my Lords? The measures that have produced the imminent perils that threaten us; the measures that have brought ruin to our doors. . . But yesterday England might have stood against the world; now none so poor to do her reverence.

"France, my Lords, has insulted you. Can there be a more mortifying insult? Can even our ministers sustain a more humiliating disgrace? Do they dare resent it? . . . Such is the degradation to which they have reduced the glories of England!

"The people whom they affect to call contemptible rebels, but whose growing power has at last gained the name of enemies; the people with whom they have engaged this country in war, and against whom they now command our implicit support in every measure of hostility—this people are now supplied with every military store, their interests consulted, their ambassadors entertained by your inveterate enemy, and our ministers dare not interpose with dignity or effect. Is this the honor of a great kingdom? Is this the indignant power of England who but yesterday gave the law to the house of Bourbon? My Lords, the dignity of nations demands decisive conduct in a situation like this; calls upon us to remonstrate in the strongest language to rescue the ear of majesty from the delusions which surround it. You cannot conquer America. In these campaigns we have done nothing and suffered much. . . You may swell every expense, pile and accumulate every assistance you can buy or borrow; your efforts are forever vain and impotent. If I were an American as I am an Englishman, while a foreign troop was in my country I would never lay down my arms, never—never—never.

"But, my Lords, who is the man that has dared to authorize and associate to our arms the tomahawk and scalping-knife of the savage, and to wage the horrors of his barbarous warfare against our brethren? My Lords, these enormities cry aloud for redress. It is a violation of the Constitution and against law. Let me ask our ministers what other allies they have acquired. Have they entered into an alliance with the king of the gypsies? Nothing is too low or too ludicrous to be consistent with their counsels."

In such strains the speech runs on, full of dignity, of strong reasoning, of cogent instances in proof of his propositions regarding the liberties of America and the rights of Englishmen in the colonies. When he came to animadvert on the proposition of Lord Suffolk to employ Indians in the war his invective is terrific. "Such horrible notions shock every precept of religion, divine or natural, and every generous feeling of humanity, every sentiment of honor; they shock me as a lover of honorable war and a detester of murderous barbarity. Spain armed herself with bloodhounds to extirpate the wretched natives of America, and we improve on the inhuman example even of Spanish cruelty; we turn loose these savage hell-hounds against our countrymen and brethren in America, of the same language, laws, liberties, and religion, endeared to us by every tie that should sanctify humanity."

The best comment on the stupid and stubborn foolhardiness of King George and his cabinet is the circumstance that this stirring speech had no practical effect, and the motion it supported was lost by a vote of ninety-seven to twenty-four. Judicial blindness had fallen upon the heavy and obstinate Hanoverian, to make him lose the sooner colonies which a word of wisdom might have kept faithful to the mother-country. In spite of warnings such as were never thundered in royal ears except by the prophets of Judah the stubborn George and his headstrong council would not yield an inch. Therefore, according to the prophecy of the greatest men of the time, they were soon obliged to give up the better half of a continent.

Lord Chatham voiced the sentiments of the rest when he said with something of hyperbole, " Events of a most alarming tendency, little expected or foreseen, will shortly happen, when a cloud that may crush this nation and bury it in destruction forever is ready to burst and overwhelm us in ruin." So far as possession of the best part of a western continent is concerned this prophecy came to pass. The lower half of North America belongs to the descendants and successors of the colonists, who are already coquetting with the northern half to remove the feud between the two sections, while Englishmen of to-day are saying, "What a pity it is that a trifling disagreement should have separated us."

With a greater Britain stretching from the Atlantic to the Pacific it is not strange that the islanders across the water should regard the obstinacy of George the Third, or, as they like to say, a threepenny tax on tea, as a poor reason for losing a western empire. But that little tax involved the right to impose every arbitrary burden; and as they were careful to insist on that right against the counsel of their greatest statesmen and orators they lost a vast domain.

XXII.

MANSFIELD—BURKE.

ONE of the most interesting inquiries in the realm of literature might be pursued with reference to the early age at which men of great attainments began to show signs of their mature ability. There are several in the field of oratory in different centuries. William Murray, afterward LORD MANSFIELD, is preëminent in this respect. Reading the classics freely at the age of fourteen, having Latin poets by heart, writing their language correctly, and speaking it with ease he gave promise of a great command of his mother-tongue in after years. This was secured by constant translation and retranslation of Greek and Roman orators, which also gave him a practical knowledge of the principles of eloquence, a study which he began to pursue with all diligence upon his entry into the university. This he continued after beginning his law studies, especially in the practice of extemporaneous speech, for which he prepared himself with such fulness and accuracy that his notes were useful to him in after-life, both at the bar and on the bench. A contemporary speaks of his historical knowledge also as appalling to the ordinary reader on account of its familiarity with the subject. Being appointed solicitor general he came into contact with Pitt in a long series of conflicts. In these his eminence as a debater was shown in the defence of his own measures and in the use of logical weapons. His was preëminently a legal intellect, clear and accurate, sound in judgment, strong in reason, and of extraordinary powers of application. He came to the bench not as one who has reached the goal of a lawyer's ambition but as one who is just starting in the race. The manner in which he discharged the duties of his high office may be estimated by the fact that out of the thousands of cases which he decided in the court of the King's Bench there were only two in which his associated judges did not agree with him.

The tribute of our own Chief Justice Story to his judicial character may be cited both as a valuable testimony and as an example of the panegyric paragraph worth repeating here: "England and America and the civilized world lie under the deepest obligations to him. Wherever commerce shall extend its social influences; wherever contracts shall be expounded upon the eternal principles of right and wrong; wherever moral delicacy and judicial refinement shall be infused into the municipal code to persuade men to be honest and to keep them so; wherever the intercourse of mankind shall aim at something more elevated than that groveling spirit of barter, in which meanness and avarice and fraud strive for mastery over ignorance, credulity, and folly, the name of Lord Mansfield will be held in reverence by the good and the wise, by the honest merchant, the enlightened lawyer, the just statesman, and the conscientious judge. His judgments should not be referred to on the spur of particular occasions, but should be studied as models of judicial reasoning and eloquence." As in duty bound, he was the king's lawyer and a defender of royal prerogative. Therefore he was opposed to Chatham and Burke and Fox as advocates of the people's rights in America. Defending the Stamp Act and the right of Parliament to tax the colonists on the ground that they were virtually represented in the House of Commons Lord Campbell, whig as he was, asserts that the logic of Mansfield's speech is unanswerable. His oratory, however, is judicial rather than partisan. He seeks to lead the minds of his hearers to the conclusions he has formed, aiding and directing inquiries rather than appealing to the emotions and wills of men, in order that they shall seem to form their own conclusions. Like our own President Lincoln his happy statement of a case was better than most men's argument. Seizing upon the strong points of the subject he kept them steadily before the mind and led his hearers step by step toward his own conclusions, in a style of speaking which resembled dignified conversation. As an example of this and to give the other side of the controversy about the right of taxing the American colonies a passage may be cited from Lord Mansfield's speech delivered in the House of Lords, February 3, 1766, when the motion was made to repeal the Stamp Act. To propitiate the king, who was opposed to this, a rider was attached declaring that Parliament had the right and power to make laws of full force to bind the colonies. This doctrine of the sovereignty of Parliament Lord Mansfield goes on to defend against the attacks of Chatham and Camden as follows:

"My Lords, I shall speak to the question strictly as a matter of right, for it is a proposition in its nature so perfectly distinct from the expediency of the tax that it must necessarily be taken separate if there is any logic in the world. I shall also speak to the distinctions which have been taken, without any real difference as to the nature of the tax, and I shall point out lastly the necessity there will be of exerting the superior force of the government if opposed by the subordinate part of it."

It will be observed here what a clear statement he makes of the case he intends to argue, rejecting and waiving what he regards as irrelevant matter, the question of expediency. Furthermore it is interesting in these days when so much is written and said upon the problems of taxation to see how the subject was regarded a hundred and thirty years ago when this great jurist said, "I shall endeavor to clear away from the question all that mass of dissertation and learning which has been fetched from speculative men who have written upon the subject of government, or from ancient records, as being little to the purpose. The constitution of this country has been always in a moving state, either gaining or losing something, and with respect to the modes of taxation, when we get beyond the reign of Edward the First or of King John we are all in doubt and obscurity. Writs were issued, some of them according to law, some not according to law." [Among the latter were calls for taxation.] Then after citing certain instances of apparent freedom from parliamentary taxation and showing that this liberty was only apparent and not real, he continues:

"The reasoning about the colonies of Great Britain, drawn from the colonies of antiquity, is a mere useless display of learning, for the colonies of the Tyrians in Africa and of the Greeks in Asia were totally different from our system. No nation before ourselves formed any regular system of colonization but the Romans, and theirs was a military one. Our colonies emigrated under the sanction of the Crown and Parliament, and were modeled into their present form by charters, grants, and statutes, but they were never separated from their mother-country, or so emancipated as to become so in their own right. There are several sorts of colonies in America; the charter-colonies, the proprietary governments, and the king's colonies." Then he shows that the charter-colonies, like Virginia, had been considered as belonging to the Crown, and that even the Commonwealth Parliament was very jealous of the colonies separating themselves from itself, and passed a law establishing the authority of England over them. Then follows the statement that the colonies have always submitted to English law, thus acknowledging their dependence. After this comes a discussion of the question upon which the whole matter of taxation turned, namely, representation in Parliament. He treats this vital point in these words:

"There can be no doubt, my Lords, but that the inhabitants of the colonies are as much represented in Parliament as the greatest part of the people of England are represented, among nine millions of whom there are eight which have no vote in electing members to Parliament. Every objection, therefore, to the dependency of the colonies which arises to it on the ground of representation goes to the whole present constitution of

Great Britain. To what purpose then are arguments drawn from a distinction in which there is no real difference, between a virtual and an actual representation? A member of Parliament represents not only the inhabitants of one place, but of others, the city of London and all the colonies and dominions of Great Britain and their interests."

It is in this speech that mention is first made by name of an American orator, the celebrated James Otis, with whose supposed speech we are familiar, beginning, "England may as well dam up the waters of the Nile with bulrushes as fetter the steps of freedom." Lord Mansfield said with characteristic fairness, "I differ from the noble lord who spoke of Otis and his book with contempt . . . who everywhere allows the supremacy of the Crown over the colonies. No man on such a subject is contemptible. Otis is a man of consequence among the people there. It was said the man is mad. What then? One madman often makes many. Masaniello was mad. Yet for all that he overturned the government of Naples. Madness is catching in all popular assemblies and upon all popular matters . . . I am far from bearing any ill-will to the Americans. They are a very good people and I have long known them . . . I dare say their heat will soon be over when they come to feel the consequences of their opposition. Anarchy always cures itself, but the ferment will continue so much the longer while hot-headed men there find that there are persons of weight and character here to justify them."

The whole speech is interesting as showing the divided sentiment in England in regard to the colonies. In the slow but constant intercommunication between them and the mother-country there were many things to continue that community of interest which belonged to the people of one race and family. Interests had not yet become separated, and the later estrangement was not yet so great as to make it common to speak of Americans as a cross between Canadians and wild Indians, and of their manners and speech and literature as something barbaric in rudeness and crudeness. Lord Mansfield meant no condescension when he said that Americans were a very good people, with whom he had begun his professional life, having managed their plantation causes in the tribunals of England, and in this way had become a good deal acquainted with them and their affairs. Therefore he was inclined to regard the disturbance as the work of a small, bad faction, which good men would soon rebuke and put down.

Among those persons of weight and character of whom Lord Mansfield speaks as justifying the Americans none was more conspicuous than EDMUND BURKE. Nor, on the whole, had they a more able advocate. His studies had qualified him to speak with authority on the American question. As early as 1757 he prepared an extensive work on the history of the British colonies, attributing their character to the spirit of their ancestors, full of enterprise, perseverance, and indomitable love of liberty. The boundless resources of the country and its irrepressible strength were obvious to his keen and prophetic observation. Accordingly when ten or twelve years after the publication of this book colonial troubles began, there was but one other man in England who had the tithe of his knowledge about the resources and determination of the colonists. That man was Lord Chatham, his senior by twenty-two years, and thirty years his predecessor in Parliament. It was eminently fitting, therefore, when Burke made his first speech, of great compass and power, on the Stamp Act that Chatham should set the approving seal of the first orator in England to this effort of his successor by saying that he himself had intended to enter into the debate, but had been anticipated with such ingenuity and eloquence that there was but little left for him to say. He congratulated Burke on his success, and his friends on the value of the acquisition they had made. Burke's reputation was established at once, affording him ample compensation for all his labors.

What those labors of preparation had been it may be worth our while to inquire. His rudimentary education was largely biblical, under the kindly instruction of a Quaker schoolmaster with whom he read the Scriptures of the Old and New Testaments, morning, noon, and night. The strong English, the imagery, the grandeur of diction, especially in the prophecies, had a lasting influence upon his style, as the positive precepts had upon his character. To the Bible in after-life he was accustomed to resort for allusions and illustrations, which distinguished him as an orator of almost oriental magnificence of imagination and expression.

In Trinity College, Dublin, a contemporary says he was a man of superior but unpretending talents, more anxious to acquire knowledge than to display it. The poets and orators of antiquity were his favorite study, together with the essays of Bacon and the plays of Shakespeare. Milton, however, was his chief admiration, on account of his boundless learning, richness of language, and scriptural grandeur of expression. In his methods of study and composition he anticipates the philosophical doctrines of Macaulay in reading history not as a record of battles and sieges, but to connect events by the causes that produced them. Intended by his lawyer-father for the bar he soon wearied of the technicalities of the law and turned to letters and philosophy. Diligent to the last degree he acquired that most useful of all powers, the ability to think at all times and in all places, and not merely when he could withdraw himself to the retirement of his study. Systematic, consecutive thought was combined with well-digested reading, and followed by daily discussions with others of whatever subject was of chief interest, giving to all his views a many-sidedness and practicality which otherwise might have given place to theories and dreams in a mind as full of exuberant fancy as his. His early works on the *Vindication of Natural Society* and on the *Sublime and Beautiful* are illustrations of his philosophical spirit rather than of its maturer form, but the language and style place those works high in the ranks of English literature. They gave the writer a celebrity and an acquaintance with distinguished contemporaries which was of the greatest advantage to him. In such congenial atmosphere his conversational powers found a field of distinction indicated by Dr. Johnson when he said, "Burke is the only man whose common conversation corresponds with the general fame he has in the world. His talk is perpetual, not from desire of distinction, but because his mind is full. No man could meet him under a gateway to avoid a shower without being convinced that he is the first man in England."

It was with such furnishings that he entered upon a political career in 1765 which was to cover three periods, that of America, India, and France respectively. The first, covering sixteen years, 1766–1782, was that in which his best oratorical work was done. At the start he encountered some obstacles by reason of his lack of rank and wealth and from the fact that he was a native of that island which to this day is a thorn in the side of England; but his talents and eloquence won universal admiration, and his devotion to the people's rights gained their hearty support. In America he was well accredited as the agent of the colony of New York for nearly four years, from 1771 to the breaking out of the war. It was in this capacity that he acquired his intimate knowledge of colonial affairs. The congratulations of Pitt on his first speech on American Taxation have already been mentioned. It was Lord John Townsend who exclaimed on the same occasion, "Heavens, what a man this is! Where could he acquire such transcendent powers!" Of his speech on the employment of Indians in the war Colonel Barré said that if it could be written out he would nail it on every church door in the kingdom, and Sir George Saville declared that he who did not hear that speech failed to witness the greatest triumph of eloquence within his memory, and Governor Johnston remarked that it was fortunate for Lords North and

Germaine that spectators had been excluded during the debate, for the excited people would have torn the noble lords in pieces on their way home.

Burke's independence was shown after his election to represent Bristol, then the second commercial city of the kingdom. The question of direction by his constituents coming up he plainly told them that his own judgment was not to be sacrificed to any set of men, and that he should vote according to his own opinion of what would best subserve their interests. The great issue which confronted that Parliament was the proposed conciliation of differences with America, a scheme calculated to weaken the resistance of the colonies by division of interests, which Burke endeavored to convert into an effective plan of real conciliation by having the colonies levy their own taxes independent of the Crown, on the principle that where there is taxation there should be representation. Upon this the great speech on Conciliation with America was delivered March 22, 1775. He spoke as if standing upon American soil. His topics were the importance of the colonial population, agriculture, commerce, and fisheries; the causes of the fierce spirit of liberty, the impossibility of repressing it by force, and the consequent necessity of some concession on the part of England. He showed that the people of the colonies ought to be admitted into an interest in representation. The tone of the speech is temperate and conciliatory toward the ministry and designed to lead the government through Lord North's scheme into a final adjustment of difficulties on the true principles of English liberty. The most finished of his speeches it is read for its richness of style and the permanent character of the political wisdom contained in it.

Of the three speeches, two on America and one to the electors of Bristol, it may be said that they compose a body of instruction in the study of public affairs which is unsurpassed. In vigorous grasp of particulars, in illustration drawn from human experience, in strong sympathy for justice and liberty they have never been excelled. Their author takes his place among the great makers of our literature in these high examples of deliberative eloquence, which are destined to outlast a multitude of efforts that have had a brief notoriety; while for the understanding of causes that produced our Revolution nothing has been written to illustrate the subject so fully and clearly. It has been truly said of his speeches that they might be the daily bread of modern statesmen and orators; and no doubt he has had an unparalleled influence upon the great forensic writers of this century, and has given a lasting stimulus to English prose literature. The secret of this may lie in his reprehension of any attempt to separate the English that is written from that which is spoken, so that his speeches have the appearance of an appeal from man to man. To a wide compass of thought, prodigality of illustration, a copiousness and fertility of allusion is joined a power of diversifying matter, placing it in new lights, and of expressing it with sublimity and an ease which give no sense of labor or display. Having the power of approximating to truth by a rapid and exact glance he also bestows upon each part of his subject its due degree of force and proper shade of color, one of the chief arts of speech. Accordingly he is a model to all who wish to say anything forcibly, naturally, and freely. Fresh, natural, and energetic in his diction he brings out the hidden power of common words and phrases without going far for strange, unusual, or outlandish words. Sonorous in his longer periods he can intersperse short, pointed, and vigorous sentences containing a wealth of philosophy; and by repetition without reiteration, but full of interpretation, he expands, contracts, condenses, and impresses his meaning too indelibly to be forgotten. In all his oratory there is something which escapes the last analysis of criticism, as life escapes the anatomist's search.

In the larger sphere of thought as distinguished from expression there were so many phases of invention as to warrant the assertion that he had great originality, if not actual genius. His intellectual independence, combined with the subtlety of a mind philosophical in its methods, dealing with large generalization and profound reasonings made him an orator to be read with interest rather than always to be listened to with attention; but for this reason his eloquence has lived long after the issues which called it forth were settled; and although he has had his critics who have censured this and that outgrowth of his luxuriant nature, still the majority of judges place him before any other orator of modern times as a parliamentary speaker.

XXIII.

SHERIDAN—FOX.

TO ONE who is disposed to look for the causes of singular concurrences an interesting problem is presented in the succession of orators who were born in Ireland. It would be too far-fetched to look for oratorical origins in that remote period of learning when Brian Boru founded schools and churches in the eleventh century, or in the remoter fourth when, after the introduction of Christianity, learning flourished to such a degree that the "Isle of the Saints," as it was called, illumined the rest of Britain. We may look for a more direct cause of eloquence, perhaps, in the temperament of the better class of the people, more Gallic than British, Celtic than Saxon, impulsive, hearty, and generous, with a volubility characteristic of southern races. But whatever may be the causes contributing to fluent and effective speech it is worthy of note that Ireland furnished a group of orators by no means of the second rate in this remarkable epoch of British eloquence. Of the chief of them, Edmund Burke, something has already been said.

Not greatly inferior to him were others who would have appeared still more illustrious if they had not been apparently dimmed by his effulgence. RICHARD BRINSLEY SHERIDAN was nearest this great luminary, and yet not totally eclipsed by him.

To note the course of his literary career would be to give something more than the life of an orator. Those who remember that he was the author of *The Rivals*, *The School for Scandal*, *The Critic*, and *The Duenna* will find it hard to adjust the great playwright to the famous oration on the Begums of India. Byron said of him, "Whatever he has chosen to do has been the best of its kind. He has written the best comedy, the best drama, the best farce, and delivered the very best oration ever heard in this country." The dramatic talents which he displayed, and by which he won a fortune, are not, however, within the province of this subject. It is his eloquence alone that is to be considered.

Gibbon had his word of praise for this, and Burke with characteristic generosity declared that the speech on the Begum charge was the most astonishing effort of eloquence, argument, and wit combined of which there was any record or tradition; and Pitt said that his speech "surpassed all the eloquence of ancient and modern times, and possessed everything that genius or art could furnish to agitate the human mind." Fox testified that all he had ever heard, all he had ever "read, when compared with it, dwindled into nothing and vanished like vapor before the sun."

After such encomiums it is safe to say that there was something more than a dramatist about Sheridan and something more than dramatic art about his oratory. The praise of the group that has been named warrants this assertion. It may be worth while to note by what steps he passed from the stage to the rostrum.

From early life he had cherished a lively interest in

politics, and having gratified his dramatic ambitions he turned toward distinction in oratory with zealous toil. Associating himself with Fox and influential whig friends he became a member of Parliament for Stafford at the same time with William Pitt, at an expense of £2,000. He came without the distinction due to birth, or the patronage of a powerful patron, things of great importance in the House of Commons. Instead he brought what was of greater harm than good, a ready-made reputation in letters, subjecting him to severer criticism in consequence.

The list of men who have been famous in literature or at the bar and failures in Parliament is a long one. Addison, Steele, Erskine, Flood, O'Connell, Jeffrey, Mackintosh, Macaulay, Bulwer, and Mill gained little by their elevation to the deliberative assembly. Grattan, Disraeli, and Sheridan are exceptions to the general fate of those who brought reputations into the national legislature. At first it looked as if Sheridan was to follow the general fortune of eminent literary men. Aiming too high he failed to enlist the sympathies of his hearers, and did not meet the expectations of his friends. Woodfall, the reporter of the House, frankly told him that it was not his line, that he had better have stuck to the drama, after his remarkable achievements in it.

But his reply was prophetic, "It is in me and it shall come out of me ;" and, as to Disraeli at a later day, the time came when he obtained a patient hearing. After this unpropitious beginning he devoted himself with diligence to the cultivation of his real oratorical ability. He had it in him as he had said—great inventive power, ready wit, perfect self-possession, a keen sense of the value of words and of their most skilful array. As a consequence he became one of the most celebrated parliamentary orators of his time. Good sense, shrewdness in detecting the weak points of an adversary, and great powers of raillery in exposing them made him an opponent to be feared, even by his great antagonist, William Pitt. How much more distinguished he might have been if he had taken the pains to inform himself thoroughly on all the points of his subject cannot be estimated. In the midst of his habitual indolence and convivialities he managed to pick up knowledge enough of leading topics to make an excellent showing when the time came for his speech. He would say to his friends, "You know I am an ignoramus; here I am, instruct me and I will do my best." And, like Mirabeau gathering up the material his friends had collected for him as he ascended the tribune, Sheridan would take the information furnished by his companions, make himself master of it, and pour out the substance of it in a form so fresh and new that it was more his own than other men's.

The great speech of his life was that on the charge against Warren Hastings. Of the first speech, advocating the impeachment, there is so little record that the tradition of it is all that remains. "The whole assembly at the conclusion broke forth into expressions of tumultuous applause," and Pitt asserted that "perhaps an abler speech was never delivered." A motion to adjourn was made that the House might recover their calmness and collect their reason after the excitement they had undergone. Twenty years later critics recalled it as a speech for which they had undiminished admiration. Fox declared that it was the "greatest that had been delivered within the memory of man."

A better report is extant of the second speech made the following year, when the actual impeachment was undertaken. It was an occasion calculated to arouse all his ambition as an orator. Curiosity to hear him was so great that Westminster Hall was crowded, and fifty guineas were in some instances paid for a single seat, yet he amply satisfied expectations and fully gratified curiosity. This one effort would have immortalized him, but when it was added to his already splendid achievements he came to be regarded as preëminent among his contemporaries. In this oration common sense and close reasoning predominate. Rhetorical passages are interspersed with dry facts to render the whole attractive as well as conclusive. In its structure it is a comment upon evidence, the evidence against Hastings of atrocities committed against the native princes of India in order to compel them to contribute treasures in his pressing want of money, and thus enable him to continue in office by relieving the East India Company from its financial difficulties. The story of his oppressions and extortions is a long one, but this is the gist of it. The public conscience was aroused, at least those men who formed the public conscience, of whom there are always a few in every nation and age. Burke was their leader and to Sheridan he assigned that part of the prosecution which related to this particular outrage.

An estimate of the speech can be justly formed only

by reading the whole of it. Even then it may be questioned if the testimony of contemporaries is not of more value than our opinion of the best of speeches in cold type. Of a poem or a romance this cannot be said, but in an oration so much depends upon the living presence before an audience in sympathy, or even in antagonism, with the speaker that a large factor has been canceled by time and distance and change. As in many other notable examples it is not possible to find the attraction that kept a vast audience spell-bound for three successive days in the great hall of Westminster. The voice, the face, the action of the great dramatic orator are gone. A contemporary says, "He had an exquisite voice, a fascinating eye, perfect self-possession, imperturbable good humor, happy audacity in speaking bold and unwelcome truths, tempered by the breeding and knowledge of the man of the world. His strongest point was his wit, which always enlivened even a wholly businesslike speech and added a charm to his loftiest eloquence. It was by no means introduced on all occasions nor to the disgust of his auditors, but when it did strike it was always opportune and effective." He cannot be called a classic orator. His oriental exuberance of imagination is Asiatic rather than Greek. With a Celtic intellect that was always in extremes, joined to a native sense of humor he could not be reckoned with the grand orators of the Demosthenean type. Impetuous and heedless he plunged into the very errors he was quick to detect and expose. But for conjuring up a storm of eloquence that should bear his hearers away from their sober sense, stirring their emotions and moving their will his magnetic and impulsive oratory was surpassed by none and equaled by few. A brief extract is given to indicate the manner of Sheridan in the use of language. His actual manner cannot be represented, for he was both actor and orator. The following is the final paragraph of the speech that has been mentioned, and it is by no means the most forcible:

"My Lords, do you, the judges of this land and the expounders of its rightful laws, do you approve of this mockery and call that the character of justice which takes the form of right to execute wrong? No, my Lords, justice is not this halt and miserable object; it is not the ineffective bauble of an Indian pagoda; it is not the portentous phantom of despair; it is not like any fabled monster, formed in the eclipse of reason and found in some unhallowed grove of superstitious darkness and political dismay. No, my Lords. In the happy reverse of all this I turn from the disgusting caricature to the real image. Justice I have now before me, august and pure, the abstract ideal of all that would be perfect in the spirits and aspirings of men—where the mind rises; where the heart expands; where the countenance is ever placid and benign; where her favorite attitude is to stoop to the unfortunate, to hear their cry, and to help them; to rescue and relieve, to succor and save; majestic from its mercy, venerable from its utility, uplifted without pride, firm without obduracy, beneficent in each preference, lovely though in her frown.

"On that justice I rely; deliberate and sure; abstracted from all party purpose and political speculation; not on words but on facts. You, my Lords, who hear me, I conjure by these rights which it is your best privilege to preserve; by that fame which it your best pleasure to inherit; by all those feelings which refer to the first term in the series of existence, the original compact of our nature, our controlling rank in the creation. This is the call to administer truth and equity, as they would satisfy the laws and satisfy themselves . . the self-approving consciousness of virtue, when the condemnation we look for will be one of the most ample mercies accomplished for mankind since the creation of the world."

The orator, without whose name even a brief enumeration of British orators would be incomplete, was CHARLES JAMES FOX. If the origin of Burke and Sheridan, Chatham and Mansfield illustrates the truth that great talents belong to no single order of nobility, the birth and training of Fox must add corroborative evidence from another direction. Reared in luxury every pains was taken by his father to make him a worthless scapegrace. Given a loose rein and plenty of money, taught to gamble, and laughed at by his father for his scruples about profligacy, the parent who wished him to become a leader in fashionable dissipation and also an orator and statesman could not complain when the son succeeded so well in the first part of his education that he contracted a half a million dollars of debts in two years' stay upon the continent. To wean him from such extravagances his father had him sent to Parliament almost two years before he was eligible by law, and in 1769 he delivered his first speech, early in his twenty-first year. Walpole speaks of his eminent abilities and his insolence. It is unnecessary to recount at length the training which enabled him to distinguish himself at such an early age in the councils of the nation. But it must be said that his was not an untutored precocity. Thoroughly grounded in the ancient languages before he was sixteen he read classic authors as he read English. Throughout life he kept up his familiarity with them, and they in turn contributed much to his Greek simplicity of taste, the terseness of his style, and the closeness and point of his reasoning. At Eton and Oxford he maintained the highest rank as a scholar by study so severe that his preceptor urged him to remit his efforts, an unusual thing for him to advise. To reading the classics and history he added poetry, oratory, and elegant literature. But all his pursuits were to his liking, and anything that was not was never allowed to trouble him. It was an early example of elective study, greatly to his disadvantage, as he afterward acknowledged when he lamented his neglect of mathematics as injurious to his mental training, and of political economy and jurisprudence at a time when Adam Smith was giving a science to the world which would have been of the greatest value to the future statesman. Worse than one-sided study was the reckless gambling which stood in the way of his preferment and removed him from a good position on the Treasury bench which he already occupied. This, with the loss of his fortune, aroused his pride and a determination to abandon the gaming table.

A change in the policy of Lord North made America at this time the great object of political interest. Fox's nature was one to respond to any complaint from the oppressed. "Alive to every kind of wrong he had an indignant abhorrence of every species of cruelty and injustice." Accordingly he began to denounce the violent and oppressive acts of North's administration, and was the first man in the House who denied the right of Parliament to tax the colonies without their consent. Contrary to his early training he now began to identify himself more and more with the sense of popular rights, "to widen the basis of freedom, to infuse and circulate the spirit of liberty." This was the inspiration of his eloquence. This he believed would strengthen and renovate the English government because, as he said, "It incorporates every man with the state and arouses everything that belongs to the soul as well as to the body of man, making him feel that he is fighting for himself, his own cause and safety, his own dignity and interest, on his own soil."

Oratorically Fox's ambition was to become a powerful debater, "one who," as has been described, "goes out in all weathers," instead of carrying with him to the House a set speech drawn up beforehand. For this was needed a ready knowledge of general principles and command of every faculty, joined with quickness and force of intellect, sharpened by constant practice. Argument was more with him than language or imagery; his sole thought how to overcome an antagonist and make out his own case. In this course he persevered until he became the acknowledged leader of the whig party in the House of Commons, no small help to which eminence was his genial and lovable disposition.

It is greatly to his praise as an orator that he has been

said to be the most completely English of all the orators in the language, plain and practical in his understanding, definite in his aims, strong and honest in his common sense. Dealing with facts in a positive way he was the practical representative of a practical people. Underneath all was a great heart full of tenderness and sympathy, expressing its emotions with sincerity and artlessness. This was one of the secrets of his power with his hearers. He was an honest, straightforward, emotional man, speaking to a nation whose character partakes largely of these qualities. He answered well to his own definition of the character of an orator, "One who can give immediate, instantaneous utterance to his thoughts." He mastered the subject and accumulated facts. How he should use these depended upon the mood of the assembly he rose to address. Such a method was much more likely to fall into a colloquial style than that of a stately rhetoric, which, it must be admitted, was largely prevalent in that day.

In his determination to convince his hearers he sometimes used language that was strong, to say the least. The king's reign he called "the most infamous that ever disgraced a nation;" the American war was "accursed, diabolical, and cruel;" the king, "that infernal spirit who really ruled, and had nearly ruined the country;" the ministers holding their office "not at the option of the sovereign but of the reptiles who burrow under the Throne;" and if the Commons took a particular course they would be "the most despicable set of drivelers that ever insulted society under the appellation of lawmakers." He acknowledged that his language was sometimes vehement and intemperate, "but I speak as I feel and no man can feel more strongly than I do the present situation of this country," was his apology. Practical as he was, he was not without that imagination which illumines a subject by the discovery of likenesses between things well known and things hard to understand. His illustrations were largely taken from literature, biography, and anecdote. In the use of the last he was particularly happy, and the effect of some of his little stories must have outweighed many ponderous arguments of an opponent. When he spoke of Pitt as "in the gorgeous attire of a barbarous Prince of Morocco who always put on his gayest garments as a prelude to the slaughter of many of his subjects," it must have taken somewhat from the effectiveness of that orator's speech. The panic caused by the principles of the French was said to have caused Russia and Prussia to seize Poland. This reminded Fox of a pickpocket who said that in a crowd he had been struck with a panic and grasped the first thing that came in his way, which happened to be a gentleman's watch. Such felicitous use of incident was peculiarly valuable to a debater, and as such he outranked all other speakers of his day. He had not every oratorical excellence and was given to faults of repetition of argument and tautology of diction, and he did not always select the best words and appropriate terms. His method was often careless, but all these things seemed to make his hearers believe that he was above artifice, and that he spoke from conviction, with clearness and force if not always with elegance. His strong point was to state the position of an adversary better than the opponent himself had done, and then seize it and tear it all in pieces. Sometimes his arguments were personal in their nature and were brought to bear upon his adversary with telling severity.

The most finished of his speeches is that on the Westminister Scrutiny, and the ablest, according to contemporary testimony, is that on The Rejection of Bonaparte's Overtures. It is in the close of this last speech that the famous peroration occurs, full of mingled argument, irony, and invective, giving a faint idea of Fox in his most effective mood:

"When, then, sir, is this war to stop? . . . One campaign is successful to you, another to them; and in this way, animated by the vindictive passions of revenge, hatred, and rancor, you may go on forever. And all this without an intelligible motive, because you may gain a better peace a year or two hence. We must keep Bonaparte at war as a state of probation. Is war a state of probation? Is peace a rash system? Is it dangerous for nations to live in amity with each other? 'But we must pause.' What! must the best blood of Great Britain be spilled and her treasure wasted that you may make an experiment? Put yourselves in the field of battle and learn to judge of the horrors you excite. In former wars a man might have some feeling or interest that would balance in his mind the impressions a sense of carnage would inflict. But if a man were present now at a field of slaughter and were to inquire for what they were fighting, 'Fighting!' would be the answer, 'they are not fighting, they are pausing!' Why is that man writhing with agony? What means this implacable fury? You are wrong, sir; that man is not expiring in agony, this man is not dead, he is only pausing. There is no cause of quarrel, but their country thinks there should be a pause—a political pause—to see whether Bonaparte will not behave himself better . . . And this is the way, sir, that you show yourselves the advocates of order. You take up a system calculated to uncivilize the world, to destroy order, to trample on religion, to stifle in the heart the affections of social nature, and in the prosecution of this system you spread terror and devastation all around you."

It should be said that Fox's diatribe had a powerful effect on the House, and, though his opponents outvoted him, in about a year and a half he saw his principles triumph in the treaty of Amiens.

XXIV.

COLONIAL ORATORS.

AMERICAN oratory of the colonial period may properly be regarded as a part of the movement and development which was taking place in the Parliament of Great Britain in the last half of the eighteenth century. So closely connected were the colonies with the mother-country in business interests and education, in its larger sense, that the influence of leaders of thought in England was as great here as at home. If the progress of colonial sentiment toward emancipation from British domination be carefully traced, it will be found that there was a great reluctance until the very beginning of the war to separate from the home government. Samuel Adams, the most radical partisan and patriot, confessed as late as 1768 that "there is an English affection in the colonists toward the mother-country which will forever keep them connected with her unless it shall be erased by repeated unkind usage on her part." Severed from English ancestral homes by weeks of voyage there was nevertheless on the part of the colonists a constant sense of the home feeling and a continual reference in their thoughts and their speech to England as their home country. The language, the traditions, the religion of the colonists were those of the land whence they were continually coming and bringing fresh news and fresh recollections with every ship-load.

A more exclusive possession was the literature of England, seeing that the colonists had little of their own; for up to the time of Benjamin Franklin's first publications there was nothing better than crude descriptions and doubtful chronicles and positive theological and polemic writings to make up a voluminous but uncritical literature this side the Atlantic. But on the other side eminent authors were writing books which the American colonists received in every returning trading vessel, and read with all the avidity of Englishmen at home, and perhaps with more care than they by reason of their remoteness from the source of supply.

In no kind of literature, however, would they be more deeply interested than in that form of it which was being created in the houses of Parliament, especially in those years when colonial affairs occupied so much national attention and legislation. Speeches came slowly across the ocean, but slowness and speed are relative terms, and ocean mails were not much behind colonial time. There was also abundant leisure to read, study, and ponder the utterances of Chatham, Burke, and Fox, until their phrases and periods should give the pitch and the measure to colonial thought and speech. These pamphlet orations as they came to cities and towns and families were not tossed into the waste-basket like the printed matter which is now mailed by the hundred weight from Washington to a fickle constituency. Instead they were carefully perused, circulated, and preserved for re-reading, future reference, and use.

Such oratory, moreover, could not fail to have its formative influence upon political leaders here, giving direction to their thoughts and shape to their expression. Now and then colonial youths were sent abroad to receive a university education, and it is not improbable that they were brought within the circle of influence whose centre was the national halls of legislation. All these circumstances together had their weight in forming a literature of oratory in the new empire of the west. It was this form of literature which first compelled attention in the old world. Our theologians and historians and biographers and poets had nothing of interest to say to their betters across the water. But when our political writers and speakers began to deal with questions which vitally affected the revenues of England and threatened to circumscribe her possessions in an almost limitless territory, then the rulers at home had to lend a listening ear. Moreover there was something worth listening to at times, when reports of unusual utterances came across the Atlantic. The material might have been what most concerned the Briton to hear, but the manner and style in which it was clothed were not without the charm of novelty and picturesqueness. They were the outcome of a stimulating atmosphere and of new political and social conditions. There was a freedom and independence of speech which wiseacres took for independence of spirit.

The first colonial orator in point of time was SAMUEL ADAMS, but the record of his speeches is not abundant. The central figure of the Boston town-meeting he fought toryism and federalism with equal vigor; but reporters did not frequent town-meetings, or think the utterances of even a leader worth preserving. For their literary merit the speeches of Adams would not have been recorded. They were the straightforward, energetic sentiments of an earnest man who had no time to choose his words. Back of these, however, was the tremendous force of a strong personal character, fired with enthusiasm for freedom. His pen served him as often as his voice, and in the people's newspaper in Boston and in the Providence *Gazette* he published predictions and opinions which both New England and Old might read, causing him to be excluded from the general offer of pardon to the patriots made by the Throne the year before the Revolution broke out. His name belongs as much to political literature as to oratory, by reason of such contributions to the public press.

Indeed oratory was not his strongest point. John Adams said of him that "in his ordinary speeches he exhibited nothing extraordinary; but upon great occasions, when his deeper feelings were excited, he threw himself into an upright dignity of figure and gesture and gave a harmony to his voice which made a strong impression on spectators and auditors."

Jefferson describes him as "logical and clear, abundant in good sense, and always master of his subject." As a specimen of his speaking may be cited his address to Governor Hutchinson after the Boston massacre, on the removal of the troops from the town: "It is well known," he said, "that acting as governor of the Province you are by its charter commander-in-chief of the military forces within it; and as such the troops now in the capital are subject to your orders. If you, or Colonel Dalrymple under you, have the power to remove one regiment you have the power to remove both; and nothing short of their total removal will satisfy the people or preserve the peace of the Province. A multitude highly incensed now wait the result of this application. The voice of ten thousand freemen demands that both regiments be removed. Their voice must be respected, their demand obeyed. Fail not then at your peril to comply with this requisition. On you alone rests the responsibility of this decision, and if the just expectations of the people are disappointed you must be answerable to God and your country for the fatal consequences that must ensue. The committee have discharged their duty and it is for you to discharge yours. They wait your final determination."

Such words exhibit the temper of the man, determined, inflexible, and daring. There is much that passes for oratory that is less eloquent than this address, almost Demosthenean in its forceful brevity.

The following sentence from a letter to the Providence *Gazette*, March 18, 1769, is interesting as the first published intimation of the possible separation of the colonies from Great Britain:

"When I consider the corruption of Great Britain, their load of debt, their intestine divisions, tumults, and riots, their scarcity of provisions, and the contempt in which they are held by the nations about them; and when I consider on the other hand the state of the American Colonies with regard to the various climates, soils, produce, rapid population, joined to the virtue of the inhabitants, I cannot but think that the conduct of Old England toward us may be permitted by divine wisdom and ordained by the unsearchable providence of the Almighty for hastening a period dreadful to Great Britain."

In point of time the name of Samuel Adams heads the roll of American orators and statesmen, and in immediately effecting the purpose they had in mind none have surpassed him. His was a practical oratory which carried its point at the time and with contemporaries, even though it has not been perpetuated as a model to succeeding generations. It ended in action, and the action which it secured was the establishment of a new and free nation on the western continent. Measured by what it accomplished it must be admitted to be among the greatest achievements of human speech, and in its final result it is as yet unmeasured.

Next to him in time and place and excelling Adams in oratorical reputation was JAMES OTIS, in his day regarded as the chief orator of the Revolution in Massachusetts. He was a type of the rotund and courtly personages who, decked with lace, arrayed in broadcloth, and crowned with enormous wigs, look out from the canvas of colonial painters. With strong voice and piercing eye he was likened by the older Adams to "a flame of fire." "With a promptitude of classical allusions, a depth of research, a rapid summary of events and dates, a profusion of legal authorities, a prophetic glance into futurity, and a torrent of impetuous eloquence he hurried everything away before him. "Every man of a crowded audience went away ready to take arms. Then and there was the first scene of the first act of opposition to the arbitrary claims of Great Britain." The reputation of his oratory is mostly a tradition, but that is of wild enthusiasm whenever he appeared. Without the discretion of Adams he was hailed with applause by a populace itself often indiscreet and inconsistent.

His five-hour speech against taxation without representation, delivered in the council chamber of the old town hall in Boston, was a masterly performance, making him famous as the bold and brilliant advocate of colonial rights. No summary or abstract of this speech can do justice to the whole, which can be estimated only by reading in its integrity. Even then how much is lost, as in the case of so many other great orators, in the lack of their presence and of the occasion which inspired them, and which they in turn made memorable. Instead of an extract from his speeches a condensed letter of his on the subject of large preparation previous to special study may be more useful in these days of specialism:

"I shall always lament that I did not take a year or two further for more general inquiries in the arts and sciences before I sat down to the laborious study of the law. Early and premature rushing into practice has blasted the hopes of many students of the profession. Those who avail themselves of the ripeness of their judgment make swifter progress than they who hasten to their life work unprepared."

Among the colonial orators of New England must be reckoned FISHER AMES, a native of Massachusetts, and graduate of Harvard at the age of sixteen. Assiduous in his study of the Latin and English classics he came to the practice of forensic oratory with much the same preparation that fitted the parliamentary orators of Great Britain for their wonderful achievements. His political essays first made his great abilities generally known, containing as they did lessons of practical wisdom conveyed in an energetic and animated style. These brought him into intimate relations with the federal school and helped him to a seat in the convention which ratified the constitution of 1788, where he made himself conspicuous by his zeal and eloquence.

A member of Congress during both of Washington's administrations he then made a fine reputation for readiness in debate and for the splendor of his speeches. At the close of one of these a member of the opposition moved an adjournment of the House, on the ground that it was not in a mood calm enough to dwell on the question under the excitement of his oratory. Massachusetts showed its appreciation of his eloquence by appointing him to deliver the eulogy on the death of Washington, and Harvard College, in recognition of his varied attainments, chose him as its president, an office which his declining health prevented him from accepting. He will always hold a place in the history of oratorical literature by reason of the general excellence of his style, although it is marked a little too strongly at times with an exuberance of imagination. At the same time it should be said that the printed speech conveys but a small portion of that power which belonged to the living speaker, the tradition of whose influence on the hearts and minds of men far outweighs the evidence of it which remains after a century of silence. He belonged to a great age and was preëminent in a time when the construction of a new order of government was going on, when men had little in the experience of the past to guide their counsels, and when the present was full of differences and apprehensions and the future administration of affairs an untried experiment. How well they builded and with what wisdom a hundred and twenty years of American history has shown.

It is time to turn from the progress of revolutionary sentiments in New England to the development of the same feeling in the South, as revealed by the oratory of the period there. The first name to command attention is that of PATRICK HENRY, an orator by nature, dealing with an uncritical people, and leaving traditions of an eloquence of marvelous power. Certainly no part of his fame is due to the meagre opportunities of education which were afforded him, or to his improvement of them, scanty as they were. A few months of such advantages as were offered in a colonial school of the poorest sort, a smattering of the classics, and less mathematics constituted the sum of his youthful instruction. But this was less attractive to him than the sports of stream and woodland. In a business enterprise he was no more successful. The country store was rather a place for anecdote and discussion than for profitable trade, and penury soon stared him in the face. As a wild venture he entered upon the profession of the law after six weeks' preparation and without a very remarkable proficiency in its first principles, as may be inferred from the promise he was obliged to give his examiners that he would apply himself to further study. However he vindicated his right to a place at the colonial bar by his famous argument in the notable Parsons' case, for which he had been retained as a mere form in a cause that had been as good as abandoned. After an awkward beginning which made his friends hang their heads for shame he suddenly rallied, his confusion passed away, a mysterious and almost supernatural change came over him. Spectators said afterward that the hitherto unknown young advocate made their blood run cold with his terrible invective, and the jury, retiring for only a moment, brought in a verdict in favor of his clients. A motion for a new trial was overruled, and "the man of the people" was caught up and borne out of the courthouse on the shoulders of a delighted multitude.

There was no lack of business or gain after this first effort. He had found his place and he made the most of it. Industry and energy characterized his labor. In the details of his work he suffered from defective study, "but in jury trials where his wonderful powers of oratory could be brought to bear upon the motives and emotions of men he far exceeded all his contemporaries. Over juries he exercised a magnetic fascination which took their reason captive and decided the result without reference to the merits of the case."

At the period now under contemplation an orator of the first rank at the bar would not long keep out of the deliberative assembly. Accordingly Henry is found in the Virginia House of Burgesses in the spring of 1765, when England was attempting to force the Stamp Act upon the colonies. The character of the assembly was determined by the two-fold sentiment of loyalty to the mother-country on the one hand and of colonial freedom on the other. The great majority were wealthy planters who were attached to England by a thousand ties of kindred blood, ancestral pride, and social alliance. They repelled the thought of separation and put off the evil day. To cut loose from Great Britain seemed like casting away their heritage of civil liberty and the established order of church and state. Accordingly they went on devising compromises and protesting and petitioning the Crown to respect their rights.

It was this conservative and loyal body which Patrick Henry threw into commotion by introducing resolutions which were deemed treasonable and incendiary. Written hastily on the fly-leaf of an old law-book they startled the staid burgesses with their unwonted tone. It was not that of renewed protest or petition. It was the declaration rather that the representatives of the people had "the exclusive right and power to lay taxes and imposts upon the inhabitants of the colony," and that "therefore the Stamp Act and all acts affecting the rights of the American colonies were unconstitutional and void." Such resolutions produced their legitimate effect. Stung into sudden and bitter hostility the House directed their invectives against the youthful member of the democracy. Patriotic aristocrats heard the resolutions with rising astonishment and treated them with a storm of opposition. Threats were uttered against their author and abuse heaped upon him. The debate that ensued was called "most bloody" by Jefferson. It was in the midst of it that Henry uttered the famous sentence, "Cæsar had his Brutus, Charles the First his Cromwell, and George the

Third—" "'Treason! Treason!" on every side—"George the Third may profit by their example. If this be treason make the most of it." In spite of all opposition the resolutions were carried, through the brilliant advocacy of a young man of twenty-nine years, who had at the same time won the reputation in the South of being "the greatest orator and political thinker" in a land filled with celebrated public speakers and statesmen. "His voice had aroused the storm, his genius had comprehended the exigencies of the crisis, and the sceptre, departing from the hands of opulent planters, was wielded by the lawyer of a country court." Thenceforward he occupied a position with the peers of the new realm that was to be.

Indeed he was by general consent the first statesman and orator of Virginia and the pride of her people. George Mason wrote concerning him, " He is by far the most powerful speaker I ever heard. . . But his eloquence is the smallest part of his merit. He is in my opinion the first man upon this continent, as well in abilities as in public virtues." He had a leading part in all the counsels of the time, he was sent to every session of the House of Burgesses, he was at the front in all conventions, and all these incidents in this portion of his life culminated in his mission as one of the deputies from Virginia to the first Continental Congress.

After a short military career as commander of the Virginia troops, in which for some reason he did not gain distinction, he was elected the first governor of his native commonwealth. This office he held upon reëlection for the first three years of American independence.

"After his descent from the governor's chair he was elected by the general assembly as a delegate in Congress, an honor which his impaired health obliged him to decline. Remaining in comparative retirement for five years he resumed the office of governor in 1784, after service in which he was once more and finally elected a deputy to the constitutional convention of 1787, in Philadelphia."

With this convention it is well known that he had little sympathy. The constitution there framed was fraught with perils to the liberty so hardly won by the War of Independence. He feared it as tending to centralization and monarchy. A president-commander-in-chief of the army looked like the possibility of despotism. Therefore in the Virginia assembly he opposed its adoption with might and main. All his eloquence was brought to bear against the concession of state rights to a consolidated government, and was exercised in favor of amending the Articles of Confederation. For twenty-three days he bore the brunt of the battle, speaking every day but five, and once making five speeches on a single day, and at another time eight, one speech alone occupying seven hours. The height of eloquence was reached just before the vote was taken, amid a scene of dramatic interest. Gathering up all his energies for a final appeal in a cause which he foresaw was likely to be lost he closed with these words : " I see the awful dangers inherent [in this constitution]. I see them. I feel them. I see beings of a higher order anxious concerning our decision. When I see beyond the horizon that bounds human eyes, and look at the final consummation of all human things, and see those intelligent beings which inhabit the ethereal mansions reviewing the political decisions and revolutions which in the progress of time will happen in America and the consequent happiness or misery of mankind, I am led to believe that much of the account on one side or the other will depend on what we now decide. All nations are interested in the determination. We have it in our power to secure the happiness of one-half of the human race. Its adoption may involve the misery of the other hemisphere." Here a violent storm arose which put the House in disorder and stopped the speaker. The scene was described again and again by witnesses as appalling. One says that "the orator, as if wielding an enchanter's wand, suddenly enlarged the arena of debate and the number of his auditors; for, peering beyond the veil which shuts in mortal sight and pointing to those celestial beings who were hovering over the scene, he addressed to them an invocation that made every nerve shudder with supernatural horror; when, lo! a storm at that instant rose which shook the whole building, and the spirits whom he had evoked seemed to have come at his bidding. Availing himself of the incident, with a master's art he seemed to mix in the fight of his ethereal auxiliaries, and rising on the wings of the tempest to seize upon the artillery of heaven and direct its fiercest thunders against the heads of his adversaries. The scene became insupportable and the House rose without the formality of adjournment, the members rushing from their seats with precipitation and confusion."

The next day the vote was taken and resulted in

favor of adoption by a meagre majority of ten. It was then that Patrick Henry showed the true nobility of his nature in complying with words already spoken, "If I shall be in the minority, I shall have those painful sensations which arise from a conviction of having been overpowered in a good cause. Yet I will be a peaceable citizen. My head, my hand, my heart shall be at liberty to retrieve the loss of liberty and remove the defects of the system in a constitutional way. I will wait with hopes that the spirit which predominated in the Revolution is not yet gone, and in expectation of seeing that government changed so as to be compatible with the safety, liberty, and happiness of the people." Of his course at this time our greatest historian says, "Henry showed his genial nature free from all malignity. He was like a billow of the ocean on the first bright day after the storm, dashing itself against the rocky cliff, and then, sparkling with light, retreating to its home."

His retreat was not to idleness. With fortune impaired by neglect of business in the service of his country he declined another election to the governorship, and set himself to making provision for his declining years and for his children. "In eight years he was able to retire in comfort and wealth from the labors of his profession." In this period his great oratorical abilities shone with undimmed lustre. In the famous cause of the British debt his learning, argument, and eloquence placed him easily at the head of his legal associates. With a preparation worthy of Demosthenes over one of his orations he came forth a perfect master of every principle of law, national and municipal, which related in the remotest way to the subject of investigation. For three days he was engaged in the delivery before a room crowded to the window seats and overflowing to the porticos.

Besides such celebrated law cases his practice led him into actions tried before juries, that have also become famous in the history of the bar. Without detailing them individually the methods of the great lawyer and orator may be given in the words of his legal biographer, Wirt, who says that "he adapted himself without effort to the character of the cause; seized with the quickness of intuition its defensible point and never permitted the jury to lose sight of it. Sir Joshua Reynolds has said of Titian that by a few strokes of his pencil he knew how to mark the image and character of whatever object he attempted, and produced by this means a truer representation than any of his predecessors who finished every hair. In like manner Henry by a few master-strokes upon the evidence could, in general, stamp upon the cause whatever image or character he pleased and convert it into tragedy or comedy at his will, and with a power which no effort of his adversary could counteract. Men might resolve to decide a cause against him, but some feint in an unexpected direction threw them off their guard; some happy phrase, some image from nature's mint struck them with surprise and melted them into conciliation, and victory was inevitable." Another critic says, "The power of his eloquence is due first to the greatness of his emotion, accompanied with a versatility which enabled him at once to assume any feeling which was suited to his ends." With matchless perfection of voice, intonation, pause, gesture, attitude, and indescribable play of countenance he united a taste that never permitted him to use an expression that was not instantly recognized as nature itself. But more than all was the intense earnestness of feeling which lay back of every word, the tremendous power of sincerity which made ordinary expressions weighty with a new meaning. His were no ordinary expressions on extraordinary occasions, as we know from such reports of his speeches as have come down to us through the imperfect stenography of the time. Neither do these latter days understand how great an orator sprung up in the revolutionary period of our history. As in the case of illustrious orators before him the record of what he said is not equal to the testimony of the manner of its saying and the ethical power of a mighty man. He lived, to be sure, in stirring times, and was both their product and exponent. He was one of a group of wise thinkers and orators of no mean attainments, viewed apart from each other; but he was easily the foremost, gifted from above with transcendental powers and with a character that gave weight to expression that in itself was most effective. Just, upright, and godly, humane, genial, and beneficent, willing to serve yet not coveting office, strong in his views of right and in his sense of duty unswerving, he stands as the everlasting memorial of righteousness in a time when men were driven hither and thither by conflicting interests and emotions. It was around such a man that men loved to rally, or against him to contend with all their might. But he lived to see his principles largely prevail and their success assured in the new nation whose character he did so much to shape.

There were other men who were with justice and propriety considered orators in the stormy period of the Revolution. For instance in the great debate upon the Stamp Act Richard Henry Lee of Virginia supported the resolutions of Patrick Henry with such ability and eloquence that the people knew not which most to admire, the overwhelming might of Henry or the resistless persuasion of Lee. Other famous speakers in the South were William Henry Drayton, John Rutledge, Edmund Randolph, the successor of Patrick Henry as governor of Virginia, a lawyer whom clients beset on his way from office to court with their papers in one hand and their guineas in the other, and crowded his office on his return. As a natural consequence he came to be first Washington's attorney-general and afterward secretary of state. Then there were speakers of no mean attainments, whose statesmanship so surpassed their oratory that the real excellence of this is forgotten in the greater splendor of their legislative, administrative, and even military renown. Alexander Hamilton, John Jay, John Adams, James Madison, Josiah Quincy, Robert Livingston, Charles Pinckney, Gouverneur Morris, Harrison Gray Otis, De Witt Clinton, and others in the grand peerage of the colonial, revolutionary, and reconstruction periods were all men of strong intellects, able to maintain their views before the world with pen and voice, and with sword if need required. It was a group created by the stirring times, which in turn they themselves inspired and guided to a fortunate termination. Viewed together it was an assemblage of wisdom and courage and eloquence such as had not appeared since the days of the Greek and Roman republics, and in many respects surpassing them, as indeed they ought to have surpassed them with the advantage of eighteen Christian centuries of history intervening. They had the inheritance of the ages and they profited by it.

XXV.

CONGRESSIONAL ORATORY.

THE above title may be applied to the efforts of a body of men who found a field of the noblest activity in the legislative halls of the nation, as distinguished from what may be called the provincial oratory of colonial days. Out of the diversity of political opinions a union and a constitution had been established; but old faiths still remained, and old prejudices survived which now and then would come to the surface to be maintained or attacked by turns. Preëminently the doctrine of states-rights would periodically appear, like an uneasy ghost, to disquiet its opponents and stir the blood of its Southern defenders. It was this dogma that made famous the successor of Patrick Henry and the predecessor of Calhoun, the man who may be regarded as the link between two generations of orators, JOHN RANDOLPH, of Roanoake. A proud Virginian, full of ambition and eccentricity, sometimes a slave to intemperance and always erratic in mind, bitter, self-conscious, and wretched, he nevertheless was a man whose reputation for eloquence will not readily perish. Of an ancient and wealthy family, having in his veins the Indian blood of Pocahontas he was a singular product of aristocratic and aboriginal life. All his days he was, as

Hildreth says, "in opposition to the exercise of authority by anybody but himself."

His entrance into Congress in the year 1800 may be taken as a convenient dividing line between the earlier and later oratory of the country, coincident as it is with the close of the eighteenth century and the beginning of the nineteenth. His career in Congress is marked by violent and acrimonious utterances. In his first debate he spoke of the officers of the army as a "handful of ragamuffins," and followed the speech by a violent letter demanding their punishment for resenting his insulting words, but was in the end censured himself. He quarreled with one administration after another, was alternately retired and reëlected. Still, during his lifetime his speeches were more generally read than those of any other member of Congress. Full of invective and sarcasm, delivered in a voice shrill and piping but under perfect command and musical in its lower tones, they recalled at times the peculiar eloquence of the earlier period. "His unquestioned courage, the cutting force of his sarcastic words, the malediction of his outstretched finger made Congress listen when he spoke and crowded the Virginia hustings wherever he appeared." His defence of slavery, to which he was opposed on principle as Patrick Henry had been before him, was rather the outcome of states-rights doctrine than something to be desired and perpetuated for the good of the South. This defence was also more after the fire-breathing-dragon order than solid or logical. Narrow and mistaken as were many of his utterances he foresaw with singular acumen the nullification of 1832 and even the civil war of 1861-5. Forty years before the emancipation proclamation he said, "There is one other power which may be exercised . . to which I ask the attention of every gentleman, who, like myself, has the misfortune to be born a slave-holder. If Congress possesses the power to do what is proposed by this bill they may not only enact a sedition law but they may emancipate every slave in the United States . . Let the gentlemen look forward to the time when such a question shall arise, and tremble with me at the thought that that question is to be decided by a majority of the votes of this House, of whom not one possesses the slightest tie of common interest or of common feeling with us." The rapid growth of the North, the ultimate destiny of the South, the abolition of slavery as a war measure, forced by a Northern majority in Congress, are here outlined, and doubtless seen in more than dim outline by this sombre prophet of an inevitable future, as they were afterward foreseen in nearer perspective by Daniel Webster. What Randolph dreaded as a "coalition of knavery and fanaticism" took the form finally as a union of all freedom-loving men in legislative halls and on fields of battle for universal liberty in a nation calling itself free from despotism of every sort.

The orator who is next in succession to John Randolph is HENRY CLAY. To write this name is to call up a long and eventful career, covering nearly half a century of American political history, in which he was more continuously prominent than any contemporary statesman. As a consequence great diversity of testimony as to his political aims and character may be expected from his enemies and his friends; some calling him a pretender and selfish intriguer, others placing him among the wisest and best of mankind. As usual the truth probably lies somewhere between these extremes, and from the point which is to be taken in viewing him as an orator the vituperation of opponents and the praise of friends need not greatly affect the judgment.

Of his early life it is necessary to observe only that he was the son of a Baptist clergyman who was noted for a fine voice and delivery. The lad inherited such a fortune as might be expected, namely, the opportunity to get his living by his own efforts and to obtain such an education as a log-cabin school might afford him in what used to be known as the "three R's," the *trivium* of country education in Virginia in the early years of this century. Then came a year in a Richmond grocery, from which he was advanced to a place in the office of the clerk of the chancery court. There he attracted the attention of the chancellor, who made him his amanuensis in recording decisions for the space of four years. By this patron's interest he was guided in his reading into historical and legal literature.

The law naturally became his profession and in a year more he was granted a license to practice. Richmond had become the capital of the state, and the society which the young lawyer was thrown into was of the best in the land. From the young men he met he formed a debating club, some of whose members became distinguished in subsequent times. In 1797, at the age of twenty-one, he struck out into the wilds of Kentucky "to grow up with the country." It was with melancholy regret that he reviewed his "imperfect education, improved by his own irregular efforts without the benefit of systematic instruction."

He opened an office in Lexington after studying his profession for less than a year and was soon engaged in a lucrative practice, due largely no doubt to a winning address and a frank, cordial manner which disarmed enmity and made him hosts of friends. He himself, however, attributes his success in life to the habit of daily reading and speaking the contents of some historical or scientific book. These off-hand efforts were sometimes made in a cornfield, at others in a forest, with horses and oxen for auditors. "It is to this early practice of the art of all arts that I am indebted for the primary and leading impulses that stimulated my progress and have shaped and molded my entire destiny," he used to say. The amusing tradition of his addressing the members of a debating club as "gentlemen of the jury" may be taken as an augury of his future career.

The road from law to politics in his case was shorter than usual. In five years from his arrival in Kentucky he was elected one of the representatives of Fayette county and was repeatedly re-chosen. It was just before his election that, at a popular gathering in reprehension of the alien-sedition laws, Mr. George Nichols, who first addressed the meeting, was applauded with deafening shouts and acclamations; but when young Clay followed in an address far more thrilling and effective the popular feeling became too deep for utterance, and he continued and closed amid profound and unbroken silence.

The year 1806 finds him in the United States Senate to serve out a fragment of a term, where he identified himself with the policy of internal improvements. Returned to the state legislature he signalized the occurrence by defeating a bill to which four-fifths of the House were understood to have been pledged before he made his speech against it.

In 1809 he again appears in the United States Senate, and in 1811 as a member of the House of Representatives where he was chosen speaker by a large majority, a distinction without parallel since the meeting of the first Congress and one which was his throughout a long career in the House of Representatives.

It was his leadership that hastened the war of 1812. He himself says, "I gave a vote for the declaration of war. I exerted all the influence and talent I could command to make the war. We had been insulted and outraged and spoliated upon by almost all Europe. We had become the scorn of foreign powers and the derision of our own citizens. . . What is our situation now? Respectability and character abroad, security and confidence at home." All this, however, he did not foresee when as a commissioner of peace at Ghent he signed what he regarded as a bad treaty, advantageous to Great Britain. On his return home he declined the offered mission to Russia and the war secretaryship, to be once more elected speaker of the House, an office which he continued to hold for fourteen years. Then followed the secretaryship of state for four years, a poor compensation for his disappointment in the presidential campaign of 1828, which was succeeded by another defeat in 1832 and again in 1844. Twelve years in the Senate were ended by his voluntary retirement in 1842 for seven years of private life. In 1849 he was again elected to the Senate, where he took an active part in the compromise measures of 1850, the last important public business in which he was involved. He died on the 29th of June, 1852, in the seventy-fifth year of his age.

Brief as this outline of his public career is it may suffice to indicate the main directions which his oratory of necessity took. It could not be other than political in its purpose and sometimes partisan in its character. But through it all ran certain qualities which have their value irrespective of the course which the current of his eloquence followed.

Chief among these is the element of sincerity which must be fundamental in all oratory that is genuinely effectual. His honest convictions underlay his best eloquence. To express these was always the purpose of his speaking. Grand as was his utterance the thought behind it was broader and deeper than his expression of it, and his sincerity added weight to both. Bold and frank in his nature he had no inclination to palter in a double sense, and no wavering in his opinions and purposes. He could not be eloquent off the line of his strong convictions. On that line he was ardent, fearless, and full of hope, with the rare power of inspiring others with his own sentiments and his own expectations. And those who could not be swayed from their personal beliefs and interests paid tribute to the honesty and sincerity of his straightforward words.

With this truthfulness of heart went as a natural sequence clearness in statement and lucidity in explanation, vastly more effective with a mixed audience than logical subtleties or rhetorical embellishments. He addressed the understanding and common sense of the people, seeing things from the average man's point of view, taking his first position by that man's side and then leading him up step by step into his own higher and wider prospect. From his lack of school and college discipline his methods were not always what the experience of centuries would have sanctioned, nor all his speeches models to be followed in every respect; but there were the natural aptitude and inborn gifts which have made the great orator in every century, a something which education may improve seven-fold, but the lack of which no training can entirely supply. In his day he was called a Western man, and his speech smacked of the freedom and unconstraint of the new settlements of the border; but it was always dignified, like the manners of the time. Even in its loftiest flights it kept within the range of consistency, and was not of the kind often associated with our national bird of freedom.

To his sincerity and lucidity must be added an earnestness which carried conviction with itself. His hearers did not always follow the intricacies of his logic, nor even its plainer syllogisms, but his clear words, delivered with tremendous energy, left no doubt as to the general purpose of the speaker. His printed speeches preserve much of the force with which they were uttered, but the traditions of his eloquence are such that we know that its power belonged largely to the living man, his majestic presence, his wonderful voice, his sweeping gestures, his bursts of enthusiasm or of wrath, thrilling, inspiring, overawing, terrifying, or winning by sweet persuasiveness. Accounts of contemporaries picture assemblies listening breathless and then breaking out in wild enthusiasm of delight, weeping and laughing in the uncontrollable storm of their emotions, overwhelming him with demonstrations of pride and affection. The testimony of the opposition is just as strong in its frequent reluctance to follow him in reply until the furor he had created should have time to subside. Contemporaries unite in throwing around him a kind of twilight atmosphere, in which he becomes a giant in the eyes of enraptured multitudes.

No critical analysis of his oratory in our time can lower the value of such testimony to his place in the ranks of the great orators of all time. He was an eloquent man in an age of eloquence and a statesman in an age of statesmanship. If he had not been more than a mere orator he would not have been an eminent one in such an age. If he had not had that *ethos* which the ancients counted so highly, a devotion to that which is right and honorable; in a word if he had not been a greater man he could not in the judgment of his own time have been so great an orator. He had his ambitions, even compassing the chief magistracy of the nation, but when he said, "I had rather be right than be president," he surpassed his own ambition and revealed the true majesty of his character. The calumnies and vituperations of that stormy time are buried with the issues which are no longer living, but the genius which dealt with them lives in history independent of the themes of its high discourse.

A name associated with Clay's is that of JOHN C. CALHOUN. Born five years later he died two years earlier than his great contemporary. Of Scotch-Irish presbyterian ancestry the Calhoun family had drifted from Pennsylvania along the Alleghany ranges into South Carolina. With scant means to obtain an education, but diligently using his limited opportunities the brightest member of this family was fitted to enter the junior class in Yale College, graduating in 1804 with the highest distinction. After a discussion with him on the origin of political power President Dwight remarked, "That young man has talent enough to be president of the United States." While in the law school at Litchfield he cultivated extemporary speaking with great success. Almost immediately upon his return home he was sent to the state legislature, and the ninth year from his graduation found him in Congress. In the measures before that body and the nation for forty years he was a prominent participator. The war policy of 1812, the national bank, the secretaryship of war, questions of tariff and nullification, and finally of slavery occupied in succession the energies of the great leader of the South. This is not the place to review the fierce struggles of those forty years. They were the decades when the United States, having declared themselves free from foreign dominion and become one in their main purpose, were attempting to adjust these separate interests and differences of race and place. It was a long and bitter struggle between individualism and unity, between rights retained and rights surrendered for the commonweal. Evermore there was the fear of a return to the monarchical or oligarchical forms of government from which emancipation had been won. On the other side it was seen that union could not be maintained if every state insisted upon privileges which made against the general welfare. It was this moil and turmoil of divergent views that tried the souls of patriots as much as the war of independence had tried those of their predecessors, but it bred a school of statesmen and orators whose equal has occurred but twice in the history of eloquence.

Although Calhoun was an orator who cannot be overlooked in any account of American oratory his mind was of the order that belongs preëminently to statecraft. He made great speeches, but they were great in the closeness of their reasoning and the plainness of their propositions, coupled at times with an impassioned delivery, oftener with a severity and dignity of manner which men respected, but over which they did not go wild with enthusiasm nor drift far from their well-formed judgments. Accepting his premises it was difficult to escape from the conclusions of his rigid logic. Whatever the sense of the speaker's profound sincerity and earnestness could accomplish was secured by the unfaltering devotion to his convictions and his unwavering persistence in imparting them to those who could not help listening with respect, though they might be far from accepting the legitimate results of his processes. Sometimes, however, he would generalize boldly, or even recklessly, and his exaggerations would run into absurdity, as may be the case with any orator overmastered by his purpose. Perhaps it was at such times that he came nearest to eloquence, as men usually count the term. But oftenest it was the qualities of massiveness and solidity, breadth and clearness of perception expressed without ambiguity and without reserve. A natural logician, acute in analysis he could expose the weak points of an adversary as well as make his own position strong. With a philosopher's sense of causes and effects he was quick to see the value of combinations which might bring about desired results.

In the manner and methods of his speech he was plain and direct. Arranging his thoughts in·his mind rather than upon paper he had his resources at ready command. A few simple, abstract propositions furnished the basis of clear explanation and illustration. Calm and impressive in sober discussion, sometimes bending forward as if in diffidence when beginning to speak he lifted himself up as the subject began to move him, and with a voice loud and shrill and eyes like fiery coals poured forth a stream of words, full of weight and power. His greatest efforts are those in which he was matched with his two illustrious compeers. In these he did not by any means always come off second. The distinction has been drawn between him and Webster, that while the eloquence of the one is inherent in his argument the eloquence of the other is extraneous to it. The eloquence of Calhoun was almost entirely in the intense and fiery energy of his logic, dense and firm in its construction, severe in its proportions, and chaste in its expression. All this the reader of his speeches would be surprised at finding in a leader of Southern men; but heredity is stronger than association, and the logical severity of a Celtic ancestry had not been long enough in its new and milder climate to lose much of its ancient and uncompromising vigor. It is in the other compeer, Henry Clay, that we find the luxuriance of expression, the ardent and fearless temperament, the magnetic and sympathetic power of communication, which is the outgrowth of a genial environment. But Calhoun was the man to set forth and maintain a doctrine that needed the relentlessness of demonstration more than the adornment of imagery or the ardor of devotion.

XXVI.

DANIEL WEBSTER.

THE tide of American oratory which had been rising for more than half a century reached its full flood in the eloquence of DANIEL WEBSTER. Whatever controversies may be waged over his legal, political, or ethical standing, his preëminence as an orator will be denied by no one but the most daring critic, one who is ready to match his private opinion against the judgment of contemporary hearers and of later readers.

An estimate of Webster's eloquence is attended with difficulties at the start. Its surpassing excellence has given it a familiarity that in most things breeds contempt. It is murdered daily in a thousand schoolrooms. Its best passages are cited and perverted as the Scriptures are by persons of poor taste. On the other hand there is a reverence begot by tradition and strengthened by history which destructive criticism has not yet banished, and the "godlike Daniel" continually comes to judgment on his critics. What would he have done with their microscopes and lancets and forceps in the days of his flesh and the years of his power? Consigned them and their manipulators to the *limbus fatuorum* and paradise of fools—the receptacle of all vanity and nonsense. Even yet his ghost is not sufficiently laid to permit much troubling, and few will undertake to offend

> ... "that fair and warlike form
> In which the majesty of buried Denmark
> Did sometime march;"

for the memory of it has not yet perished from the earth.

To trace the causes which made his name synonymous with eloquence supreme has been the privilege of one biographer after another, each better than his predecessor as the art of investigation has been developed. In one sense the story is a simple one of a farmer's son struggling with poverty, of heroic sacrifice in the family to give him the meagre best that the remote district afforded, of self-help in securing an education, of recognition by elders, of brightening prospects in wider fields, of success in his profession, then competence and eminence, and finally honors at the capital and throughout the land.

It is not a story of industry alone, for others have been as diligent as he was. Neither is it the record of genius alone, for there have been as great geniuses in their way. But the inborn gift which is bestowed through a man upon his age and the working habit of a sturdy generation together produced the perfect flower and fruit of deliberative oratory after a century of growth. Fortunately the scope of this sketch admits of nothing more than a presentation of the chief characteristics of his eloquence. As it was adapted to different purposes and occasions it will best be considered with reference to them. A chronological order will not make an unnatural sequence.

To those who believe in the old saying that the boy is the father of the man in things intellectual a line or two from the biography of Webster's boyhood will confirm them in their opinion. A mastery of the greatest number of verses from the English Bible, in a prize contest at the district school, may be taken as a prophecy of his mental power and of the kind of words in which that power should find expression in future years ; while the purchase of a handkerchief on which was printed the newly adopted Constitution of the United States may stand for a sign of the direction in which his intellect was to move with largeness and freedom. His entire life was the development of these three things which appeared in his boyish days, mental power, familiarity with the best English words, and acquaintance with the principles embodied in our constitutional union. And yet he loved the sport of stream and woodland enough to keep him from becoming a book-worm. Even the paradoxical prophecy of failure on the first appearance to "speak in public on the stage," which has befallen many orators in their boyhood, came to him when he attempted to recite the verses at Exeter Academy which he had read so well to Boscawen teamsters.

He found his tongue again at Dartmouth, where his native gift of speech, enriched by careful study and meditation, gained him good repute and gave promise of a brilliant future. His acquisitions in college were chiefly in ancient and modern literature and his most noted performances were in the line of oratory, but every one saw that there was more in him than the general reader or the public speaker. His first speech outside of college walls before the citizens of the college town was in the direction of his future achievements, and considering his youth and the temptations of the Fourth of July to a college orator it was not unworthy the future statesman. Whatever its absolute worth it was considered by the town fathers good enough to print.

It has been truly remarked of his style in this oration that it was florid, inflated, and heavy, after the manner of the eighteenth century. But it must be said also that the year was 1800 and the orator but eighteen. The seventeenth century English of the Bible had not been much improved by his reading of Addison, Pope, Watts, and *Don Quixote*, together with such other classics as the student could find in a college library in the closing years of the last century. If he had not shown the good sense to improve upon some of his models in the direction of simplicity and straightforwardness his oratorical "coming out" would have been less like his later masterpieces than it was.

The usual period of enforced silence which follows upon the graduation of even the most promising students was broken only by another Fourth of July oration. Loyalty to the principles of the Constitution is the burden of his discourse at Fryeburg, Maine, as it had been at Hanover, New Hampshire.

These were years of gathering material rather than of much speaking. Law and literature were his studies; his associates the ablest advocates, jurists, and statesmen in New England. It was four years before the courts had need of his services in a way to give him distinction. Men had seen in him the indications of a promising future and they prophesied that Ebenezer Webster's boy would be greater than the paternal judge of the local court.

But the oratory of the Boscawen days smacked somewhat of academic artificiality and floridity. The style was a little strained and stilted, perhaps because his growing thoughts could not readily adapt themselves to simple words, but associated more naturally with large expressions. The thoughts, however, were great and the views profound which the young lawyer had to express, and they were fast drifting toward wider and higher fields of national politics. Another Fourth of July address marks his advance in style even more than in thought. It was now 1812 and at Portsmouth. The companionship of Jeremiah Mason and of Christopher Gore, in whose office he had glimpses of Theophilus Parsons, Samuel Dexter, and Harrison Gray Otis, had been to him what the graduate course is to the latter-day student, and more. William Plumer, governor and senator, was almost his first antagonist at the bar in Portsmouth. From him the youthful advocate received a wholesome snubbing which lowered a conceit that was growing with his sense of power. At the same time he was gaining skill and strength by contests with these giants in our heroic age of jurisprudence at the beginning of this century. From them he learned that a valuable fact needs little else than perspicuous statement and that too much adornment is no ornament to a truth. The Greek temple and the Greek statue do not need Asian pigments to set off their perfections. The affected falseness of expression which comes from striving after an unnatural ideal is found no longer. Contact with reality in things and men has banished indistinct theories in thinking and generalities in speaking. His words no longer vaguely embody an unformed, immature conception nor include a dozen more for which he has no immediate need. There is not, indeed, such a diversified vocabulary as has been possessed by writers of greater linguistic attainments and of wider literary pretension, who have studied expression for its own sake. On the other hand no master of English has surpassed him in making the ordinary words of our mother-tongue do manifold service by their emphatic placing and skilful combination. Like the man himself his language is plain but full of power. There is no waste, no display. Terse and clear his lucid statements are obscured by no needless refinements and qualifications and weakened by no amplifications unnecessary to their plain meaning. His statement of his case was often its best defence, making further discussion seem almost superfluous. His language was plain and clear enough for the ordinary juryman to understand. One did not need to be translating technical terms into homespun English, thus becoming diverted from the course of the great advocate's argument. Herbert Spencer's theory of sparing the listener's available mental force by as little demand for attention as possible was exemplified by Webster's practice. He talked to his twelve men as a man with his neighbor, as one juryman with another about this particular case now in their mutual keeping, trying to place fact with fact, circumstance with circumstance, sign with sign, to see if they would all point to some conclusion or square with some hypothesis.

In this monologue in conversational tone there was the appearance of natural growth and sequence from point to point, each step so taken by the leader of their thoughts that there seemed to be no other or better way than to follow in his tracks. It is not certain that a New Hampshire jury of farmers would have resented the imputation of following him as their sheep followed the bell-wether of the flock. Not to follow him was to assume a wisdom greater than Daniel's. It was often to deny what was as good as the testimony of their own eyes and ears. So it seemed to them when he talked to them. For every occurrence he pointed out the cause. For every cause he showed the only legitimate effect.

This sympathetic address and reasonable dealing is illustrated in all its bearings by the defence of the Keniston brothers, reluctantly undertaken in a time of great fatigue "because the neighbors thought he would not allow two humble but innocent men to suffer from the wiles of a scoundrel." This defence is worth reading as a reflection of the advocate's attitude toward his fellow citizens in that state which he remembered with fondness and gratitude, though at this time he had moved on into the larger arena of a metropolis. It also illustrates his method of dealing with legal transactions in all his professional career.

A more striking instance of his skill in criminal causes is afforded by the celebrated Joseph White murder case. The deprecatory opening of the argument to remove a prejudice which had been raised against the prosecution and its methods of procedure; the vivid portrayal of the midnight assassin and his bloody deed, as if seen by the speaker himself; followed by his lucid statement of the essential points to be established— "Was there a conspiracy? Was the accused a party to it? Was he one of its executors? What motive impelled him to become an accomplice?" The answer, and the exhibition of folly in weaving about himself a network of entanglements from which his efforts to escape only involved the accused more surely and fastened upon him the inevitable conclusion that the aiding and abetting this dastardly crime made him as guilty as its principal,—all this marshaling of facts, interpretation of circumstantial evidence, casting aside of irrelevant matter, linking together of remote coincidences, bringing truth out of mystery, indicated a legal acumen second to none in the history of criminal jurisprudence.

In the superior courts of different states and in the supreme court of the United States the same principles were exemplified when he came to engage in their larger fields. He had a comprehensive grasp of the whole case in hand, saw what was irrelevant in the mass of material that gathers about any disputed question, and had a marvelous insight to discern at once the decisive points of fact and law. Then he would exhibit with the greatest clearness the proofs and reasonings from facts. And to all he added the force of an emotional appeal as from one who regarded right and wrong not as abstractions but as elements in human life which made for the welfare or the woe of his fellow-men.

An occasion when these powers were notably exhibited was in the celebrated Dartmouth College case. Without recounting its complicated history and tracing its course from the local courts to the supreme court at Washington it may be said that the claim to be defended was "that the college was an institution founded by private persons for particular uses; that the charter was given to perpetuate such uses; that misconduct of trustees was a question for courts; and that the legislature by its interference transcended its powers."

In arguing the case Webster pretended merely to put together the arguments furnished by his colleagues; but he had that quality of a commanding intellect which in combining the results of other men's labors stamped the final product with its own mint-mark. His was an originality which many will aver is the only originality possible in these latter ages of human thought and experience, namely, that of rearranging and recombining old material. It was not a case in which the great advocate felt that he could rely entirely upon the strength of a purely legal argument. There was another side which had its supporters even on the bench before him. Accordingly he attempted to carry the fortress by storm and to appeal to the court as men subject to human feelings and human prejudice; as men who had fond memories of some *alma mater* of their own and who would therefore respect and defend the cause of sound learning. It was with this in view that, casting aside his legal logic, he said in closing,

"This, sir, is my case. It is the case not merely of that humble institution, it is the case of every college in our land. . . . You may destroy this little institution. . . . but if you do you must extinguish one after another all those greater lights of science which for more than a century have thrown their radiance over our land. It is, sir, as I have said, a small college, and yet there are those who love it." The scene in the courtroom at this point has been graphically described.

Judge Story used to say, "For the first hour we listened to him with perfect astonishment, for the second hour with perfect delight, and for the third hour with perfect conviction." Stoical judges were moved to tears and the audience was spellbound by his affecting peroration, in which the hard and sharp forensic argument had passed into loving reminiscence. It may or may not be regarded as legitimate dealing with the points at issue, but it was the beginning of gaining a case that appeared to be hopeless at first. Two judges only out of seven favored Webster's side, notwithstanding his eloquence, but this partial support was the basis of a successful campaign conducted through another year and resulting in a decision in favor of the college.

Other arguments followed this, in which his legal eloquence is maintained by his sure grasp of the vital point of a question, and his recognition of every cardinal principle and estimate of every fact and circumstance at its intrinsic worth, and by a reasoning which was cogent, leading to conclusions that were irresistible. Added to these main features were his skill in concentrating his strength upon the weak points of his opponent's position and his carefulness not to be betrayed into untenable ground himself. He knew what not to undertake, and combined the sagacity of a prudent general with the valor of a wise one confident of his resources and knowing his occasion. Altogether he will be reckoned as one of the three or four greatest advocates that the world has known.

It has been said that the exclusive practice of the law is not considered the best preparation for public life. There are minds, however, which cannot take narrow views and are destined to find wide fields for their legitimate and natural action. This was true of Daniel Webster. The Portsmouth oration led him into a political convention and the writing of the *Rockingham Memorial.* This is turn placed him in Congress at the age of thirty-one, among a company of stalwarts. He kept tolerably quiet for the first session, but in the second he made a speech against the bill to encourage enlistments, which was worthy of his new dignity. The academic dress of his thoughts is dropped. Short and direct his sentences fall like hammer-strokes. "Give up your futile projects of invasion. Extinguish the fires that blaze on your inland frontier. Establish perfect safety and defence there by adequate force. . . . Unclench the iron grasp of your embargo. . . . If you are seriously contending for maritime rights, go to the theatre where alone those rights can be defended. Then the united wishes and exertions of the nation will go with you. Even our party divisions, acrimonious as they are, cease at the water's edge."

A tone worthy of his new sphere is discernible. It is at this period that his success in the larger domain of statesmanship begins to be recognized by those who hitherto had known him as a lawyer only. In the Massachusetts constitutional convention his advocacy of conservative action was conducted with great ability and skill, calling out many prophecies of his future career, among them one by Judge Story concerning the possible presidency. Accordingly when he was returned to Congress from Massachusetts after a retirement of six years for professional reasons, he is fairly in the field of deliberative oratory. It is here that the greatness of his intellect appears and also of his labors and triumphs. He was preëminently a statesman, with a large grasp of principles to which he committed himself with all the devotion of a great intellect and soul. He had the wisdom to view things in their true relations, uncolored by imagination or sympathies.

Of broad and comprehensive views he did not attempt the ideal or the impossible, but only what was attainable in any given situation. He embraced the whole nation in his outlook and cultivated a national rather than a sectional spirit. Being in the political minority he could for this reason be free to exercise generous views and a high national spirit. Such breadth and comprehensiveness were the best foundation for a lofty and majestic eloquence, which was displayed from time to time during the forty years of his public service.

The best comment on this oratory is suggested by the careful reading of it, as has been remarked of the works of our greatest dramatist. What, however, is true of one example of it is true in a measure of all, making allowances for differences of occasion and interest. The speech in reply to Hayne will be considered as the best exposition of the cardinal principles around which clustered and crystalized the system of political wisdom that distinguished him. Its nucleus is the integrity of the Constitution and the preservation of the Union. Around this idea, as around a fixed and double pole-star, all other political theories revolved.

The reply to Hayne was itself a twofold production on two different days in answer to two speeches from the South Carolina general, but the first reply is so overshadowed by the magnificence of the second that its existence is almost forgotten. The occasion of the speech was the introduction of a resolution of inquiry as to the sales and surveys of western lands. Senator Foote, of Connecticut, must have been surprised to see how great a fire his little match had kindled, and the uninformed reader would be puzzled to know what there was in that resolution to provoke the greatest parliamentary contest of modern times. But it is not the spark that explodes. The air was full of irreconcilable elements and the "irrepressible conflict" was beginning. The powers of that Constitution, which seemed to be little more than articles of confederacy in 1789, had still a double meaning to the nation. There was a south side on which "State Sovereignty" appeared to be written, and a north side inscribed with "Sovereignty of the Union"; not always clear, however, to all northern people. But in this great debate Webster made it clear to the understandings of all men that the nation is greater than any state and all the states. A generation later the logic of events established the solidity of his position. Passing over the first reply, which would be a remarkable effort from any other man of that time, the second may be taken as an exhibition of Webster's characteristics as a parliamentary debater.

It should be borne in mind that in Hayne's first speech it had been groundlessly charged upon New England that she had shown hostility to the West. This charge was repelled with such vigor as to provoke another bitter attack upon New England, Massachusetts, and her senator, accompanied by a declaration of nullification doctrines and the sovereignty of South Carolina, with threatened resistance to the Union and the laws of Congress. On January 26, 1830, the great reply to Hayne was delivered. Intimations of the approaching encounter had gone abroad, and men were gathering from every quarter, with sunny and hopeful faces from the South, while apprehensive and dejected countenances marked the anxiety of New Englanders. On the eventful morning the Senate chamber was crowded with notables from every state and dignitaries from abroad. It was an assemblage worthy of the discussion of the cardinal principles of our nationality by the greatest of our constitutional lawyers and the chief orator of the land. Amid breathless silence he began the famous exordium: "Mr. President:—When the mariner has been tossed for many days in thick weather and on an unknown sea, he naturally avails himself of the first pause in the storm, the earliest glance of the sun, to take his latitude, and ascertain how far the elements have driven him from his true course. Let us imitate this prudence, and before we float farther on the waves of this debate refer to the point from which we departed, that we may at least be able to conjecture where we now are. I ask for the reading of the resolution before the Senate."

His quiet manner and tones had relieved the tension of strained suspense, and the House took breath during the monotonous reading of the resolution and then adjusted itself for four hours of listening to what, all in all, is by general agreement the greatest speech of modern times. To follow its outline will reveal in a convenient, if not in a logical, order the great orator's method of treatment of men who opposed him and of principles to which he was opposed, or, again, of principles which he espoused. In his opening sentences he obeyed the first principles of address in starting from the level of ordinary thought and feeling, or, in this instance, of bringing his hearers back to their normal condition before leading them up to the heights he proposed to ascend. His next rhetorical and argumentative necessity was to deal with the personalities with which his opponent had seen fit to assail him. He treats these with a dignity, enlivened by a pleasant humor, that belongs to assured power and conscious rectitude. He disclaims resentment or the slightest feeling of unkindness for the adversary who had been betrayed into a personal attack. He simply informs him that his arrows failed to reach their mark, that, in fact, they had not disturbed his sleep; but he does protest against the intended disparagement and the lofty assumption of superiority, and he recalls his opponent to a sense that this is a Senate of men possessing honor, character, and independence. It has been said that Webster was not a witty man; he was something better and greater. His dignified irony gave him an advantage over his persecutor that could not have been won by the crossing of rapiers. While, however, he good-naturedly parries the thrusts of his adversary he informs him that there are blows to give as well as to take, and commends him to a prudent husbandry of his resources. The weight of those blows appear later.

In the following paragraph is displayed Webster's command of allusion, as great apparently in the English classics as in the English Bible. Hayne had lugged in Banquo's murder and ghost to illustrate the "murdered coalition" with infelicity of application. Webster's discernment of its inapplicability is even surpassed by his correct statement of the dramatic incident and the readiness with which he turns the true situation upon his opponent, quoting line after line of Macbeth. His familiarity with Latin authors is also evinced by his skilful introduction of phrases, according to a custom which was more prevalent in his day than in ours. The Bible also is a source of allusion in which he is much more at home than most modern speakers. Touching upon the slavery question early, as underlying all this controversy, he passes with dignified humor over his alleged attack on South Carolina and to his famous eulogium of the Revolutionary heroes of that state and their comradeship with Massachusetts men. It is in the encomium on both sections that he exhibits the comprehensive patriotism for which he is justly renowned and also that eloquence which came from a heart big with emotion when the daring heroism of the Revolutionary sires rose up before him. That which stirred the fountains of feeling in the Dartmouth College case and in the Bunker Hill oration was thrilling the heart-strings of Massachusetts and South Carolina men alike when he said, "Shoulder to shoulder they went through the Revolution; hand in hand they stood round the administration of Washington." And with these words was coupled a personal sympathy with such devotion to a common country that it lifted him above the spirit of sectional jealousy and recrimination which had forced him into a declaration and a defence of his all-including patriotism.

It was a fit prelude, however, to what was to follow, best stated in his own words: "There yet remains to be performed, Mr. President, by far the most grave and important duty which I feel to be devolved on me by this occasion. It is to state and to defend what I conceive to be the true principles of the Constitution under which we are here assembled."

He had come to what was also the great business of his life and to a task which no one before or since could so well accomplish as he. With a modesty as becoming as his authority was great he proceeds to state his sentiments "without challenging for them any particular regard, with studied plainness, and as much precision as possible." First he states his opponent's position; states it so fairly and clearly that it might seem as if he were going over to that side and about to surrender his own. It was his usual practice. He could afford to be generous with his adversary. He ascertained the full strength of his own position by going into the length and depth of the enemy's intrenchments. He never was surprised by difficulties which he had not faced in advance of the battle. It had always been his habit to reckon beforehand with the foe, and here he knew the strength of the stronghold he was about to carry.

Having exemplified his habitual candor and clearness in stating the claims of the opposing side he next gives us an illustration of another oratorical phase in his masterly argumentation concerning "The origin of this government and the source of its power." Is it of the state or of the people? He employs the most convincing of methods. He assumes two hypotheses, only one of which can be true ; he reduces to the absurd ; he distinguishes between a pleasant theory and an unwelcome fact ; shows the difference between an impatient, regretful wish and a retained right, between making and breaking a contract; and states the origin of all power in words that have been perpetuated in Lincoln's paraphrase, "It is, sir, the people's constitution, the people's government, made for the people, made by the people, and answerable to the people." Other forms of deliberative reasoning succeed to these, by example from history at home and abroad, by testing syllogisms in their major or minor premises and in conclusions unwarrantably drawn. It is safe to say that there are few forms of applied logic that may not be found in this speech. Yet it may be said of him as he himself said of Samuel Dexter, but with a profounder meaning, that "aloof from technicality and unfettered by artificial rule a question of constitutional law gave opportunity for that deep and clear analysis, that mighty grasp of principle, which so much distinguished his higher efforts. His very statement was argument, his inference seemed demonstration. The earnestness of his own conviction wrought conviction in others. One was convinced, and believed and assented, because it was gratifying, delightful, to think and feel and believe in unison with an intellect of such evident superiority." This was all the truer of the author of this tribute because he was the greater man. The directness of his purpose, the irresistible sweep of his argument, his perspicuity and energy, his dignity and simplicity, his unimpassioned statements and his forceful appeal, his vigor of reasoning and felicity of diction, his luxuriant but chastened imagery, his masterly power of condensation, and under all and over all the unvarying fitness to the subject and the occasion—the very essence of oratory, an adaptation to persons, times, places, and the theme under consideration—all these, and added to these the ethical element which pervaded all like an atmosphere of purity and truth, made him a living example of Cato the Elder's definition of the orator, *Orator est vir bonus dicendi peritus.*

The difficulty in writing of such a man is to omit much that is closely related to his speech. Personality, character, presence, and the element that has lain back of every great orator and refused to be transmitted with his words, the subtle magnetism of a great man over all persons within the sight of his eye and the sound of his voice, all this must be hurried over. So, also, must the history of a life full of action and thought and devising and purpose, now crowned with success and rewarded with approval, again saddened with failure and darkened by disappointment and ingratitude and desertion. Many words of explanation, which become possible and obligatory as time clears the air of the dust and smoke of battle, must be left unsaid by reason of the limits set by the point of view when oratory alone is to be considered. Even this must be contemplated in a fragmentary manner and from afar. But enough can be discerned in the outlines of the heroic forms which are projected on the shadowy past, like the majestic spectres of the Brocken, to distinguish them from the multitudes among which they mingled in their daily life. Generally they have been in most respects exalted characters. This one was such a character with one great purpose and one great ambition. The ambition was doomed to failure; the purpose succeeded, but in the way that Webster feared and not in the way that he hoped. Yet the thoughts that he wrought out into clear, forcible, fitting, and effective speech place him in the foremost rank of eloquent men and crown him as the chief of American orators. If impartial judgment could be secured, as it may be in the far future, it is possible that, estimated by absolute standards, he will be considered, all in all, to be the perfected fruit of twenty-four centuries of oratorical culture.

XXVII.

OCCASIONAL ORATORY.

THE impulse that was communicated to American oratory by the great triumvirate whose deliberative eloquence has been described did not cease its movement on the death of the latest survivor. The direction which it took, however, was one in which Webster was particularly distinguished. Mention of it has been omitted in order to incorporate this phase of his public speech with its proper topic of occasional or demonstrative oratory.

This has been defined as the kind of speaking in which "no defined end is directly proposed, but rather a general impulsion toward noble, patriotic, and honorable sentiments and toward a large and worthy life." Taking an anniversary, a great historical event or character, a celebration, or occasion of any sort as a starting point, it permits either a close adherence to the original subject or the widest latitude of treatment. "The field is a broad and inviting one, promising easy success. But the facility of saying something is counterbalanced by the difficulty of saying anything worth hearing." Many an oration which had great fitness to the occasion when delivered has been so occasional in its character that it could have no permanent value. Webster, however, was accustomed to link the immediate lesson of the hour with truths so large and enduring that his utterances acquired an abiding worth and interest. In his Plymouth oration, after touching upon the event to be commemorated and the men who made it historic, he discourses at large upon liberty, education, humanity, and the Constitution. A succession of great themes was treated in a grand and inspiring manner, suggesting the majestic march of a classic procession around the frieze of an Ionic temple. His delivery reminded his hearers of the music of a full-toned organ. Readers of the printed speech found it a literary production of the first grade; some at this day regarding the Plymouth oration as the finest of all his efforts in this field. Five years more, however, added enough to his experience and power to enable him to produce a finer finish if not a profounder thought in the Bunker Hill oration.

The directness of his plain, strong words; the massiveness of his short, clear sentences; the due proportion of simplicity, force, and beauty; the wonderful adaptation to the occasion, the subject, and to his own personality make it altogether the masterpiece of commemorative eloquence. Familiar as household words to our educated youth it has done much to inspire them with reverence for ancestral devotion and to inculcate the first principles of citizenship consecrated to freedom and an undivided nationality. How much these examples of patriotic eloquence have done to perpetuate noble speech in later orators it is impossible to say. There are a few of them who, like nine out of the Attic Ten, would have been seemingly greater if there had not been a greatest. But they are too illustrious to be passed over on this account.

The one who comes nearest to Webster in time if not in ability is EDWARD EVERETT. Only twelve years his junior he was Webster's life-long friend and political ally. Much of their political careers was in the same field, with similar sympathies and purposes. But Everett, like his compeer, had a distinctive character of his own, personal, literary, and oratorical. As the one was preëminently a lawyer so the other was first of all a scholar. Entering Harvard College at the age of thirteen and graduating with the highest honors at seventeen he rivaled the best of parliamentary orators of Great Britain in his precocious attainments. Like them he was an accomplished reader of the ancient classics, and the tradition of his ability as a writer lingered long after his graduation. The next year he delivered a poem before the Phi Beta Kappa Society on American poets, and within two years was winning great admiration in the pulpit of the Brattle street church in Boston by the eloquence and power of his discourses. Very soon he was called to the chair of Greek literature in Harvard, and to further qualify himself he spent three years abroad in travel and study. Lectures upon Greek literature and ancient art, delivered in Cambridge and Boston, were the immediate fruit of this experience. Added to such labors was the editing of the *North American Review*, which he imbued with a thoroughly national tone, defending the country with great spirit against the shallow and flippant attacks of several foreign travelers of a class not yet extinct.

He was thirty years of age when he made his first essay in that department of demonstrative oratory in which he afterward became distinguished. It was before the same society that listened to his poem twelve years previously. An immense audience had been drawn together by his growing fame to hear him speak upon *Circumstances Favorable to the Progress of Literature in America*. Twenty-five years later one of the audience wrote: "The sympathies of his audience went with him in a rushing stream as he painted in glowing hues the political, social, and literary future of our country. They drank with thirsty ears his rapid generalizations and his sparkling rhetoric. As with skilful and flying hand the orator ran over the chords of national pride and patriotic feeling every bosom throbbed in unison, and when the fervid declamation of the concluding paragraph was terminated by the simple pathos of the address to Lafayette, who was present at the orator's side, his hearers were left in a state of emotion far too deep for tumultuous applause."

The scholar and the speaker was now launched on an oratorical career which was to be followed more exclusively by him than by any predecessor. Others had made it the by-play of legal, theological, or political life, with, most often, the ephemeral reward that goes with diversion. Everett, on the contrary, may be said to have made occasional oratory the business of his life and all other speaking a departure from his chosen vocation. Elected to Congress in this very year he became a frequent but not obtrusive debater, and was distinguished for the ability and tact of his diplomatic papers in his high official stations, as notably at the court of St. James; but it is as the orator of some great occasion or the commemorator of an anniversary or the eulogist of an illustrious patriot that he will be best remembered. Perhaps he more than any other man is responsible for the large number of orations and speeches which have been delivered here and there in the country founded upon the Declaration of Independence and the national Constitution. Although their literary life has been short they have served to keep alive the spirit of loyalty to the Union and of devotion to the ideals which were set up by Revolutionary patriots. Everett himself delighted in nothing so much as to inspire a deep veneration for our hero-statesmen, to draw from our past lessons for our future, to awaken a thoughtful, intelligent enthusiasm for constitutional liberty, to champion American worth, and to encourage home-born virtues. In this labor of his best days he performed a service of education among a people who have been said to "present the anomaly of being political in their tastes and habits without having a political education." This cannot be averred with so much truth now, when every college has its course in political science. Yet before these days no people could be without instruction in the profoundest political wisdom, among whom the speeches of Webster and Everett were as familiar as the reading books of the common school could make them. Boys knew them by heart, as they did the catechism, long before they understood their meaning. But the time came when whole regiments of those boys knew their import well enough to fight and to die for the principles they once learned by rote.

Nor is it any qualification to the oratory of Everett that it is the work of a rhetorician. He lived in a time when our American youth needed the inspiration of a master in English style. It was the age between the formative and the reformative epochs in our national life. In literary activities we were still under the dominion of the mother-country and had but few creditable authorities to which appeal could be made at home. In this period of comparative quiet and of commercial occupations the opportunity for the education of the American people in polite letters had come. It was particularly fortunate, therefore, that a man of the best culture and of the most refined taste could from time to time as occasion after occasion arose stand before the best audiences in the nation and give object lessons in literature and English composition and oratory as well as in the principles of liberty under the laws. It was the fortune of many distinguished men in the last generation to receive an impulse early in life from the classic purity and grace of such English as Everett knew how to construct out of the wealth of his resources. To the most varied culture he added an immense and diversified learning, a retentive memory, so much valued by the Hellenic orators, great facility and felicity of expression, a ready wit, a conciliating humor, a dexterity in turning the sharp corners of discussion, and always a sense of fitness which is both the essence and the safeguard of good style. Beyond all the excellencies of its form he had also the power of oratory; imagination enough for illustrating and emphasizing his thoughts, the kindling sensibilities without which eloquence, though perfect as an Apollo Belvidere, becomes as lifeless as a statue, and a ready perception of the progress that his discourse was making in the minds of listeners. Of what is called magnetism, so often the one thing lacking in otherwise effective speakers, he had an abundance. It came out in an emotional voice, of large compass and full of melody, sometimes grave and even melancholy, but able to rise from moving pathos to thrilling and triumphant tones. And everywhere and always there was the unfailing harmony between the speaker, his subject, and the occasion, which leaves no vulnerable place for criticism and keeps the orator at his best advantage and on his highest ground. Harmony is the characteristic which pervades all his work. The symmetry and fitness and finish are in general so complete that they leave strong, individual traits to be discovered rather than to reveal themselves. Sometimes a homely phrase or an ill-balanced sentence might be pardoned for the relief of its variety, but such phrases and sentences would be as impossible in Everett's pages as gravel stones in Pentelic marble. His composition is a work of art, to be sure, but it is high art. It would be a great natural orator indeed who should produce out of his native abilities equal effects. If the best work of nature results in fitting correspondencies, this art of his comes very near the finest achievements of nature. His words seem the only words that can exactly match his thoughts, and no syllable can be spared from the rhythm of his best passages. Yet he was not a mere rhetorician. His good sense kept him from sacrificing anything to mere expression, his large knowledge delivered him from bondage to the symphonies of speech on every occasion. He knew when magnificent declamation was in place and also when plain and practical discourse was equally imperative. The sense of fitness never deserted him.

The criticisms which his oratory has received are incurred by the optimism of a hopeful and charitable temper and by an artistic sense which sometimes led him into a poetic use of imagery for its own sake, just as his admiration for his country sometimes made him oblivious to its perils and defects which appeared to less sanguine spirits. But the evil day which they foresaw had not yet arrived, and to this bright and cheerful representative of a prosperous age of wealth and learning, of art and literature, it would have been an incongruous thing to be a prophet of evil.

As the result of his labors for a lifetime we possess what one of the old Greek orators might have left, an assemblage of occasional orations. As literature they approach nearer the Hellenic standard in form and body than any collection from the days of the famous Ten to our own. What he might have done in the way of historical or political writing to leave as a memorial of his learning and his wisdom it is not pertinent to consider here. What he did leave in his great masterpieces of eloquence is of immeasurable worth in the history of that art which he so assiduously cultivated. It constitutes a special department of public speech and approximates closely to the ideal of oratory as an art, yet having a high purpose withal and an object, noble and definite, of inculcating lessons of patriotism by recalling the virtues of patriots and the love of learning by exemplifying what knowledge can become in the mouth of an eloquent man.

The next name in the succession of orators who won distinction in the first half of the present century is that of RUFUS CHOATE. Only five years younger than Everett he was yet old enough to be associated with Webster, or opposed to him, in legal conflicts. The three together may fairly be considered as forming a triad of New England men representing, each in his own way, the ruling ideas of the province without narrow provincialism. One stood for profundity and strength, a second for learning and polished diction, a third for broad culture, brilliant wit, and impetuous eloquence.

It is much the same story in the matter of his early training as with the other two. Whatever New England may have lacked it has had as good schools as the education of the people could furnish from the colleges which are scattered here and there from east to west through her territory. Now and then a farmer has thought it a pity that a boy who could lay a stone wall as well as Rufus Choate should be spoiled for such work by going to college, but the transfer to the larger field has generally been made and also been justified, as in his case, by the result. Sent over the New Hampshire line to Hampton, the academy nearest his home in Ipswich, he in some way drifted into Dartmouth college in those stormy years of litigation when there were two colleges, one of them "without buildings, without libraries, without apparatus, without resources." But law, and law mixed with politics, were at that time thicker than the river-fog in Hanover. The cloud soon spread over the state and finally cast a shadow over every college in the land, until the question of collegiate rights was settled through Webster's efforts in the Supreme court at Washington. This legal contest turned the mind of Choate to the study of law, and the most eminent lawyers of a pre-eminently forensic age were his exemplars and his inspiration. From the greatest of them may have come the impulse "to become a national man," with large thoughts of the country, the Union and the fathers of the republic. At all events these college days gave promise of great vigor and grasp of mind, of richness and expressiveness of style, and of a strange fascination of eye and voice.

The traditions of his valedictory oration correspond to those of his later achievements in persuasive eloquence. The law-school at Cambridge and the law-office of William Wirt in Washington widened his views of law and politics. Then followed the years of waiting for clients and business. They were also years of acquisition and of study in letters and philosophy, as well as jurisprudence. By and by his first case came and with it the beginning of his reputation as a forensic orator. A contemporary writes: "There had been giants among us, some of national fame and standing, but no such giant as this had appeared before at the Essex bar—such words, such epithets, such involutions, such close and powerful logic all the while, such grace and dignity, such profusion and waste, even, of everything beautiful and lovely.

No, not waste; he never wasted a word. It was a new school of rhetoric, oratory, and logic, and of all manner of diverse forces, working steadily and irresistibly in one direction to accomplish the speaker's purpose and object."

His eloquence at the bar soon found a wider field in Congress, to which he was elected at the age of thirty-one. His speech on the tariff, begun to a house almost empty, brought members from lobbies and committee-rooms by the charm of its irresistible persuasiveness until the hall was filled. He closed amidst the enthusiasm of his hearers, and his position as a parliamentary orator was established. In a later session he made a speech of which an old-stager in politics from Kentucky said, "In accordance with my custom I took my hat to leave, lingering a moment just to notice the tone of his voice and the manner of his speech. But that moment was fatal to my resolution. I became charmed by the music of his voice and was captivated by the power of his eloquence, and found myself wholly unable to move until the last word of his beautiful speech had been uttered." At this time his eloquence was characterized as exuberant, fervid, and of a new variety, not commonly accepted at the bar at first, but gratifying at length a taste which it created. On the lecture platform and on the floor of Congress it found a greater variety of hearers and a more catholic taste than in a Massachusetts court-room, where his vehement gestures and wealth of imagination sometimes seemed exotic and oriental in the midst of hard facts and hard-headed lawyers and juries.

Ten years after he entered the House of Representatives, where he served four years, Choate was elected to the Senate to succeed Webster, the latter having been appointed secretary of state under President Harrison, who died one month from the day of his inauguration. Choate's eulogy in Faneuil Hall upon one whom the nation loved was a sincere and eloquent tribute to his many virtues. In less than a month the new senator was receiving warm commendations from all parties for his defence of the government's policy in the then famous M'Leod case, involving complications with Great Britain. In a later discussion on the same general topic he exhibited a generous statesmanship, resting upon the inviolability of the Constitution and expressed in strong and forcible language. Other measures were discussed in the two years which remained of Webster's uncompleted term, at the expiration of which Choate returned to his professional labors in Boston. He had won for himself an enviable reputation as a deliberative orator in the golden age of American eloquence among the great congressmen of that notable age. But he had little taste and less fondness for political life and no aptitude at all for the drudgery by which party eminence is gained and party favor kept. He cared little for this sort of success. He counted it as a hindrance to the cultivation of professional and literary tastes, and could therefore hold fast to those conservative opinions which tend to keep a person in the retirement of a minority.

In making an estimate, therefore, of his oratorical achievements it will be fair to consider his forensic and occasional efforts, for the most part. In the first, when he addressed a jury he began in an easy, natural way, with that conversational manner which he might have caught from some of his eminent contemporaries at the bar. The same clear and definite statement of the case which has been noticed in other great lawyers was his also. This he followed by minute analysis of the evidence, taking care incidentally to broach his theory of the case and introduce or insinuate his main propositions often enough to get them well before his hearers, who were often unconsciously forming an opinion, as they thought, for themselves. In the exordium his well known sweetness of temper and courtesy of manner served him admirably, as in other and more trying places. He conciliated by overcoming prejudices with fairness and kindness and won smiles by his gracious pleasantry and the keen wit for which he was always famous. He made his audience willing and delighted to hear him. If a juryman grew sleepy he would wake him up with a story from the vast collection in a memory that retained everything which touched it. His ludicrous representations and exaggerations that were almost sublime always had a purpose as well as an efficacy which argument often fails to have with "twelve honest men and true." There was no fault to be found with his logic. It used to be supposed, on account of the marvelous beauty of his rhetoric, that this was his chief power. Very likely it was what caught the public ear when the common understanding did not trouble itself with his reasoning processes. These, however, were strong and irrefragable as a chain of triple links. The massiveness of his argumentation was equaled only by the brilliance of his rhetoric. Indeed with him they were not two processes, but one and indivisible. It was the whole thought, in its spirit and its body, that he presented.

He had, moreover, what is equally valuable, the skill to arrange his arguments in the most effective order. He massed his forces at the proper point, the strong against the weak, his own weak places covered by the strong or artfully concealed. But the entire effect was cumulative, argument upon argument, figure upon figure, an overwhelming flood carrying everything before it at last. Still, impassioned as were his addresses to the jury his arguments before the bench were deferential, quiet, and precise. In a clear, musical voice, without much gesture or change of position he would deliver a long argument full of legal knowledge and acumen, but without pretension or artificiality. Through it all the driest technicalities were relieved and illuminated by narrative and illustration, by imagination and humor. In those trying positions to which the advocate, of all men, is oftenest subjected he seldom lost his presence of mind or quickness of wit to meet the unexpected turn or to get out of an awkward dilemma.

Logical, however, as he was, he was known among contemporaries as a magician in the open and occult forces of expression. He would have been termed a rhetorician if he had dealt with words and sentences instead of weightier matters through their instrumentality. Gifted beyond most men with the powers of speech he had added to his talents "by trading with the same." He was always a student of literature, full of appreciation and sympathy for men of letters, especially fond of the classics and of imaginative authors. In his busiest professional days he would manage to steal an hour, too often from sleep or exercise, for an ancient or modern classic. Philosophy, history, and poetry were devoured by turns, sometimes without much order; but as from the notorious jumble of papers in his desk he could quickly find a document desired, so from the heterogeneous stores of his memory he could summon the fact or the figure he wanted, and when he wanted it most. By gift and by acquirement he could not help being a master of the high art of public speech. Given such a man as he was, with such audiences as he was likely to have, communication from him to them and responsive sympathy from them to him were as certain and as free as electric currents. Charged with thought, alive with emotion, possessing the open vision and the ready word he was as delighted to speak as they to hear. The one qualification seems to have been that when the thought began to flow forth it became so full and so abounding that no sentence of ordinary length could contain it. Yet the idea was so exact that fewer words could not express its manifold character as it lay before the enlarged prospect of the orator. Others would have seen less and said less; but for him, thinking with marvelous rapidity and intensity, the product must be delivered complete and entire. Still his long sentences were so framed that the ordinary hearer caught their meaning and strength as one discovers the higher peaks on the horizon, while through his discourse as a whole there ran a stateliness and a dignity which was always kept in spite of an exuberance that he knew as well as anyone was more permissible in a speaker than in a writer. By no means were all of his sentences long. In a paragraph that happens to be on a page opened at random there are short sentences where they are needed to gather up the substance of the paragraph. The last one has but four words, the two next to the last occupy one line each. But he could make a sentence rivaling the philosopher Kant's, and keep its proportion and balance and periodic structure subservient and tributary to clearness and force and beauty.

It is in the whole discourse, however, that we look for the constructive power and manifold art of the orator. The disposition of every part to contribute toward perfected unity, the sense of proportion and harmony, the distribution of facts and reasons and inferences, a just appreciation of the enlightening and illumining power of imagery, these are the criteria of eloquence. Judged by these and by the effects of his speech upon his hearers there is no room for doubt that his rank as a forensic and an occasional orator is among the first. Had he confined himself to literary studies and to the lecture platform he would have been preëminent as an instructor of the people by that method which prevailed in the third quarter of this century, the lyceum lecture. Such addresses as that on *The Eloquence of Revolutionary Periods* and similar ones growing out of our early history are alive with instruction and moving power. They contributed largely to the stock of controlling ideas which have gone with the New Englander to every section of the country and have helped to strengthen its stakes and lengthen its cords. The day of such public instruction has passed with the generation that listened and the men that spoke, but when its story shall be told one of its pioneers and illustrious orators will be recognized in this brilliant man of letters and of law. Much of his greatness will be lost to posterity by reason of the volatile nature of that power which depends upon a living presence and an impressive personality, but enough remains for the historic faculty to build upon and for the historic imagination to restore to something of its original proportions the fabric of marvelous strength and beauty which Rufus Choate raised in his life of laborious study, of conscientious endeavor, and of brilliant success.

XXVIII.

CHARLES SUMNER.

FOUR men, who have the distinction of being both deliberative and occasional orators, were born within the thirty years from 1782 to 1812. The last of these, CHARLES SUMNER, was twelve years the junior of his predecessor, Choate, as Everett was by the same number of years the junior of Webster. Accordingly they may be regarded as a group of Massachusetts men having much the same interests and associations, both state and national. On the other hand the difference in their defence and advocacy of common principles and policies was as diverse as their own strong personalities could make them, strengthened and emphasized by the march of events and progress of public sentiment. As this progress was greatly hastened in the lifetime of the last of the group one may expect to find a wider separation between him and his predecessor than could exist between the other three. It will also be harder on this account to separate the oratory of this man from the issues with which it deals, for we are approaching the time when the long strife of words is to flame into civil war, and Charles Sumner may be regarded as the exponent of this stormy transition period.

It is true that he gave little promise of such a distinction in early years. A Boston boy, educated at the

Latin school and Harvard, and also by such schoolmates as Robert C. Winthrop, George S. Hillard, James Freeman Clarke, Wendell Phillips, and such elders as President Quincy, Professors Channing and Ticknor he lacked no advantages of learning. Those which he made the most of were the classics and *belles lettres*, writing at first in a manner that was somewhat heavy and pedantic with undigested learning. But his knowledge was wide in its scope and acquired with great readiness. It was after he left college that he began to develop rapidly by laborious days and nights of study and by listening to lectures, orations, and legal arguments and by converse with the jurist Story, his idol. To be a jurist and not merely a lawyer naturally became his ambition. To this purpose he devoted six morning hours, but afternoons and evenings were reserved for classics and literature. These were the days when he was laying up stores of knowledge for future use in a memory that retained everything and re-presented everything at need. The productive period came later. Just now there were legal articles and editing and lectures at the Harvard law-school and in popular courses on professional topics. Not yet an orator he was, nevertheless, laying deep and broad foundations. His ambitions were divided, his purposes not fully established; both were waiting for an inspiring motive to arouse and direct them. European travel followed as a broadening educator, opening a large mind to wider views and the social world to a spirit that was eager to be cosmopolitan.

He was thirty-five before his first famous oration inaugurated the period of his occasional oratory. It was delivered before the city of Boston, assembled in state on the Fourth of July, 1845. The memories of Bunker Hill and of the war of 1812, with the prospect of a Mexican war, did not tend to make his subject in harmony with the occasion; for peace was the burden of the address in the *True Grandeur of Nations*. But it was in harmony with the sentiments of the speaker, and his task was to bring his auditory into sympathy with himself. That he failed to do this was owing to the spirit of that age more than to the lack of eloquence in the orator. He was in advance of his generation, full of enthusiasm, which the elders called youthful and visionary, but they also recognized the power and promise of the man. Personally he was tall and commanding in stature, possessing a voice of great power and compass and a mind full of learning and the wisdom of the ancients, with which he illustrated the science of modern times. His discourse was freighted with allusions from every department of knowledge. History, mythology, literature of fiction and the drama, the poets and orators of every country were woven into the fabric of his speech until it became a very cloth of gold and gems in its barbaric splendor. It was what might be expected as the outcome after years of continuous storage. These accumulated riches were poured forth with a lavish hand, as if it were the first and last occasion for their use. Jewels of silver and jewels of gold were cast into this molten image, which has never lacked its contingent of worshipers among youth whose studies and aspirations have upon them the dew of the morning. Even the older heads must revere the massiveness of that lore upon which the structure rests. A liberal education is essential to its comprehension. Within the turning of a leaf are contributions from Plutarch and Livy, from Homer and Dante, from Demosthenes and Cicero, from Virgil and the Troubadour, from Hobbes and Sir Thomas Browne, from Bacon, Vattel, and the great jurists in every nation. Another turn brings up Hesiod and Anacreon, Herodotus and Froissart, Sismondi, Montesquieu, Liutprand and Muratori, and the historians of every century. The dicta of the Christian fathers, the superstitions of mediæval doctors, the comedies of Moliére and the dialogues of Plato, the discourse of Brantome and the sayings of Malte-Brun, the epistles of Augustine and the letters of Madame de Sévigné are drawn upon in turn to embellish this Boston oration. And not these alone, but the authorities and authors that are the furniture of each man in his own profession and calling all belonged to this young lawyer and man of letters, whose first public appearance in his native city was a prophecy of his approaching public life, with its distinctions and oppositions. For there were friends who did not fail to express their surprise and enemies who did not wait to declare their antagonism to his views. Still both friends and foes admitted that another prophet had arisen among them. As with the prophets of Israel, however, the burden was not of a kind to appeal to their taste. For awhile his orations were mainly literary and almost academic in their character. A lecture on the *Employment of Time* before the Boston lyceum is full of examples of diligent workers in many fields and has all the interest of personal narrative. Then follows the oration of July 4, 1846, a eulogy upon the lives and characters of four illustrious men, Pickering, Story, Allston, and Channing, personifications of scholarship, jurisprudence, art, and philanthropy. Yet underneath all his tributes ran the strong current which was rising in his soul against war and slavery and war for slavery, for it was within a twelvemonth of the incursion into Mexico. The occasion was academic, the Phi Beta Kappa anniversary at Harvard, the subject as inoffensive as a memorial of departed worth, but living and approaching issues were mingled with retrospective thoughts. It is of this memorial discourse that John Quincy Adams wrote the author, "I trust I may now congratulate you on the felicity, first of your selection of the subject, secondly of its consummation in the delivery. The pleasure with which I listened to your discourse was inspired far less by the success of the present moment than by the vista of the future which was opened to my view. Beyond my time I see you have a mission to perform. I look from Pisgah to the Promised Land; you must enter upon it. *Delenda est servitus.*"

Edward Everett thanks Sumner for his "most magnificent address of unsurpassed felicity and power. Should you never do anything else you have done enough for fame." Chancellor Kent wrote, "You have raised a noble monument to the four great men who have adorned your state, in a production glowing with images of transcendent worth and embellished with classical and literary allusions drawn from your memory and guided by your taste with extraordinary force." Such are a few of the sympathetic criticisms of distinguished contemporaries upon this early work of Sumner's. They also contain, as can easily be seen, a foreshadowing of the transition from literary to political discourse which soon followed. In a similar vein were a few succeeding efforts with a still stronger expression of his hatred of war and slavery in some of them, as in his Tremont Temple speech of 1846, and his lecture in 1847 on *White Slavery in the Barbary States*, with an eye upon black slavery in the United States. In this year came the oration before the literary societies of Amherst College entitled *Fame and Glory*, written in true academic style, opening with mention of the last work of the Roman orator mentioned by Valerius Maximus upon the same subject. The next allusions are to the *Æneid* and the *Iliad*, to Dion Cassius, the *De Officiis*, to the *Mabinogion* and the *Chronicles of the Cid*, to the *Divine Comedy* and Montaigne, to Carneades and Chrysippus, to Epicurus and Diogenes, to Pliny and Tacitus, to Milton and Pascal, to Mansfield and Burke, to historians and statesmen, to orators and poets, to explorers and generals. From them all he extracts their views of fame and glory to show, in one way or another, that they do not consist in the victories of war and bloodshed and that "all war is fratricidal." More than this he calls in Rabelais to help him degrade pagan heroes by making Alexander a mender of old clothes in the Elysian Fields, and Hannibal a poor tinker, and Arthur's knights ferrymen of Phlegethon and Lethe, Styx and Acheron. Then follows his own estimate of greatness and glory. "There is another and higher company that thought little of praise and power, whose lives shine before men with those good works which glorify their authors — Milton bating not a jot of heart or hope ; Vincent de Paul, the fugitive slave who devoted himself to the spread of amity and peace; Howard illumining dungeons as with an angelic presence ; Clarkson, inspired in college with the supreme duty of a crusade against the African slave trade. Such are exemplars of true glory. Without rank, office, or the sword they accomplished immortal good and teach the universal lesson of magnanimous duty. We must reverse the poles of worship in the past. Farewell to the dismal phantom of martial renown ! . . . . Good works ! Such even now is the heavenly ladder on which angels are ascending and descending, while weary humanity on pillows of stone slumbers heavily at its feet."

It is only a sentence here and there that has been quoted, but the moving force is evident in all the oration. Throughout the stately and sometimes lofty style there runs the enthusiasm of reverence for his ideals in friendship and of devotion to an ideal future in which freedom and peace shall go hand in hand. His diction is a scholar's, his imagination historic if not poetic, his spirit that of a crusader against established wrongs. It is the spirit and the letter together that make these addresses orations indeed in the classic sense. Even in the semi-political speeches that fell in those years from lips accustomed to other than political phrases there was the same readiness of allusion to the remote in time or place, which was nevertheless near in essential relation. In the Worcester convention of whigs in 1847 he calls in the powers of India to condemn American slavery as they had already done by the Ganges, and Constantinople by the Bosphorus, and the Barbary States by the

Mediterranean. He compares the slave power to Enceladus struggling beneath Etna, causing eruptions of evil, threatening a deep, abiding, unutterable curse from the existence of a national wrong imbedded in our Constitution.

It is time to contemplate his oratory as taking on something more than a scholastic complexion. The cosmopolitan man of letters, the lawyer who had composed fewer arguments than legal papers and delivered fewer arguments than orations, the man who loved literature and art and converse with the best in the society of two continents was being drawn into advocacy of a cause which would make him an exile from the social world and take him out of the academic walks he loved. A sense of the inconsistency between the boasted freedom and the cherished slavery in the nation grew stronger each day in a soul which could see nothing but the absolute truth. No coloring of partisanship or convenience or custom or general sentiment tinged his vision. Moreover he could never understand why every one else did not discern the ugliness of injustice and crime and see its enormity as he saw it. Furthermore for him to see was to follow. If there was a crime against humanity, a standing crime, it became his business to put it down as if he were clothed with omnipotence. Consequences were not thought of, obstacles were unconsidered, the sentiments he held were the only ones to be contemplated. With such a single-heartedness, and almost simple-mindedness, it is not hard to understand what sort of speech would follow. Add to this a sublime confidence in his own power and a strange misapprehension of the power and prejudices of others and there may be expected words of sincerity and soberness, sometimes of inconsideration and unsparing severity.

To understand the conditions and formative influences of his oratory we must go back fifty years. Half a century is sufficient in uneventful times to make a former age incomprehensible. But the changes in the last half of this century have been marvelous. In 1850 any allusion to the sin of keeping one-sixth of our population in bondage was dangerous in the South and unwelcome, to say the least, in the North. An uneasy feeling, bred of a consciousness of wrong, kept men busy with compromises, but they knew that they were living over a powder-mine. Accordingly neither North nor South were tolerant of what they called firebrands. For the most part abolitionists were at first of the class which is ready for any break with the existing order, extremists in all other things, hard to deal with, radicals who are not helpful to the genuine reformer. But the cause was too good and the issue too vital to be destroyed by the factions and whims of its early defenders. Still it was not an illustrious company in which Sumner found himself, and his companions must have been much prouder of their leader than he of his followers. These soon increased in number and value after the passage of the Fugitive Slave bill in 1850. The South threw the match and the North was shortly in flames. The ancient and honorable whig party contributed of its best, the new free-soilers, and democrats not a few, helped to swell the ranks of the growing anti-slavery army. Charles Sumner was its candidate for the vacant senatorial chair, in which he took his seat in the thirty-second Congress in 1850. Against what political odds may be inferred from the fact that up to this time the Southern party, numbering less than one-tenth of the nation's voters, had placed in office from two-thirds to three-fourths of the presidents, presidents of the Senate, speakers of the House, Supreme court judges, and attorney-generals, with a corresponding majority of smaller national officials. With him stood only three famous defenders of liberty, Seward, Chase, and Hale. With no parliamentary training and late to enter political life he came into his high position to maintain the cause of freedom and to attack the usurpations of slavery. These two sides of a single question filled his vision so completely as to shut out all secondary issues, blinding him to considerations of policy and person. His spirit was that of a Cromwellian Ironside, but his port and mien was that of Ithuriel with his spear or the traditional St. George in conflict with the dragon.

For eight months he kept a silence which, though enforced by the tactics of his foes, began to disquiet his Massachusetts constituency, and then one day when his vigilant enemies were off guard he offered an amendment to an amendment with an unlooked-for clause, "which said Fugitive Slave act is hereby repealed." Upon this amendment he spoke for nearly four hours, beginning as follows :

"Painfully convinced of the unutterable wrong and woe of slavery, profoundly believing that according to the true spirit of the Constitution and the sentiments of the fathers it can find no place under our national government; that it is in every respect sectional and in no respect national; that it is always and everywhere creature and dependent of the states, and never anywhere creature and dependent of the nation; and that the nation can never by legislative or any other act impart to it any support, under the Constitution of the United States—with these convictions I could not allow this session to reach its close without making or seizing an opportunity to declare myself openly against the usurpation, injustice, and cruelty of the late intolerable enactment for the recovery of fugitive slaves." This was new talk in senatorial ears, and hands that had just joined in burying a live question and voices that had chanted the requiem of compromise over the grave were now raised in angry remonstrance. Webster had staked his last political chance upon a final effort to put off the evil day and Henry Clay had tottered out as Charles Sumner came in, but the survivors were men who had conquered and made their own terms with the North. Who was this new-comer, so unskilled in parliamentary fencing and broadsword that he was not even condescending to preliminary conciliation in his speech, but going right on to add, "The discussion of slavery will proceed wherever two or three are gathered together, by the fireside, on the highway, at the public meeting, in the church. Even now it is gathering its forces, soon to be felt everywhere. The movement against it is from the Everlasting Arm. It may not be felt yet in the places of office or power, but all who can put their ears humbly to the ground will hear and comprehend its incessant and advancing tread."

Then followed his masterly argument showing that slavery was sectional and unsupported by the Constitution. "And, by implication, nowhere can the nation, by legislation or otherwise, support slavery, hunt slaves, or hold property in man."

It is not easy at this day to estimate the wrath which such speech aroused on the Southern side. But it also excited admiration. A pro-slavery senator said, "I did not know it was possible that I could endure a speech for over three hours upon the abolition of slavery. But this oration of the senator from Massachusetts has been so handsomely embellished with poetry, both Latin and English, is so full of classical allusions and rhetorical flourishes, as to make it much more palatable than I supposed it could have been made." If this was Southern testimony it is easy to imagine what came from Northern and even European friends. The speech was another landmark in the progress of liberty. It did for abolitionists what Webster's reply to Hayne had done for union-men twenty-one years before. It placed them upon the solid ground of the Constitution instead of the uncertain foothold of personal conviction. Right was henceforth might.

It also placed Sumner in his own proper position of a prophet who should not hold his peace until this righteousness should finally triumph. Henceforth there shall be no less learning and cultivation of its graces, but they will be consecrated to the one cause and tributary to its success through the speech which convinces and persuades. Oration will follow oration, each more earnest and direct than the last. The speaker will become more and more oblivious of consequences. When the opposing faction assail him with bitter words they will be repaid in their own coin with interest. Argument will end in indictment, invective in malediction. Not inspired by personal animosity, but by a hatred of slavery so deep that nothing can stand in its shadow without seeming to be a part of it and to fall under its curse he exclaims, " From the depth of my soul, as a loyal citizen and as a senator, I plead, I remonstrate against the passage of this [Kansas-Nebraska] bill. I struggle against it as against death; but as in death itself corruption puts on incorruption and this mortal puts on immortality, so from the sting of this hour I find assurance of that triumph by which freedom will be restored to her immortal birthright in the republic."

The next day, after the midnight passage of this bill, Boston saw Anthony Burns returned to slavery from her streets and all New England binding itself with an oath to the destruction of slavery. Hear Sumner speak to his state three months later: " In doing this deed of woe and shame the mayor of Boston was converted to a tool, the governor of the commonwealth to a cipher; the laws, the precious sentiments, the religion, the pride and glory of Massachusetts were trampled in the dust, and you and I and all of us fell down while the slave power flourished over us." Over the orator himself it flourished political billingsgate. "A miscreant, a madman, a serpent" were parliamentary refinements of epithet, to which he replied with the contempt and scorn that filled his soul for the abettors of bondage and for Southern chivalry. The impending war was preceded by words as sharp as swords, words which were followed often by the click of pistols and at last by the blows of the bludgeon upon the head of Sumner, after he had delivered his great speech on *The Crime Against Kansas*, May 19-20, 1856.

This oration may be regarded as the climax of a series of attacks upon the slave power. Its struggles for domination were recounted; the apologies for the crime characterized as imbecile, tyrannical, absurd, and infamous; the remedies he styled those of tyranny, folly, injustice, and civil war, as contrasted with the remedy of justice and peace. Such is the faintest outline of an argument which occupied two days in the delivery and covers one hundred and twelve octavo pages. Some extracts from it would be misleading, and any single paragraph would fail to give an idea of the magnitude of the issue and the fearful odds that existed against it. It was the protest of an outraged public sentiment at the North against the extension of the power that had hunted its victims in the streets of Boston, aided by the authority and resources of the national government. Its spokesman was a senator who was learned, logical, and fearless, able to return every malignant epithet with a more forcible equivalent; able, also, to interpret history truly, to unite fire and fervor with irrefragable logic, and throw over all the grace and charm of classic elegance. It is the burning force, however, that is most apparent here. The deadly earnestness is beyond all other qualities, great and eminent as they are. Nothing can stand in its way; it hesitates at nothing. Right on over ancient prejudices, over vested right so-called, over intrenched wrong, over slave-holding senators from the South and their obsequious henchmen from the North this majestic orator strides with no thought of anything but the wrong which is to be righted. His unconsciousness is sublime. "Mr. President, I mean to keep absolutely within the limits of parliamentary propriety. I make no personal imputations, but only with frankness such as belongs to the occasion and my own character describe a great act, now enrolled in the Capitol. Sir, the Nebraska bill was in every respect a swindle of the North by the South . . . a swindle of God-given, inalienable rights. . . It is everywhere a swindle. No other word will adequately express the mingled meanness and wickedness of the cheat."

Men fared no better at his hands than the measures they had advocated, but it was because they were advocates of the wrong he hated and not because he hated them. Yet he could never understand why they should be offended, nor why, if in their senses, they should not see the evil he had plainly pointed out.

All his later speeches upon domestic themes are in the strain of the two which have been noticed. He was essentially an orator devoted to the reform of that anomaly in our nation which was the taunt of critics at home and abroad. It fell to him to lead the forces opposed to it in the final struggle in Congress, where an unequal war had been carried on by skirmishing for thirty years. Hitherto truces had followed wordy conflicts and compromises had ended great debates. But debates now were no longer discussions and the day of compromises was over. The next measure was to be war, and the words exchanged over the issue were desperate with determination, on the one side for justice with peace if possible, on the other sovereignty at all hazards.

There have been greater orators than Sumner in the direction of native ability and of acquired art, but they have been few. Some have been devoted to their respective causes with a similar earnestness, but they have been fewer still. If, however, one be sought for in all the illustrious succession who has combined surpassing talent for public speech with wide learning, profound convictions, and uncompromising surrender of self to a righteous purpose, none will be so able to stand the test as this man, who was deaf to every solicitation to swerve from the single aim of his public life. This is the secret of his oratorical power—the whole heart was in it, the entire life was given to it. His opportunity was great, and his strength was equal to his opportunity. Equally great was the moral power, the ethical force, the strongest element of all, buttressing and fortifying every other. As the generations of men draw away from the culmination of a long series of conflicts in our legislative assembly at Washington, as they see more clearly the historical relations of that stormy period to those compromising times that preceded it and the bloody years which followed it, the worth of Charles Sumner and his speech will be more and more appreciated as the power which comforted the discouraged few, confirmed the wavering many, and finally inspired crusading hosts to follow to the utmost verge in the direction he himself had already gone before.

XXIX.

WENDELL PHILLIPS.

AS SUMNER was the advocate in Congress of liberty to all the inhabitants of the land, so WENDELL PHILLIPS became the great agitator in the same cause among the people. There was nothing, however, in his antecedents to warrant a prophecy of such a mission. By birth, social surroundings, education, and natural affinities it might have been expected that he would keep his place in that sphere of eminent respectability and conservatism into which he had been born. His ancestors had amassed wealth, founded academies, become eminent in learned professions, and been distinguished in the state. His home was a colonial mansion, abounding with all that refines and cultivates. Books, pictures, statuary, and above all the atmosphere which goes with the traditions of an honorable family contributed to make gentle and noble the children who grew up among such influences. His companions were of the same class. Motley was his nearest playmate, Wendell Holmes his kinsman, the Appletons lived near by. Revolutionary traditions were the most dangerous influences around him. Bunker Hill was in sight and the church tower where Paul Revere hung his lantern. Brattle street church, Old South, and Faneuil Hall were not far away. At the Boston Latin school, famous for its illustrious sons, he followed Sumner by a year. There also it was that he recited the classic eulogies of brave men and martyrs for freedom, and became the chief object of interest on declamation days. From such triumphs among his schoolmates he would go out to listen to Daniel Webster, Harrison Gray Otis, Edward Everett, and other "masters of assemblies," his real teachers in the art in which he was to be their peer. Harvard College classmates remember him as an excellent scholar and an orator preëminent among the graduates of the time. Handsome in form and feature, with superior elegance of manners, of rare conversational ability, and a character upright and transparent there was no lack of anything which might make his start in life prosperous and his ultimate intellectual and social position assured.

Harvard law-school was the next natural step in the predestined course of a gilded youth, and then admission to the bar, followed by a practice which soon became absorbing. It was in the midst of his studies in his office at the beginning of the second year of his legal practice that an event occurred which gave a new direction to his energies and altered the purpose of his life. A mob was dragging a man, bare-headed, with a rope about his waist, toward the city-hall with cries of "Hang the abolitionist! Lynch him! Kill him!" Phillips, going on to the street, asked who the man was. "Garrison, the abolitionist; they are going to hang him." He was sent to jail for safety from the "mob in broadcloth," but the occurrence showed the young lawyer that law was of little account when it stood in the way of popular prejudice. The thoughts which this outrage suggested found an opportunity for utterance about two years later, on the occasion of a public meeting in Faneuil Hall to denounce the murder of Elijah P. Lovejoy, of Alton, Ill., who was mobbed and shot while protecting his printing press, from which had issued a denunciatory editorial on the burning of a negro alive in St. Louis for killing an officer who had attempted to arrest him. The freedom of the press had been assailed in a free state and a free man had been shot down like a dog; it was not yet time to pay much attention to the burning of a negro. Conservative Boston was slightly stirred and the old Cradle of Liberty was filled with a crowd a good deal mixed in its character. Among the speeches that were made, generally sympathetic in tone, was one by the attorney-general of Massachusetts which was intended to defeat the object of the meeting, and at its close the protest was likely to end in an endorsement of mob law. With this prospect impending Wendell Phillips sprang from the audience to the platform. His self-possession, his dignified bearing, his marvelous voice compelled the silence of wonder and then of respect. It was his first opportunity to prove what years of education had done with native ability. But something greater than either was back of talent and culture. It was his purpose to secure the passage of resolutions in sympathy with freedom and against lawlessness on the border. In the quietest tones he said:

"We have met for the freest discussion of these resolutions and the events which gave rise to them. I hope I shall be permitted to express my surprise at the sentiments of the last speaker, surprise not only at such sentiments from such a man, but at the applause they have received within these walls. We have heard the drunken murderers of Lovejoy compared to the patriot fathers who threw the tea overboard. Is this Faneuil Hall doctrine?" Then he went on to refute the sophistries of the attorney-general, who had based his justification of a murderous mob upon the resistance of the Revolutionary patriots to British tyranny, and continued with the words: "Sir, when I heard the gentleman lay down principles which place the murderers of Alton side by side with Otis and Hancock, with Quincy and Adams, I thought those pictured lips (pointing to the portraits in the hall) would have broken into voice to rebuke the recreant American, the slanderer of the dead. . . . For the sentiments he has uttered, on soil consecrated by the prayers of Puritans and the blood of patriots, the earth should have yawned and swallowed him up."

It is said that the scene that followed was beyond description. Delirious enthusiasm seized upon the audience. The opposing faction attempted in vain to create a stampede from the hall, but the orator enchained the throng. Waiting for silence he pursued his victory uninterrupted to the end of what he had to say and was greeted by a whirlwind of applause. He had the pleasure of seeing the resolutions carried by an overwhelming majority. The speaker's reputation was made at the start. Whatever Boston might think of his discretion and worldly wisdom it knew that another prophet had arisen in the city who was worthy to wear the mantle of her best orators. None of them had sprung full-fledged into the arena as he had. On the other hand none of them had dared place himself at such odds against the great power of general opinion. As they had climbed step by step into eminence, so they had espoused causes which were dear to the heart of the majority. This man had sided with a handful who were regarded as sentimental fanatics, but his defence of them and their principles was a surprise and an astonishment to friends and foes alike.

An absence in Europe was followed, after his return, by his next opportunity to speak for his adopted cause, when a protest against slavery and an appeal for their fellow-countrymen in America to join the abolition movement came from seventy thousand Irishmen abroad. It was this speech in Faneuil Hall that O'Connell pronounced the most classic short speech in the English language, and declared the young American orator to be without an equal. The purpose of the petition failed. The times were not yet ripe, but they were ripening slowly. Webster had taught the country to reverence the Constitution. Phillips in 1842 began to denounce it as a pro-slavery document which needed amending. He would not practice law under its provisions, he would not participate in national affairs even by voting. In consequence he brought down upon himself the rage of both the South and the North. His skill in persuasion and his ability as an organizer, however, called out the beginnings of a movement which was to sweep over the land.

By this time Phillips came to be what was characterized as an agitator. Such a designation he himself rejoiced in, and in agitation he saw a final result of better things. The platform was his arena and the people of cities and towns throughout the North were his audience. It was in the palmy days of the lyceum lecture and no course was considered complete without Wendell Phillips. Lecturing became his calling in large places and small wherever the people would listen to him, first on the arts or literature or biography, and having won attention and stimulated the thirst for more he would return when again invited with some discussion of the slavery question. He believed in the ultimate decision of an enlightened public conscience and in the power of a nation to eradicate evils that were rooted in dishonor. He used to say, "The people always mean right, and in the end they will do right. I believe in the twenty millions to arrange this question of slavery. . . . Drag it from its concealment and give it to the people; launch it on the age and all will be safe. But there must be no half-declaration of the issue, no compromise with convictions, no concealment of an ugly fact." In accordance with this sentiment he was most plain and uncompromising in his utterance. Truths for which the people were not ready were proclaimed with remorseless clearness and received by them with corresponding expression of disgust and sometimes of horror. And then the speaker would proceed to demonstrate with invincible logic that his positions were based upon solid ground, however far from the present attainment of the multitude. He would have been called a leader if he had not been too far in advance to secure an immediate following. A few did indeed follow him close, and more afar off, but the common crowd of conservative respectability looked upon him as a foolhardy fanatic bearing the excelsior banner up dangerous heights which they had no inclination to climb. By and by the logic of events hurried this same multitude on to overtake him and establish themselves on his uttermost outpost.

Meantime the aggressive orator went on with his ceaseless warfare against bondage of every sort in every place. In his own city he brought the exclusion of colored children from the public schools before the authorities until they were compelled to yield the point. With equal success he appealed to the legislature to compel railroads to admit colored travelers to the cars their tickets entitled them to enter. When fugitive slaves were hunted in Boston Phillips was active in aiding their escape, or if captured and remanded to slavery he was the man to call citizens into Faneuil Hall to hear words that branded with eternal infamy the city where Crispus Attucks, a negro, was first to fall in the struggle for American freedom in Revolutionary days. In the fight over the admission of California and the opening up of the territories to slavery Phillips did more to inform the people of impending dangers than the congressmen whose speeches were heard in Washington but not always read by constituencies. He was educating future electors of congressmen while representatives and senators, even from Massachusetts, were patching up compromises. Indorsing and supporting fugitive slave laws did not, however, rescue these legislators from a political grave, while the growth of the heresies which Wendell Phillips preached sent other law-makers to take their places, who in turn repealed compromises and amended the Constitution until it became the consistent expression of the doctrines it professed to uphold.

By 1853 abolitionism was merged in the rising tide of anti-slavery sentiment, which began to flow into every valley north of the Ohio river. In May of that year Phillips was before a great audience in New York city, cheered by some and hissed by others in one sentence, and cheered by all in the next when he turned the hisses to the credit of an antagonist. Two weeks later he was in Boston defining the difference between a reformer and a politician. "The reformer is careless of numbers, disregards popularity, and deals only with ideas, conscience, and common sense. He feels, with Copernicus, that as God waited long for an interpreter, so he can wait for his followers. He neither expects nor is anxious for immediate success. The politician dwells in an everlasting *now*. His motto is 'success,' his aim votes. His object is not absolute right, but as much right as the people will sanction; his object is not to instruct public opinion, but to represent it."

From New York and Boston he went to other cities and towns, everywhere disseminating the claim for an absolute and unqualified freedom for all, irrespective of race or class. Events were helping him. The dastardly assault upon Sumner, the repeal of the Missouri Compromise, the Dred Scott decision, John Brown's raid, secession, and the attack upon Fort Sumter marked so many stages which gave new phases to discussion and a fresh impulse to his speech. In all these stages the orator was the same self-contained, all-commanding power. He was a man never to be forgotten by those who had the privilege of seeing and hearing him. In form he is said to have closely resembled, by actual measurement, the Greek Apollo. Graceful in pose and gesture "every change of attitude was a new revelation of manliness." His presence was conciliatory without a shadow of self-depreciation, full of repose, combined with supreme action. His voice was smooth, sweet, and penetrating, with a modulation which expressed every shade of thought. His tones were seldom above the middle notes, although the lower ones were impressive. It is said that no other speaker, here or in Europe, put such intense feeling into so small a compass of voice and into a colloquial manner. What he lacked in range he made up in distinctness of enunciation. One by one, without hesitation or artificial elocution his words came as in dignified conversation with the multitude before him. You might be expecting a burst of eloquence, so-called, which never came, and yet you were not disappointed. You went away feeling that he might have flown higher and yet were glad that he did not. It pleased you more to know that there was still a mighty reserve force which was not drawn upon. The speaker always seemed greater than his audience. The phrase "an host in himself" was more than once demonstrated to be true of Wendell Phillips. No man of this century had such elements to deal with who mastered them as he did. There were great speakers who could sweep an audience along with them, there were none who could turn the tide rushing against them as he invariably did. It was because he kept his composure when the contagious fury that sometimes seizes upon a public assembly ran away with it. He could always rule the storm.

The colloquial style which was so varied as not to tire was equaled and surpassed by the matter of his speech. This was never heavy nor dull. In the first place his logic was irresistible. He convinced men against their own convictions. They were sure that there were flaws in the reasoning or in their own conclusions, possibly in their inherited prejudices, and for the time it seemed that Phillips must be right. It is probable that for the moment they saw the law of eternal justice and humanity on which he based all his logic rather than on the sophistry which makes the worse appear the better reason. He tore away the disguises of pecuniary interest and political advantage which so long obscured the living issues of the mid-century, and brought men face to face with righteousness. He knew on what his premises were based, and when those should begin to be admitted he had no fear for the conclusion nor the consequence. This iron logic was not, however, cast-iron. It was alive with electric charges of wit, glowed with picturesque description, abounded in anecdote, thrilled with personal appeal, bristled with epithets which were characterizations in themselves. "Vesuvius in full eruption in the calm of a summer day" is the report of a Northern hearer, while a Southern newspaper said, "Wendell Phillips is an infernal machine set to music." He usually spoke without notes, as he composed his speeches without pen. This does not mean without preparation. He was always preparing and storing his memory with facts, pursuing fallacies, linking chains of argument that seemed to have no weakest link, gathering anecdotes, culling illustrations that found their own places when and where they were wanted. Above all for years he cultivated the habit of thinking on the platform and off, and was never so effective as when apparently the most extemporaneous. His own explanation seems simple enough : "The chief thing I aim at is to master my subject. Then I earnestly try to get the audience to think as I do." Many orators, however, might have as laudable aims without his success. It is the constantly recurring reason, that the character and soul of the man was in all his speech with persistent earnestness. He was the incarnation of the cause he championed.

If we should recall the great speakers who made the second and third quarters of the century the golden age of American oratory it would be found that each had some excellence in a superlative degree and that one who should combine all these virtues would be an impossibility. But if the criterion of eloquence be the ability to hold all sorts of audiences in rapt attention for one hour, two hours, and more, in all sections of a broad belt from ocean to ocean, audiences hostile and amicable and sometimes both at once, then the palm must be awarded to Wendell Phillips. He fought his way up through obloquy and opposition, and carried with him the burden of an unpopular cause to its final triumph. He did this without a following or support that in the beginning was of more advantage than disadvantage to him, but in the end a nation was on his side by virtue of its acceptance of the principles which he advocated at the start. Therefore for every word of detraction and calumny which he endured in the early years and in later years the judgment of the future, looking back as he looked forward, shall return him a thousand words of praise.

XXX.

GEORGE WILLIAM CURTIS.

IT WAS a maxim of the best Hellenic orators that a composition should not be closed with a climax, but rather that the aroused interest and emotion of the audience should be allowed to decline toward the normal level of ordinary quietude. Perhaps it would be according too much to the subject of the last chapter to place him at the top of the ladder, and too little to the subject of the present one to place him much below the other. Those who have had the good fortune to hear both will follow their recollection in forming their judgment, and those who have not will appeal to the printed speech and contemporaneous testimony here as elsewhere. In the remote future any such comparison will doubtless be of individual qualities rather than of degrees of excellence in several of our recent orators. This last one was something besides an orator, and in his capacity as a man of letters and a journalist may represent an age of transition, or possibly of combination, in which the public speaker and the public press are working together for the welfare of communities. Let it be observed here that it is a narrow and one-sided view which places these two agencies in antagonism or asks which is greater in its influence. Each has its own sphere which the other cannot fill, but each is the complement and fulfilment of the other's limitations. The orator's audience is multiplied a thousand-fold, and the printed page is suffused with something of the light and heat which belong to the spoken word. Together the platform and the press offer a field to the thinking mind more inviting and wider than any which previous centuries have afforded for the dissemination of useful truths. GEORGE WILLIAM CURTIS was a man to discern the equal value of both agencies and to employ both with equal effectiveness. The restrictions of the subject, however, confine consideration mainly to his oratorical achievements.

It was in the political campaign of 1856 that he delivered his first important speech, a fair example of that form of oratory by which he made a distinctive reputation. In it the academic and the political elements are found side by side, as might be expected from its title, *The Duty of the American Scholar to Politics and the Times.* Delivered before the literary societies of Wesleyan University the oration touches fondly upon the charms of intellectual pursuits and the delights of a scholar's life. From this pleasant contemplation the speaker turns to say in effect that studies are but a selfish indulgence unless consecrated to the service of something broader than personal gratification. Material success has its dangers for the state as for the citizen, and unless there be a class of men who shall form the public conscience disaster will surely come. "This is the class of scholars. The elevation and correction of public sentiment is the scholar's office in the state. If, then, such be the scholar's office, if he be truly the conscience of the state, the fundamental law of his life is liberty, liberty of thought and liberty of speech." Later he adds, "Brothers, the call has come to us. I bring it to you in these calm retreats. I summon you to the great fight of freedom. . . . I call upon you to determine whether this great experiment of human freedom, which has been the scorn of despotism, shall by its failure be also our sin and shame. I call upon you to defend the hope of the world."

In this beginning of his oratorical career it is plain what is to be its character. It will represent devotion to freedom, inspired at first by a young man's enthusiasm, tempered later by a broad view of impending issues and dangers. The ballot and the widening influence of the emphatic word, spoken or printed, became the instrumentalities of reform, which he advocated with no apparent thought at the outset of violence on either side. The power of the educated class to wield a control out of all proportion to their numbers was uppermost in his mind, and the final resort in which he put his trust. Therefore his appeal was to this class, particularly to the young men who were going forth from the colleges of the land in a time full of momentous questions.

His first speech had been under every favoring circumstance that can gather around a literary anniversary in a New England college. Another was delivered three years later amidst the hootings of a rabble rout, threats of violence, and the danger of incendiarism. The topic was *The Present Aspects of the Slavery Question*, and though repeated attempts were made to drown the speaker's voice and to break up the meeting he kept on with undisturbed self-possession. The stormy assemblage of such elements as came together in Philadelphia in 1859, when the irrepressible conflict was coming on, found that the accomplished scholar and the elegant man of society and of letters was also a man of heroic spirit and intrepid resolution. These were qualities which had to be added to the customary qualifications of an orator in that decade. As a time to bring out all a speaker's skill, his self-control, and command of a turbulent throng it has seldom been equaled. The rude times that are called the Dark Ages and the stormy scenes of the French Revolution furnished similar demonstrations, but for persistent and frantic attempts to silence free speech one must turn to sundry cities of the North between 1850 and 1865, and, as the most successful of any the world over, to Liverpool when, appealing to the Englishman's love of fair play, Henry Ward Beecher attempted to state the cause of the North. Something, therefore, ought to be credited to the oratorical ability of such speakers as were eloquent not only in the piping times of peace, but who were also masters of assemblies that were mad with rage, or like the mob at Ephesus, "full of wrath, some crying one thing and some another, but the more part knowing not wherefore they were come together."

In the next year there was another occasion of the same kind but differing in the character of the assembly, which was the Republican National Convention at Chicago, met to announce the platform and nominate the candidate of the party for the presidency. The advanced element desired to insert among its avowed principles the preamble of the Declaration of Independence, containing the assertion of equal and inalienable rights, a doctrine which at that time was in advance of the actual condition of human freedom in the nation. It was a resolution looking to the limitation and final extinction of slavery, and was rejected by vote of the convention eleven months before the first gun was fired upon Fort Sumter. Curtis at once moved to renew the motion. His voice was drowned in the clamor of the men who feared to alienate possible supporters by the radical sentiments of 1776 pushed to their legitimate conclusion. "Gentlemen," said he, "this is the convention of free speech, and I have been given the floor. I have only a few words to say to you, but I shall say them if I stand here until to-morrow morning." Again the yells of a faction shook the roof of the wigwam, but pluck and serenity were mightier than the throats of Thurlow Weed's henchmen, and a hearing was granted at last. Then he "dared the representatives of the party of freedom to reject the doctrine of the Declaration of Independence affirming the equality and defining the rights of man." When he had finished the resolution was adopted "with a shout of enthusiasm more unanimous and deafening than the yell with which it had been previously rejected."

Let these two exhibitions of personal power remove any impression of uniform mildness that may be associated with one who is known more widely through the graceful emanations from an editor's chair. The reserve forces of such men as Curtis are among the inspirations of biography.

In those unquiet years such a speaker found abundant opportunity to voice the sentiments of a large and growing body of sympathizers in what he named the *American Doctrine of Liberty*, in the title of an oration which he delivered at Harvard University in the summer of 1862, and repeated forty times in Northern states during the ensuing year. It was the year of the emancipation proclamation, and the liberty for which he demanded the service of all Americans was a grade higher than that which any nation had yet achieved. "Seated in the temperate latitudes of a new continent, with free hands, free hearts, free brains, and free tongues, we are called to a destiny as manifest as the great heroism and the lofty principle that made us a nation. That destiny is the utmost development of liberty . . . not in any single direction, political, social, or moral, but in all the ample and jubilant splendor of its spirit and promise . . . the absolute personal and political freedom of every man to think, speak, and act, subject to the equal rights of other men, protected in their exercise by common consent or law." This definition of the new doctrine of liberty he unfolds and amplifies by contrast with the narrow conceptions and realizations of freedom in former times and in our own land hitherto.

In the emancipation of the slave population he saw a fulfilment of the declaration of the natural equality of human right to life and liberty which the fathers had considered the corner-stone of the new republic. Consistency was the key-note of his argument. His ideal was no higher than the declaration of 1776. He demanded no more for all men than the rebels against British tyranny had demanded for themselves.

The inconsistency which made this declaration a half-truth he denounced in a lecture entitled *Political Infidelity*, delivered more than fifty times in the years 1864 and 1865. In the midst of a war which was not yet terminated he asserted that republican principles of government are not necessarily a failure nor impracticable, that war is the result of disregarding and denying the fundamental truths on which our nationality was based, and that enduring peace can come only by returning fidelity to original principles. In this oration he arraigns the attempts to limit the power of public opinion by silencing debate, also the mincing and sneaking subserviency of the North, the confident arrogance of the South; and shows the reason of England's contempt, and the general demoralization of the country. In this arraignment the scholar's obligation is not forgotten, as it never was by Curtis. "How true is it," he remarks, "what Theodore Parker wrote to me eight years ago: 'If our educated men had done their duty we should not now be in the ghastly condition we bewail.'" And then follows a peroration which is a bugle-note of inspiration and a clear strain of prophecy: "Let the security of free discussion be maintained and jealously defended by all parties in the land, north, south, east, and west, at every country cross-road and in every city and state, and the Union and government are forever secure."
. . . "To the American republic belongs the national domain. To the American heart belong the national

principles of liberty and union. To the American flag belongs the national victory which shall secure those principles from sea to sea."

When the war was over speeches followed on *The Good Fight* and *The Right of Suffrage*, and similar discussions of reconstruction issues. In 1877 came the oration at Union College on *The Public Duty of Educated Men*, and one on *The Leadership of Educated Men*, delivered before the alumni of Brown University in 1882. Education and patriotism, learning and loyalty to the nation was evermore the recurring theme.

It was the same high thought that appeared when he delivered a eulogy upon Charles Sumner at the request of the legislature of Massachusetts. This new phase of public address gave him a new opportunity and added a new lustre to his fame. Hitherto he had spoken of abstract truths and of personal convictions; now he was to put himself in another's place and give a fair interpretation of another's views of truth and duty, by no means so easy a task to perform. To mingle praise and its qualifications duly, to reconcile the real man of ordinary, commonplace days with the ideal and possible man of the rare and high occasion, to estimate character by the strain it will bear and the latent force that is in it, to see how it avoids the pitfall and seizes the grand opportunity, above all to judge justly of the average and sum of attainment according to gifts and environments is an undertaking in which there is seldom the likelihood of unqualified approval and often the chance of but partial success. That he would be likely to succeed was the opinion of the assembly which invited him; that he did fulfil the obligation of honor and friendship completely is the testimony of his auditors and of the eulogy itself. One paragraph may stand for all:

"During all that tremendous time, on the one hand enthusiastically trusted, on the other contemptuously scorned and hated, Sumner's heart was that of a little child. He said no unworthy word, he did no unmanly deed; dishonor fled his face; and to-day those who so long and so naturally but so wrongfully believed him their enemy strew rosemary for remembrance upon his grave. . . . This is the great victory, the great lesson, the great legacy of his life, that the fidelity of a public man to his conscience, not to party, is rewarded with the sincerest popular love and confidence."

Another masterpiece of commemorative discourse, that on Wendell Phillips, has these among its closing words: "The radiant figure passing swiftly through these streets, plain as the house from which it came, regal with a royalty beyond that of kings; the ceaseless charity untold; the strong, sustaining heart of private friendship; the eloquence which, like the song of Orpheus, will fade from living memory into a doubtful tale; the surrender of ambition; the mighty agitation and the mighty triumph with which his name is forever blended; the consecration of a life hidden with God in sympathy with man; these, all these, will live among your immortal traditions, heroic even in your heroic story. But not yours alone. As years go by and only the large outlines of lofty American characters and careers remain, the wide republic will confess the benediction of a life like this and gladly own that if, with perfect faith and hope assured, America would still stand and 'bid the distant generations hail,' the inspiration of her national life must be the sublime moral courage, the all-embracing humanity, the spotless integrity, the absolutely unselfish devotion of great powers to great public ends which were the glory of Wendell Phillips."

Curtis' memorial addresses upon Bryant and Lowell bring out his twofold appreciation of patriotism and letters, so preëminently illustrated in the lives and writings of these two distinguished men. Of the first he said, "Here, then, we leave him with tender reverence for the father of our song, with grateful homage to the spotless and faithful citizen, with affectionate admiration for the simple and upright man." And of Lowell, "Intellectual excellence, noble character, public probity, lofty ideals, art, literature, honest politics, righteous laws, conscientious labor, public spirit, social justice, the stern, self-criticizing patriotism which fosters only what is worthy of an enlightened people; such qualities and achievements, and such alone, measure the greatness of a state, and those who illustrate them are great citizens. They are the men whose lives are a glorious service and whose memories are a benediction. Among that great company of patriots let me to-day reverently and gratefully blend the name of Lowell with that of Washington."

The mention of Bryant and Lowell recalls the literary sympathies and aptitudes of Curtis, for the consideration of which there could be no place here were it not that he must be regarded as the man who united in his personality and activity the power of the platform and the press. In the discourse upon Bryant he paid tribute to a fellow-worker in the broad field of journalism, and in the editorship of a great newspaper in the metropolis he recognized an agency for wielding a wide and constant influence. While Curtis least of all editors had reason to underrate the advantages of a personal presence and the living voice on great occasions, he also knew that the echoes of noble speech are carried by the press beyond the remotest hills. Accordingly he found in his own *Easy Chair* and in his weekly editorials a way to reach thousands who might never come within the sound of his voice. For nearly forty years he discoursed of literature and science, art and politics in a style so simple and colloquial that none would suppose that the pen he used was often scarcely dry from writing rhythmical periods of orations that held multitudes entranced. It was the talk of a sympathetic man with his neighbor at his elbow, and there was no snobbish inquiry about who his neighbor might be. What he sacrificed for such editorial labor, that might easily have gone into the field of elegant literature, it would be idle to discuss. He had higher purposes and devoted to them the noblest resources of public speech and the familiar forms of conversational prose. His was the grand opportunity of the occasional orator; the continuous instruction of the periodic press was also his. With voice and pen, with pen and voice, he alternately gave renewed impulses or steadily followed them with unceasing pressure. Therefore it is probable that, taking all his working years together, with all his hearers and all his readers, he reached more minds and hearts, more souls and consciences than any other orator of his time, and must always be remembered as the representative of the closing years of the nineteenth century, when words may not only be fitly spoken but also widely published.

It was eminently appropriate that toward the end of his days his devotion to the cause of educated manhood, as well as to universal freedom and political reform in official stations, should be recognized by an election to the chancellorship of the University of New York, in 1890, to say nothing of academic honors from different colleges seven times conferred. Passing from the stage in 1892 he was the last in the stately procession of American orators who were actors in the latest Reformation. The lessons which he left to youth of kindred aspirations were first that nothing should be spared in the preparation for public speech, even to the perfect memorizing that has all the force of extemporization without its inevitable blemishes of repetition and disproportion, of things better left unsaid, of good things arriving too late to be uttered, and a general deterioration in the speaker who follows it exclusively. Then there is the inspiration of a lofty ideal and profound sense of duty and an unswerving devotion to convictions. These were the strong foundations on which he built a fabric of sweet persuasiveness that was itself the natural expression of a gracious and noble character. The charm of manner, the musical and flexible voice, the engaging countenance were elements that made for peaceful assent with his hearers. Their hearts might not be rent nor their judgments swept away by stormy eloquence, but the sound sense, the high range, the clear reasonableness of his utterances commended them to what was best and broadest in his audiences. Not that he did not often rise to the upper levels of speech in form and in thought. He commanded all the reserves of the language. He knew where its dynamics abide, but he also knew what they are for and that their power depends upon the rarity of their use. A friend's testimony is true that "for a certain sustaining elevation and dignity, for uniformity of grace and unruffled fulness and richness he had few peers;" and again "the perfect symmetry and completeness of the whole, no part obtrusive and no part deficient, and all permeated with such consummate ease and grace of delivery that no room was left for any emotion but that of admiration and delight."

In speaking of Curtis as the last orator of the group whose chief representatives have been noticed it is not to be supposed that there were no contemporaries who, in their several ways, were not as great or greater than those who have been mentioned; and the same is true in all the ages here reviewed. It may be doubted, however, if any enumeration of names entitled to great distinction would be deemed complete by those whose memory runs back of the half-century line. There have been great speakers, in the old Greek sense of the word, in this age and country as in every other, whose light has been dimmed by the effulgence of greater contemporaries. Men like Chapin and Beecher and Phillips Brooks in the pulpit, Corwin and Winter Davis in Congress, Douglas and Lincoln in the political arena, and some whose continued life forbids present mention, great speakers all, or who could make a great speech upon occasion; such names will be recalled by one and another as fit to be enrolled among those that have been emphasized in these pages. Some who were young in the palmy days of the lyceum lecture will recall oratorical efforts unsurpassed in interest even by the present spectacular shows of high and low degree. But after all is said the greater orators will always hold their preëminence like fixed stars in the firmament, though sometimes outshone by planets less remote in time or place. The verdict of the future, if not of the present, will determine here, as in Athens of old, who shall be enrolled among the Immortal Ten.

In regard to the present condition of oratory it is not necessary to suppose that the former times were better than these in order to account for the general low estate of it that has prevailed for the last twenty-five years. To say that the preceding age was worse is a better explanation. The wave of discussion over a vital question rose high and higher until it broke in a clash of arms. Prolonged for a while it receded at length and comparative silence followed. A reconstructive period for legislators and a commercial one for the public at large is not favorable to eloquence. Questions of ways and means of doing what all agree should be done inspire nothing beyond heated discussions. Therefore oratory is at its ebb, as it has been a hundred times before. It has also been at the flood again as often. The wave-law of succession holds true here as in light and sound, in winds and waters, in growth and decay, in decline and revival. Crests may be near together, or so far apart as to be spanned by generations, but so sure as history repeats itself, so truly as a time of adversity is followed by a time of prosperity, so surely will the temporary depression of eloquence be followed by a renewal of interest in it. The problems of the future may not be of such magnitude as those in the immediate past, but they are likely to be important enough to call for such a personal appeal of the wise to the unwise, of the educated to the uninformed, as nothing but the voice can make with head and heart behind it. When that time of need shall come, eloquence will come with it.

Are there indications of a renewed interest even now? If it is true, as has often been observed, that the universities are the first to catch returning light, it may be that the revived interest in public speaking among students can be taken as the harbinger of a revival of oratory. For thirty years academic debate has languished. The open society hall has been closed like the temple of Janus Quirinus in times of peace. Now once more keys are turning in rusty locks, there is a dusting of furniture long unused, and a lighting of council fires afresh. Intercollegiate debates are arranged in the East; interstate oratorical contests and discussions are held in the West. Heads are not used solely as battering rams, nor voices for college yells alone, greatly as these exercises may contribute to vigorous disputation, or indirectly to effective speech. Long journeys are made and distant libraries consulted in preparation for literary contests. Living issues are studied with an interest which leaves no doubt that the men of the future will meet intelligently the questions that are likely to confront them, and that one of the chief factors in the solution of these problems will be the power of instructive, reasonable, and persuasive speech. For from these academic performances it is not a long step to the court-room, the pulpit, the town meeting, the representative assembly, to the people's platform and the commemorative occasion. Not far again, and in consequence, to a restored oratory and a revived eloquence, as it may not be far to a time when both shall be needed, as they have been ever and anon century after century in the past. When that time comes men will turn instinctively to hear what their leaders will have to tell them, and leadership may depend largely upon the manner of the telling.

A retrospect of oratory during twenty-four centuries is not unlike a glance along the horizon line of a mountain range with its elevations and depressions; for the history of eloquence, like that of liberty its companion, is marked by diversified fortunes. On this horizon there are lofty peaks showing where volcanic fires reared their monuments; there are lesser heights beside them and low table lands and shadowy valleys and sunless gorges. The mountain tops upon which light perpetual lingers are named for the Greek Demosthenes and Cicero the Roman; for John of Antioch and Tertullian of Carthage and Ambrose of Milan; for Savonarola of Florence, Peter of Picardy, Jaques de Vitry and his successors at the court of Louis the Great. Westward there is a giant group in England, and across the ocean another group upholding the honor of free and fearless speech in the remotest West.

A more deliberate view also reveals eloquence and liberty going hand in hand from the Orient to the Occident; in Greece amidst Hellenic resistance to Asiatic despotism, at Rome in a long warfare against imperialism, in the early Church against papal usurpation, in mediæval ages against the sacrilege of the Saracen, at the Reformation in protest against ecclesiastical corruption, in France against the dominion of Satan in high places, and later against the grinding oppression of the people by kings. In England voices are lifted up for authority tempered with justice and generosity, in America for equal rights of all subjects of the Crown, and afterward for general liberty under the laws, with the natural sequence of freedom to all the inhabitants of the land.

In all this movement there can also be observed diverse phases of expression in different ages and countries: Attic simplicity and strength running into Asian splendor, degenerating at length into barbaric tawdriness, followed by a restored severity not untainted with the finery of a later time, passing into an almost savage crudeness, uncouth and grotesque, to be refined at last by the revival of letters to a style blending the classic and romantic tendencies, which henceforward will fare on together according to the temperament of each nation, age, and orator as the subject, the issue, and the occasion shall demand. In all the long procession there is also a similar variety of method and manner and form, the same repetition of unchangeable principles in a diversity of manifestation that prevails in material and immaterial nature throughout the universe, so far as observation has reached; variety in unity, diversity of form amidst uniformity of law, changing phases of expression, but ceaseless persistence of purpose toward larger truth, a better liberty, and a nobler life. Until, however, these are more completely attained it cannot be affirmed that the movement which has continued so long with various degrees of acceleration will wholly cease, or that there will be no need of the speaking man in the future. Therefore the necessity still remains of gathering up the lessons left by masters of the art in the past, that, profiting by their successes and their failures, the men of the present and the future may know how they can best instruct, convince, and persuade.

INDEX.

A

Aaron, spokesman to Is-
rael 28
Abelard and Bernard.... 195
Abolitionism 376, 384
Abusive words............ 385
Academies, French...228, 231
  Italian 211
  Plato's, Aristotle at.... 81
  Cicero on.............. 113
Acheron 378
Action, oratorical...... 111, 269
  following speech...309,
                   355, 392
Actors, stage............67, 70
Adam of St. Victor's hymn 188
Adams, John Quincy..309, 377
Adams, Samuel...304, 306,
               307, 309, 392
Adaptation of discourse ..
  57, 76, 249, 256, 258, 358
Addison in Parliament ... 292
  in *Spectator*............ 339
Admiration for speaker .. 125
Advocates in New Eng-
  land 339, 340
Ældred 193
Æneid 200, 378
Ætna 30, 380
Æschines, with Demos-
  thenes................. 56
  with Gorgias........... 41

characteristics 67
  at Rhodes 105
  his style............... 106
Æschylus and contempo-
  raries.................. 33
  at Syracuse............. 30
Afer, Domitius, Quintilian
  on..................... 141
Affectation, at Rome...127,
                   132, 137
  elsewhere 213, 341
Africa 162, 166, 281
Aix 243
Africanus, Julius......... 141
Afterthoughts added to
  sentence 52
Agitator 389, 393, 394
Albertus Magnus 198
Alcibiades with Gorgias.. 41
Alexander 79, 104, 228, 378
Alexandria and Athens... 91
  and Tarsus 147
  and Athanasius 152
Alexandrian library...... 179
  schools 107
Alfred the Great, trans-
  lator.................. 178
Alliteration 225
Allston, W. 377
Allusion, understanding of
  by Greeks......78, 288, 384
Ambrose of Milan......165-sq.

419

420   INDEX.

and Augustine---------- 168
  eulogist ------------- 167
  preacher ------------- 166
  mentioned also---223, 417
Ames, Fisher------------ 310
America-266, 269, 283, 361, 417
Amherst College--------- 378
Amiens, Peter of-------- 190
  treaty of------------- 303
Amplification, Cicero's-117, 126
  other instances-238, 257, 258
Anacreon---------------- 376
Analysis, Aristotle's ---81,
    82, 83, 89, 334, 354
Anaximines, as an orator- 54
  rhetorician----------- 83
Anecdote, Andocides' use
  of-------------------- 54
  Fox's--200, 201, 202, 204,
    300, 301, 417
Andocides-----------51-sq.
  criticisms of -------- 53
  excellencies --------- 54
  traits --------------- 54
Anglo-Saxon element in—
  English language----- 120
  in taste------------- 107
Anne of Austria ------231, 233
Animation in discourse--- 260
Anselm... -------------- 192
Anthony of Padua ----- 196
Antioch, Chrysostom in 153
    159, 161, 416
Antiphon ------------ 39-sq.
  legal and political ora-
    tory----------------39, 40
  Plutarch on---------- 53
  rhetorician----------40, 42
  style --------------- 41
  strong point--------- 40

also-------60, 62, 68, 174, 175
Antisthenes, with Gorgias. 41
Antoninus Pius---------- 137
Antonius-----------111, 114, 137
Antony, Mark-88, 100, 101, 111
Apollinaris ----------- 137
Apollo-------200, 261, 362, 376
Apollonius of Rhodes---- 108
Appeal, personal-------- 288
Appropriation ---------- 258
Applause and hisses----- 376
Archias------------- 108, 116
Argumentation-37, 56, 57,
    96, 233, 299, 302, 343,
    345, 346, 353, 369, 399
Aristides -------------- 33
Aristotle-27, 31, 33, 78, 80,
    81, 82, 83, 84, 87, 88, 90,
    91, 92, 104, 110, 113,
    138, 140, 145, 208
Arpinum ---------------- 116
Arraignment------------- 407
Arrangement----------52, 369
Arrian------------------ 146
Art concealed--------43, 66
Arthur------------------ 228
  his knights----------- 378
Artificiality ---------- 199
Asia-----101, 104, 116, 281, 417
Asianism --------------- 104
Asiatic style-----102, 104, 105
Athanasius--149, 151, 152,
    174, 196, 223
Athens, 42, 45, 60, 70, 71,
    82, 91, 94, 101, 105, 106,
    107, 108, 147, 242
Attic style-104, 106, 109,
    115, 119
Attic Ten------------ 358, 363
Attica ----------------- 175

INDEX. 421

Atticus 112
Attucks, Crispus 395
Audiences 197, 262
   violent 403, 405
Augustan age............. 96
Augustine... 169, 174, 219,
            223, 230, 376
Augustus, Cæsar.104, 139, 147
Aurelius, Marcus...... 137, 146
Authoritative speech.165,
     194, 195, 249, 272, 352
Avicebron 189
Avicena 189

B

Backsliding, comparison... 202
Bacon 376
Bacon's Essays 87
Barbary States, slavery in 379
Barré, Colonel 286
Basil of Cæsarea.155, 156,
              174, 219
Bailey's dictionary........ 268
Barbaroux................ 248
Barot, Odillon 260
Barrow 268
Bede, the venerable... 178-sq.
Beecher, Henry Ward 404, 414
Begum charge 291
Belhaven, Lord........... 268
Bellerophon.............. 200
Bernard..175-sq., 193, 194, 195,
          196, 216, 219
Berenice, Queen.......... 138
Bible.203, 204, 210, 230,
          284, 338, 351
Biel, Gabriel............. 201
Billingsgate 385
Biographies.............. 69
Boëthius................. 177

Bonaparte .... 248-sq.
Bonaventura 198
Boniface 182
Borgia, house of......... 214
Bossuet 229-sq., 237
Boston 358, 369, 391
Boulogne, Counts of...... 190
Bourdaloue ...229-sq., 233, 240
Brantome................ 376
Brescia 211
Bristol 287
Brocken, spectres of the. 355
Brooks, Phillips.......... 414
Brown, John 396
Brown, Sir Thomas....... 376
Brown University........ 408
Bruno of Aste........... 193
Brutus............... 111-sq., 315
Bryant, W. C. 410, 411
Bucer 222
Buddha 152
Buffoonery 199
Bulwer 292
Bunker Hill 375, 389
   oration 358
Bunyan, John............ 162
Burke, Edmund...72, 283,
        285, 294, 297, 305
Burgesses, House of..314, 378
Burns, Anthony.......... 385
Byron 291

C

California 395
Cæcilius 141
Cælius 114, 115
Cæsar, Julius.93, 114, 141, 315
Cæsarea................. 159
Calhoun, J. C..323, 332-sq., 334
Callidus............. 114, 115

INDEX.

Calvin ---------- 222, 228
Calvus ---------- 114, 115, 141
Cambridge, Mass. ---------- 365
Camden ---------- 279
Canada ---------- 267, 283
Canterbury ---------- 180
Carlyle ---------- 24
Carbo ---------- 114
Carneades ---------- 378
Carthage ---------- 173
Cassius, Dion ---------- 378
Cassiodorus ---------- 177
Catiline ---------- 149
Cato ---------- 95, 96, 114, 174
Catullus ---------- 171
Celtic ---------- 290
   traits ---------- 295
   ancestry ---------- 335
Celsus ---------- 134
Centralization ---------- 316
Cerberus ---------- 200
Cethegus ---------- 96
Chæronea, battle of ---------- 48
Chaldee beliefs ---------- 152
Chalmers ---------- 126
Channing, W. E. ---------- 374, 377
Chapin, E. H. ---------- 414
Charlemagne ---------- 177, 228
Charles I. ---------- 267
Chase, S. P. ---------- 382
Chatham 102, 268, 270, 279
   284, 297, 305
Chaucer ---------- 92
Chesterfield ---------- 268
Chicago Convention of 1860 404
Chios ---------- 45
Choate, Rufus ---------- 364-sq., 373
Christianity 152, 162, 165, 220, 290
Chroniclers ---------- 177, 190

Chronicles of the Cid ---------- 378
Chrysippus ---------- 378
Chrysostom 153, 154, 155, 174, 178, 223, 230, 416
Church, early, Chapters XI. and XII. *passim*
   mediæval, Chapters XIII. XIV. *passim*
   reformation, Chapter XVII. *passim*
   Gallican, Chapter XVIII. *passim*
   Brattle st. Boston ---------- 389
   Old South ---------- 389
Cicero ---------- 43, 49, 62, 92, 100, 103, 107, 108, 109, 110, 112, 113, 114, 116, 117, 124, 130, 138, 141, 142, 147, 149, 209, 238, 376, 416
Cineas ---------- 94
Citizen advocates ---------- 36
Citizenship, Greek ---------- 35, 179
Clagny ---------- 236
Clairvaux ---------- 196
Clarke, James Freeman ---------- 374
Clarkson, Thomas ---------- 379
Classics, classical literature and learning 156, 181, 201, 210, 230, 298, 311, 370, 374
Clay, Henry 325-sq., 335, 383
Clearness ---------- 262
Climax ---------- 205, 206, 401
Clinton, De Witt ---------- 321
Collaborators ---------- 244, 293, 344
Collard, Royer ---------- 256
Colloquial discourse 66, 397, 398
Cologne ---------- 191

INDEX. 423

Colonies of Great Britain.
280, 281, 283
Columbus. 214
Comines 228
Commemorative oratory..
239, 358, 409
Commendation 250
Commonplaces 87
Common sense....94, 250,
261, 294, 330
Commonwealth 281
Comneni 190
Compactness 201
Comparison 197
Composition, practice of.. 67
Compromise-314, 381, 387, 396
Conciliation with America 287
Conciliatory speech-24, 29,
117, 287, 396
Conciseness 127, 128
Conclusion............43, 57
Condé 223
Connecticut........... 348
Conscience, public 394
Conservatism 395
Consistency 406
Constant, Benjamin...255, 256
Constantinople....72, 161, 379
Constitution of the United
States 338, 339, 348
Contests, mock......... 139
  literary 27
  oratorical 416
Conversation 286
Conviction....56, 125, 126,
329, 334
Copiousness 99
Corneille 230
Corwin, Thomas........ 414
Cotta 111, 114

Courts of law ---35, 43, 49,
57, 58, 59, 61, 69, 70, 71,
278, 344, 364
Creative power 99
  age 80
Cranmer 194, 222, 223
Criteria of eloquence..192,
199, 371, 399
Critics and criticism-50, 53,
58, 66, 67, 68, 76, 79, 82,
91, 115, 117, 151, 192,
210, 331, 336, 362, 363,
377, 414
Crispus, Vibius 141
Cromwell 315
Crusader spirit 379
Crusades 190, 195, 207
Culture 113, 269
Cumulative effects....245, 379
Curatii 200
Curio 100, 114, 115
Curtis, George William.401-sq.

D

Dalrymple, Colonel..... 308
Damiani ....186-sq.
Dance 157
  the devil's way 200
Dante 93, 311, 376
Dartmouth College...338,
344, 345, 352, 364
Davis, Henry Winter..... 414
De Barzia 203
Debate and debaters..299,
311, 326, 327, 359
  intercollegiate 415
Declamation-108, 134, 137,
170, 327, 363
De Claris Oratoribus 112
Delaying action........ 258

424 INDEX.

Deliberative oratory---68, 347
Delivery---------103, 111, 141
Demetrius of Phalerum -- 70
Demonstration ---- 56, 191, 245
Demosthenes ---55, 56, 57, 58, 62, 67, 70, 73, 74, 75, 76, 77, 80, 92, 105, 106, 107, 108, 119, 122, 128, 156, 159, 192, 240, 268, 270, 319, 376
Denunciation ------------ 65
De Officiis---------------- 378
De Oratore--------------- 111
De Republica ------------ 79
Descartes --------------- 228
Descent of man---------- 156
De Serre------------253, 255
Description-------------- 54
Desmoulins-------------- 248
Despotism and oratory --- 148, 208, 209-sq.
Devil and the dance--200, 221, 225
Dexter, Samuel---------- 354
Deza, Maxmilian--------- 205
Dialectics-------68, 82, 83, 189
Diction---90, 112, 119, 120, 121, 166, 238, 284, 285, 288, 289, 379
Dignity---63, 102, 150, 154, 165, 201, 413
Diligence --------48, 285, 292
Dio Chrysostom---------- 146
Diodorus of Tarsus------- 155
Diogenes of Apollonia---- 23
Diogenes Laertius-------- 378
Dionysius of Halicarnassus 61, 65, 79
Dionysius of Syracuse---- 44
Directions, marginal----- 199

Directness ---------192, 207
Discouragement --------- 211
Discourse, divisions of---- 110
Discursiveness---------- 223
Discussions, oral--------- 170
Display ---------------- 200
Disposition-----------87, 371
Disraeli ---------------- 292
Dissipating influences---- 297
Divine Comedy, the------ 378
Diversity --------------- 418
Division of subject-84, 114, 253, 254
Domitian --------------- 138
Don Quixote------------ 339
Douglas, Stephen A. ----- 414
Drama and oratory----27, 375
  English --------------- 228
  Greek ----------------- 26
Dramatic action--------- 295
Dramatic interest-------- 316
Dramatic style--------27, 136
Drayton, W. H. --------- 321
Dred Scott decision------ 396
Druids ----------------- 178
Dublin ----------------- 284
Dumont ---------------- 244
Dunstan---------------- 162
Dupin------------------ 260
Duroveray-------------- 244
Dust, sermon on-------- 206
Dwight, President------- 322
Dynamic words--------- 413

E

Earnestness------201, 220, 271, 386
East India Company----- 294
Eccentric eloquence---199-sq.
Editors -------------255, 411

INDEX. 425

Education and politics 408
Educational advantages .. 312
   lack of 312, 330
Educated class, power of. 403
Edward I. 280
Edward VI. 224
Elective studies 298
Eliot, Sir John 268
Elizabeth, Queen 265
Elocution 232
Eloquence, American 367
   Attic 68
   British 267
   commanding 399
   commercial age, of a ... 414
   decline of 107
   deliberative 288, 356
   dignified 122
   eccentric 199
   famous passages of 262
   freedom and 34
   impetuous 364
   moving 191
   patriotic 358
   patristic .... 159-sq.
   perpetuity of 101
   precocious 229
   prophetic 28
   primeval 27
   reputation for 323
   road to honors 94
   single-minded 388
   storm of 295
   susceptibility to 36
   turbulent 164, 263
   vigorous 231
England. 189, 194, 223, 225,
   253, 266, 267, 268, 278,
   304, 314, 417
English language 93

English literature 285, 305
English oratory .. 300, 305, 306
Enthusiasm. 195, 221, 259,
   331, 392, 405
Epaminondas 72
Ephesus 161, 242, 404
Epic poetry 25, 95
Epithets 96
Epicharmus 30
Epigrammatic style 259
Epicurus 378
Epos 23
Erasmus 222
Eratosthenes 44
Erudition in oratory 93
Essays, political 311
Escape from eloquence 311
   331, 392
Essex bar 365
Ethical element in oratory
   72, 140, 141, 272, 331, 398
Ethos 68
Eton 298
Euclid 190
Eulogy. 167, 311, 367, 376,
   377, 390, 408
Euphiletos 57
Euripides 33
Euthalus 108
Everett, Edward .. 358-sq.,
   373, 390
Exaggeration 117, 333
Exeter Academy 338
Exordiums ... 115, 199, 238,
   254, 313, 343, 350, 391
Exposition 204, 213
Extemporization, and writ-
   ten speech 262, 412
   Clay's 332
   Fox's 299

426   INDEX.

Mansfield's 277
Mirabeau's 245, 246
Phillips' 398, 399
faults of 246, 412

F

Faber, Matthias 202
Faction 257, 392
"Fame and Glory," 278
Fanaticism 295
Fashions, literary 139
Faneuil Hall 367, 389, 391, 395
Fastidiousness in style ... 127
Fathers, the Christian 376
Faust tradition and Empedocles 31
Fearlessness 246
Fees of ancient rhetoricians 108
Ferrara 208, 209
Fervor 201
Feudalism 189
Field practice of oratory .. 327
Fifth century B. C. 32
Figures of speech and—
  thought, Antiphon's 52, 53
  Greek and Roman use of 125
  Bede's treatise on 182
  Demosthenes' use of 106
Fimbria, orator 100
Fitness and harmony . 361, 362, 363
Five principles, Corax' ... 43
Florence, Savonarola in 175, 199, 209, 212, 214, 216
Flood 292
Fluency, Tiberius Gracchus' 99
Foote, Senator 348

Force, Demosthenes' .. 106, 246
Formalism 221
Forty years' discussion ... 332
Fourth of July orations . 339, 340, 375, 376
Fox . 279, 294, 297-sq., 298, 299, 305
Foy, General 253, 255
Franklin, B 270, 305
Frankness 329
France .. 195, 242, 269, 301, 417
Free-Soilers 381
French language and
  Greek 92
  in America 267
  orators 228
  Revolution 241, 242
  Norman French 120
Friars, preaching 200
Friendships, Cicero's 130
Froissart and Herodotus 26, 228, 376
Fronto's "Praise of Dust and Smoke," 137
Fugitive-slave act 381, 382
Fulness of treatment 128
Funeral sermon 239

G

Galba, orator 97
  emperor 138
Garrick 269
Garrison, W. L. 390
Gaul 139
Geiler 219
Gelo, tyrant 39
Genius and orders of nobility 297
  in groups 265

INDEX. 427

Genoa 194, 212
Genseric................ 173
George the Third.265, 275, 276, 315
Georges of Hanover, the.. 265
Gerbert of Rheims....... 189
Germaine, Lord.......... 287
Germany 194, 195, 223
Gesture, in Roman oratory 141, 320, 331, 396
Gibbon's praise of Sheridan 291
Girondists 247
Gnosticism 152
Good sense.............. 363
Gore, Christopher........ 340
Gorgias ....21, 41-sq.
  methods.59, 68, 106, 147, 175
Gorgias 21, 41
Gothic invasion........... 165
Gracchi, The, orators..98, 100, 114
Gracchus, Caius 93, 99
Gracchus, Tiberius....... 98
Grace of Hyperides...... 67
Roman came late....93, 413
Grasp of subject......271, 343
Gratian, eulogy upon..... 167
Grattan 292
Great Britain 282
Greek classics studied by orators 167
Greek declamations...... 108
Greek fathers, their eloquence............146, 148
Greek language-32, 92, 101, 138, 193
Greek treasures in Italy .. 209
Greek manners........... 101
Greek teachers.......... 147

Greek unpopularity at Rome 101
Gregory the Great....175, 177
Gregory Nazianzen-155, 157-sq.
Gregory of Nyssa........ 155
Gregory's pastoral 178
Guarric of Igniac 193
Guizot.................. 261

H

Hall, J. P. 382
Hamlet, quoted......... 337
Hamilton, Alexander..... 321
Hamilton, Sir William, on Aristotle.............. 82
Hancock, John........... 392
Hannibal 97, 378
Harrison, W. H. 367
Harshness of early Roman oratory 100
Hartung Philip von...... 203
Harvard Law School..374, 390
Harvard University...311, 358, 375, 377, 379, 390, 406
Hastings, Warren 293, 294
Hayne's speech.......... 349
  reply to speech......... 348
Hebrew prophecy and song 28
  poetry................. 34
Hellenist rhetoricians.... 108
Hermogenes' criticisms 52, 53, 66
Henrietta of England 233
Henry the Eighth........ 224
Henry, Patrick....312-sq., 323
Henry of Sens........... 193
Hercules 200
Hermagoras, rhetorician.. 104, 111
Heredity 335

Herodotus, imputed
  speeches 23
  historian...26, 33, 42, 60,
        80, 94, 156, 249
Hesiod.................155, 376
Hexham.................... 181
Hiero, patron of letters..30, 34
  tyrant 39
Hincmar 178
Hildebert of Tours........ 193
Hildebrand 189
Hildreth, Richard......... 324
Hillard, G. S. 374
Hisses.................... 396
Historians, early Roman.. 92
Hobbes.................... 376
Holmes, O. W. 389
Holy Land 191
Holy Sepulchre............ 190
Homer..........55, 92, 209, 376
Homeric speakers.......... 29
Homilies 182
Horace 93, 181
Horatius.................. 200
Hortensius...100, 102, 103, 108
House of Commons 299
House of Lords............ 269
Hutchinson, Governor..... 307
Hyperides..............66, 106

I

Idealists................. 247
Ildefonse 177
Iliad................200, 378
Illustration-52, 96, 255, 288,
    300, 301, 362, 369, 378
Imagery..233, 261, 299 363,
            371, 376

Imagination...99, 144, 259,
    261, 271, 300, 311, 362, 379
Imitation.............63, 96, 210
Imitators 107
Imperturbability 259
Impetuosity...99, 100, 295, 309
Impressiveness........196, 334
Impulsiveness 192
Independence 306
  declaration of............ 405
India...................... 379
  princes of 294
Indians 274, 283
Industry.................. 337
Inheritance 67
  cases of..............57, 59
Innocent II. 193
Inspiring occasions...247, 412
Institutes of Oratory 140
Interpretation, mystical .. 193
Intuition................. 271
Invective....117, 164, 168,
  173, 313, 318, 324, 331, 385
Invention......41, 109, 110, 273
Ireland, learning in...179, 290
Irony..................... 351
Irrelevancies 343
Isæus 49, 55, 56, 57, 58,
       59, 62, 70, 83, 159
Isaiah 156
Isidore 177
Islam 191
Isocrates 42, 44
  Cicero, on 45
  Socrates, on...62; 68, 82,
          110, 159, 175
Issues, living............ 416
Italy 209, 212, 214, 215
Ithuriel.................. 382
Ivo of Chartres 193

INDEX. 429

J

Jacobins ... 247
Jarrow ... 181
Jay, John ... 321
Jeffrey ... 292
Jerusalem ... 190, 191, 192
Jest ... 124
Jester ... 201
Job, speeches in book of ... 28
John of Antioch ... 153-sq.
John of Damascus ... 177
John, King of England ... 280
Johnson, Samuel ... 285
Johnston, Governor ... 286
Journalism ... 411
Journalist ... 244, 401
Judaism ... 147
Judgment of posterity ... 355, 400
Judges ... 345
Julianus ... 137
Juries, addresses to ... 341, 342
Jurisprudence ... 93
   heroic age of ... 340
Jurist ... 371

K

Kaiserberg ... 219
Kansas-Nebraska bill ... 385
Kempis, Thomas à ... 198
Kenedy, Abbot ... 227
Kent, Chancellor ... 377
Kentucky senator ... 366
Knights Templars ... 193
   Arthur's ... 378
Knox, John ... 226

L

Labor ... 124
Lafayette ... 259-sq.
Lamech's defence ... 28
Lanjeunais ... 189
Language, English 338, 339 341
   French ... 228, 229
   Greek ... 104, 105, 119, 161
   Latin ... 92, 95, 103, 113,
      155, 162, 210, 214
   abusive ... 67
   plain ... 341
   strong ... 300
Languedoc ... 196
Latimer ... 223-sq.
Latin poets ... 277
   literature ... 180
   race ... 93
Law ... 190, 285
   and politics ... 313, 327,
      346, 364
   skill in ... 342
Leaders ... 394, 395
Learning, in Britain ... 178, 180
   Greek ... 180
   pagan ... 204
   stagnation of ... 189, 223,
      361, 394
Leo the Great ... 171-sq., 174, 177
Leonidas' supposed speech 134
Lethe ... 378
Letters, decline of ... 179
Liberty, Greek ... 34, 48, 107
   and oratory ... 208, 299, 403
Liege ... 192, 194
Lincoln, Abraham ... 279, 353, 414
Lindisfarne ... 181
Litchfield, Conn ... 332
Literature, Christian ... 164
   classical ... 156
   English ... 305, 339
   French ... 228
   Greek ... 95, 115, 146, 190
   Roman ... 179

of oratory ------ 240, 288, 370
Liutprand ---------------- 376
Liverpool, Beecher in ---- 404
Livingston, Robert ------- 321
Livy ------------- 147, 249, 376
Logic. 82, 83, 220, 233, 234,
    278, 285, 330, 333, 334,
    346, 369, 386, 394, 398
Logographers --------- 50-sq.
Longinus ------------- 76, 123
Lorenzo de Medici ---- 210, 214
Lottery system ----------- 256
Louis XIV. --------------- 167
    age of --------- 229, 233, 236
Louis of Granada --------- 199
Louvet ------------------- 248
Lovejoy, E. P. -------- 391, 392
Low countries ------------ 204
Lowell, J. R. ------------ 410
Loyalty, colonial ----- 304, 314
Lucian ------------------- 146
Lucidity ----------------- 330
Lucretius ---------------- 181
Luther, Martin --- 162, 194,
    219, 222, 223-sq.
Luxury ------------------- 208
Lyceum, Boston ----------- 376
    lecture ---- 371, 372, 394, 414
Lycurgus, character of ---- 65
    style ---------------- 64, 65
Lysias -------------------- 43
    style ------------------ 44
    orations-- 44, 49-sq., 106, 175

M

Mabinogion, the --------- 378
Macbeth ---------------- 351
Madison, James ----------- 321
Magnetism, personal -- 150,
    167, 174, 196, 252, 313, 362

Maine -------------------- 329
Malherbe ----------------- 228
Malte-Brun --------------- 376
Mansfield... 277, 278, 279,
    283, 297, 378
Manuel ------------------- 258
Macaulay --------- 268, 285, 292
Marat -------------------- 248
Marchant ----------------- 204
Marcion ------------------ 163
Mariano ------------------ 210
Marlowe ------------------- 55
Mary of Guise ------- 226, 227
Mason, Jeremiah ---------- 340
Massillon ---- 167, 229, 237,
    238, 239, 240
Massachusetts --- 349, 352,
    366, 369, 373, 385, 395
Mausolus, panegyric of, 27, 46
Mavilus ------------------ 164
McLeod case -------------- 367
Medici, Lorenzo de ------- 210
Melancthon ---------- 218, 222
Memory --------- 141, 361, 370
Menot, Michael ----------- 200
Metaphors ----------------- 74
Metellus, Quintus --------- 96
Method ------------------- 301
Methods, literary ----- 151, 330
Mexican war --------- 375, 377
Middle Ages -------------- 177
Milan ------------ 169, 174, 194
Millennial year ------- 187, 189
Military oratory ------- 25, 249
Miltiades ----------------- 33
Milton --------- 34, 49, 285, 378
Mirabeau-243-sq., 246, 248,
    257, 293
"Mob in broadcloth," ---- 390
Moderation --------------- 260

Modesty, Demosthenes'.. 124, 352
Mohammedan cities 189
Monasticism 177, 219
Montaigne 228, 378
Montesquieu................ 376
Moliere....................... 376
Moral element in oratory 68, 70, 72
Mortality 206
Moses, poet, prophet— speaker 28
Moslem 190
Motley 389
Movement......... 126, 271, 389
Muratori 376
Mystery plays 190
Mysticism 170
Mythology.................. 375

N

Nævius 94, 95
Napoleon.... 249, 252, 258, 282
Naples 282
Narration 37, 43, 56
Nature and art.............. 125
  improved by study..... 62
Natural gifts........ 67, 68, 330
Naturalness 54, 78
Nerva........................ 135
New Hampshire....... 339, 364
New York City............. 396
Nicæa......... 135, 149, 155, 159
Niebuhr 96
North American Review- 358
North, Lord...... 286, 298, 299
Northumbria 180
Nullification........... 325, 332

O

Occasion, power of. 75, 89, 358
O'Connell 127, 292
"Old man eloquent,' 49
Olympic festival, oratory at.................. 44, 49
Opposition, the--- 315, 334, 353, 392, 399
Optimism 363
Orations, classic........... 399
  commemorative, 360, 377, 410
  crown, on the........... 75
  making orations flat..... 90
  aggressive 395
Orators, comparison of... 431
  compared to statues.... 256
  defined 112, 131, 300
  greater, the............. 414
  living 414
  natural 312
  obscure.................. 73
  press and orators... 401, 402
  qualifications of 87, 111
  rhetoricians and......... 42
  self-educated 67
  their times, and...... 98, 192
  American....... 304-sq., 324
  English......... 128, 129, 358
  French........... 228-sq.
  Greek- 32, 33, 48, 90, 106, 160, 363
  Irish 290
  Roman 91, 144
Oratorical art.......... 363, 364
  formative influences.... 381
  methods 319
  power..... 107, 173, 192, 397
  purpose 389
  studies 339
  rules 213

INDEX.

styles ------------------ 240
training ------- 140, 143, 298
Oratory, adroit ---------- 256
  beginnings of ---------- 33
  Christianity and ------- 147
  colonial, --------- 304-sq., 323
  commanding ------------ 260
  congressional -------- 323-sq.
  deliberative ------- 64, 86, 242-sq., 323-sq.
  demonstrative --------- 359
  despotism and ------ 34, 133
  drama in ------------ 26, 27
  early Christian --------- 147
  eccentric ---------- 199-sq.
  effective ---------- 105, 327
  emotional --------- 250, 345
  erratic ---------------- 241
  evolved from laudation. 22
  forcible ---------------- 253
  forensic in Sicily - 30-sq., 64, 133, 366, 368, 371
  future of --------------- 416
  gentle ------------------ 98
  Hebrew ------------------ 29
  history in ---------- 23-sq.
  impassioned ------- 190, 311
  impetuous --------- 246, 256
  Institutes of ----------- 138
  liberty and -------- 34, 133
  literature in ----------- 376
  military --- 24, 93, 94, 249-sq.
  natural -------- 50, 51, 62, 94
  occasional - 356, 363, 371, 374, 413
  parliamentary ------ 265-sq.
  patristic, Greek ----- 148-sq.
  patristic, Latin ----- 161-sq.
  poetry in early --------- 23
  political --------------- 64

  plain ------------- 172, 181
  practical --------------- 37
  practice of ------------- 41
  preferment and - 311, 313, 416
  primeval --------- 27, 29, 38
  retrospective ---------- 134
  revival of ------------- 415
  rewards of ------------- 136
  rude ------------------- 192
  sacred --------- 176, 177, 178
  sensible --------------- 254
  scholastic -------- 134, 386
  showy ------------------ 105
  southern --------------- 312
  treatment, historical - 5, 6, 22
  unique ----------------- 247
  vigorous --------------- 98
Origen -------------------- 230
Originality, age of - 91, 223, 344
Ornamentation ------------ 135
Orpheus ------------------ 261
Osorius, John ------------ 204
Otis, Harrison Gray --- 321, 340
Otis, James ---- 282, 309-sq., 392
Ovid --------------------- 147
Oxford University ---- 268, 298

P

Paganism ----------------- 208
Palestine ---------------- 195
Panathenaicus ----------- 48
Panegyric -------- 118, 136, 164
Papacy --------------- 193, 211
Parker, Theodore --------- 407
Parliament --- 281, 287, 304, 305
Parliamentary oratory, 265, 267
"Parson's case, the," ----- 313
Parsons, Theophilus ------ 340
Parthenon, the ----------- 159
Party favor -------------- 367

INDEX.

Pascal 229, 378
Paterculus, Velleius 49
Pathos 67, 68, 76, 101
Patriotism 363
Patristic age 158
Patristic oratory 148-188
Paulus 147
Paulinus' preaching 178
Paul's cross, sermon at 224
Pegasus 200
Pennsylvania 332
Père de Neuville 231
Periclean age 32, 33
Pericles 26, 29, 33, 60, 62, 72, 159
Peripatetic school 33
Peroration 37, 70, 115, 254, 345, 379, 407
Persecution 148
Persia 71
Personalities 350
Personality 215, 354, 399
Personification 106
Perspicuity 80
Persuasion 56, 125, 129, 271, 412
Peter the Hermit 175, 190, 192, 193, 195, 213, 216
Peter of Leon 193
Petition of Right 268
Pevensey 67
Phædrus of Plato, the 44
Phi Beta Kappa orations. 358, 377
Philip of Macedon 128
Philip of Narni 199
Philip of Neri 175
Philippics 117
Phillips, Wendell 389-sq., 409, 410

Philo the Academic 108
Philosophical mind 289
Philosophy 113, 190, 209, 370
Phlegethon 378
Pickering, Timothy 377
Pinckney, Charles 321
Pindar 30, 33
Pisa 194
Pisistratus 33
Pitt, William, Lord Chatham 266, 268-sq., 277, 291, 293
Plan 74, 117, 125, 238
Plato 21, 31, 33, 44, 79, 81, 82, 92, 376
Platonism 113
Plato's Academy 33
Plemyrium 36
Pliny the Younger 378
Plumer, William 340
Plutarch 53, 96, 376
Poetry 30, 93
Points, essential 343
Poland 301
Polemarchus 42
Political education 360
Political and academic elements 402
Politician 45, 396
Politics 367, 376
Politics and religion 226
Pollio 134
Polycrates 54
Pope 339
Portsmouth bar 341
Power, personal 405
  in reserve 406
Preachers 177, 201
  of crusades 189
  early .... 146-sq.

eccentric 199-sq.
French 228-sq.
mediæval 177
plain 201
university 179
Preaching, bold 165, 168
effective 216
expository 204, 213
long 205
mission 204
mystical 204
open air 224, 226
plain 202, 219
realistic 204
topical 204
sensational 200
Preëminence in speaking 270, 284, 294, 315
Premeditation 224
Preparation 101, 263, 313, 318, 319, 412
Precision 52
Precocity 298
Presence, personal 68, 331
Presentation, variety of 118
Presidents and officials from the South 382
Press, the, and oratory 53, 255, 256, 401
freedom of 391
Priests, hedge 200
Principles, general 82, 88
five of Corax 36, 39
Private causes 57
Probable, the doctrine of 40
Proclamation, emancipation 325, 406
Proem 37
Proof 43, 84, 85, 117, 271
Prophecy 407

Prophets, Hebrew 223, 376
political 211, 307, 317, 325
of evil 363
Proposition 288, 371
Prose, among Romans 93
poetic 132
Prosper of Aquitaine 177
Prosperity 363
Proserpine 95
Protagoras 108
Protest 385, 386
Protestants 207
Providence *Gazette* 307
Proxy, arguing by 49
Prussia 301
Pulpit 172, 174, 178
Purpose, singleness of 123, 125, 363
Pygmalion 175
Pyrrhus 94

Q

Quebec 267
Quincy, Josiah 321, 374, 392
Quintilian, rhetorician 137-sq,
his place 139
purpose 139
criticisms 113, 141, 145
follows Aristotle 140
knowledge of rhetoric 143
on Cicero 122, 139
on Latin writers 119, 136
on orators 145, 147, 238
Quotations inadequate to represent an orator, 151 and *passim*.

R

Rabanus 178, 189
sermon 184
Rabble 403, 404

INDEX. 435

Rabelais 228, 378
Radicals 381
Raillery 118, 293
Raleigh 34
Randolph, John 323, 325
  Edmund 321
Ratramn 178
Raulin, John............. 201
Reading 140, 348
Reasonableness........... 413
Reasoning.....25, 56, 343, 353
Reductio ad absurdum.... 353
Redundancy............... 126
Reformation.....207, 218,
           221, 223, 417
  in England....218, 222, 223
Reibaz 244
Refinements, scholastic... 220
Repetition................ 301
  of history............... 415
Reputation 292
Reporting 320
Republics............247, 322
Restoration, orators of.... 253
Resources, dependence upon........43, 45, 70
Restraint.............76, 99
Retrospect 416
Revere, Paul.............. 389
Revision, Plato's--79; 230, 272
Revolution, American-288,
             389, 395
Revolutionary heroes..... 351
Rhetoric, Aristotle's-82, 83, 88
  art of 5, 109
  definitions of........47, 84
  importance of........... 139
  kinds of 42
  philosophy of........5, 90
  place of........84, 136, 177

  precept of 23
  primer of................ 36
  professors of, ancient
    41-sq., 78-sq., 104-sq.,
     165, 168, 169, 369
  rules of 41, 83, 117
  schools of............... 101
  science of.....5, 37, 125, 137
  scope of 144
  theoretical 97
Rhetorical instruction.... 138
  methods 190
  study......108, 138, 145, 169
  systems 84, 94
Rhetoricians of Asia,..... 108
  professional....137, 361,
           363, 369
Rhine, the..........191, 220
Rhodes 100, 105, 107
Rhythm 59, 67, 206, 238
Ridicule 123
Ridley 226
Rights, citizen's......... 395
Rivals, The.............. 291
Robespierre 248
Roger of Sicily........... 194
Roland 248
Roman empire............. 177
  literature 91
  orators, see "Orators,"
Romancers 190
Rome-148, 169, 171, 173,
   174, 175, 181, 194, 199,
           205, 417
Rude diction...........93, 94
Rufus, Rutilius........... 97
Rugged style 103
Rules 117
Russia 301
Rutledge, John 321

S

Sacerdotalism - 220
Sæculum obscurum - 187
St. Aurelian, church of - 222
St. Bartholomew massacre 227
St. Helena - 253
St. George - 382
St. Paul - 128-sq.
Saracen - 417
Sarcasm - 66, 195, 324
Satan - 417
Satire - 95
Saturn - 248
Saville, Sir George - 286
Savonarola - 175, 195, 199, 208, 211, 213, 214, 215, 289-sq., 417
Saxon school at Rome - 180
Scævola - 100
Scapula - 164
Scholasticism - 170, 189
Schools of Charlemagne - 187
  of Isocrates - 106
  Peripatetic - 104
  Rhetorical - 107, 127, 139, 365
  Rhodian - 104, 105
  Boston, Latin - 374, 389
  New England - 364
Scholar, the - 358
  American - 402
Scotland - 226, 268
Scott, Walter - 38
Scotus, John - 178, 193
Scipio Africanus Major 96, 99
Scipio Africanus Minor - 97, 98
Scriptures, Holy - 182, 336
Scythian tribes - 93
Sects and divisions - 152
Seclusion - 208

Secundus - 136, 142
Sedulius - 181
Self-possession - 293, 391, 396, 397
Self-complacency - 130
Self-confidence - 380
Seneca - 14, 135
Seneca the elder - 139
Senate of U. S. - 328
Sentences, short and long 142, 186, 346, 358, 370, 371
Serenity - 259
Sermons - 183, 186, 383
  before Louis XIV - 235
  eccentric - 199-sq.
  funeral - 232
  long - 205
  powerful - 215
  thoughtful - 201, 202, 203
  to fishes - 198
Servius Sulpicius - 141
Sevigné, Madame de - 376
Seward, W. H. - 382
Shakespeare - 38, 55, 88, 175, 244, 265
Sheridan - 290-sq., 292, 293, 294, 297
Shrewdness - 293
Simile - 204
Sincerity - 63
  in an orator - 130, 192, 207, 214, 329
Sibylline books - 200
Sicily - 30, 34, 134
  courts in - 36, 37, 40
  literary resort - 35
  rhetoric in - 68
Sismondi - 376
Sixtus, pope - 211
Slavery - 377, 379, 381, 384

INDEX. 437

Slave trade............... 379
Smith, Adam............. 298
Sobriety.................. 102
Socrates 21, 33
  on Isocrates............. 44
Solidity, logical.......... 334
Solon................... 33, 112
Sophists............. 26, 59, 68
Sophocles 33
Sophron 300
South Carolina...332, 348,
               349, 351, 352
Southern party........... 382
Spain, teachers of rhetoric
             138, 139, 199
Speaking, public, labor
                of. 144
Speech, first words of..... 102
  severe................... 162
  sonorous................. 123
  reflection of character.. 25
  writers .... 39-sq.
  writing............... 49, 244
Speeches, frequent........ 316
  long............310, 316, 382
  plain.................... 240
  short.................... 393
  interesting.............. 263
Spencer, Herbert......28, 341
Spenser, Edmund.......... 92
Stage Instruction......67, 213
Stamp Act................ 284
Standards of eloquence...
                 242, 363
Stanhope, Earl of......... 268
Statement ...... -330, 341, 352
Statesmanship....93, 333, 347
States rights..........323, 348
Stephen of Paris.......... 193
Story, Joseph 345, 347, 377

Strafford, Earl of.......... 268
Strength 244, 364
Studies, elective.......... 298
Style.........68, 96, 221, 230
  abrupt 90
  adaptive................. 232
  ancient and modern..... 136
  Asiatic....102, 104, 105,
                  295, 417
  Attic..104, 105, 106, 109,
             115, 119, 417
  beauty of................. 67
  brilliant................. 263
  careful.................. 102
  clear 10, 53, 231, 341
  colloquial..226, 300, 342, 411
  concise....126, 127, 128, 129
  conversational......259, 263
  dignified 371
  diversified 96, 106
  earnest................... 52
  easy..................... 271
  energetic................ 311
  English 361
  epigrammatic 253
  exuberant............... 366
  fervid................... 366
  figurative............... 125
  finished 132
  flexible................. 118
  florid................... 339
  flowing 129, 136
  forensic 61
  forcible................. 174
  free.................100, 330
  French 263
  Greek and Roman..125, 346
  grand 43
  grotesque............... 417
  inflated................. 339

438 INDEX.

ornamental ------------ 106
  plain ----- 43, 53, 68, 106, 244
  quiet ------------------- 67
  rhetorical, early -------- 43
  round ----------------- 122
  rude ------------------ 95
  severe ----------------- 105
  simple ------ 62, 133, 231, 244
  splendid -------------- 375
  stately ----- 129, 300, 371, 379
  sublime --------------- 122
  tawdry ---------------- 417
  terse -------------- 298, 341
  thoughtful ------------ 174
  truthful --------------- 52
  turgid ---------------- 174
  uncouth -------------- 417
  vehement -------------- 76
  vigorous ----------- 62, 132
  vivid ------------------ 62
Stories, amusing ------- 201-sq.
Styx -------------------- 378
Suasorial pieces --------- 134
Subject and object of speech --------------- 86
  mastery of subject ------ 300
Subsidiary remarks ------- 43
Success and failure ------ 418
Suggestion -------------- 204
Sulpicius -------- 100, 111, 114
Sumner, Charles -- 373-sq., 374, 381, 396
Sumter, Fort ------------ 396
Sunday ----------------- 184
Superstition ------------ 185
Sybaris ------------------ 42
Symbolism -------------- 187
Symmachus ------------- 116
Sympathy ---- 54, 239, 300, 342, 359, 370, 375

Syracuse -------- 30, 34, 35, 39

T.

Tacitus, as an orator ------ 136
  his style --- 136, 137, 230, 249, 378
Talents improved -------- 370
Tarsus ----------------- 147
Taste, laws of ----------- 105
  Greek -------------- 78, 104
Tasso ------------------ 93
Tautology ---------- 301, 311
Taxation --------------- 310
Teachers, the best at first- 144
  of style -------------- 361
Temporizing and delaying legislation ---------- 259
Ten, the Attic ---------- 414
Tertullian -------- 162-sq., 416
Testimony, value of contemporary --- 150, 232, 295, 377
Tetralogies -------------- 39
Tetzel ------------------ 219
Themes ----- 133, 137, 170, 358
Theodectes --------- 27, 54
Theodore of Tarsus ------ 180
Theodosius ------------- 167
Theology -------------- 190
Theopompus ------------ 27
Theosophy ------------- 146
Theremin -------------- 240
Thermopylæ ----------- 134
Thiers ----------------- 263
Thoughts, connection of-- 244
  basis of rhetoric ------- 369
Thoughtfulness --------- 234
Thrasybulus ------- 35, 36, 39
Thrasymachus ----------- 54

INDEX.

Thucydides, imputed—
speeches.24, 25, 26, 33, 38
his frankness............ 38
on Pericles.24, 26, 29, 60,
62, 68, 94, 156, 230, 249
Thurii 42
Tiberius, Cæsar........... 134
Ticknor, George 374
Timoleon................. 36
Tisias 42
Town meeting............. 306
Townsend, Lord John..... 286
Trachalus 141
Training, oratorical....... 298
Trajan............93, 136, 164
Transition, orators of a.
27, 97
Treves 174
Trivium and *Quadrivium* 177
Tudor, Mary.............. 226
Tusculum 95
Tyranny.................. 242
Tyrants, the thirty........ 42
Tyrian colonies........... 284

U

Ulysses' bow............. 174
Uncompromising speech.. 394
Unconsciousness, sublime 387
Unfavorable conditions... 415
Union, the...........349, 364
Uniformity 418
Unity in composition..... 418
University, Cambridge... 222
of New York........... 412
Oxford............268, 298
Universities 190, 219
and oratory........... 415

Uproar 404, 405
"Upsetters, The,"........ 169

V

Vagueness of thought.... 341
Valentinian.............. 167
Valerius Maximus........ 378
Valley of Wormwood 193
Vandals 171
Varennes................ 248
Variety 199, 398, 418
Vattel 376
Vergniaud............... 247
Variety in discourse. -75,
149, 204, 255, 418
Vehemence...94, 123, 135, 245
Veneration for past...... 360
Venice 205
Verbosity 121, 127, 128
Versailles 235
Versatility...235, 264, 271, 320
Vespasian............108, 138
Vesuvius 398
Vexilla Regis............ 188
Views, broad............ 347
Vigor 93, 119, 219, 365
Villehardouin........... 228
Vincent of Lerins....... 177
Vincent de Paul........ 379
Viret 222
Virgil....93, 171, 181, 219, 376
Virginia 281, 315, 316
Vision, singleness of..... 380
Visions and dreams...190,
191, 211
Vitry, Jaques de......... 417
Voice...45, 67, 68, 99, 166,
220, 232, 268, 270, 320,
324, 326, 331, 358, 362,
369, 391, 397, 412, 415

W

Wags, pulpit 202
Walpole, Sir Robert..268, 269, 297
War 377
Washington, George..260, 321, 352, 395, 410
  eulogy on 311
Watts, Isaac 339
Wave law of revival and decline 415
Wealth 69
Wearmouth Abbey 178
Webster, Daniel..267, 325, 334, 336-sq., 356, 362, 364, 383, 390, 393
Webster, Ebenezer 340
Weed, Thurlow 405
Wesleyan University 402
Westminster Hall 294, 295
  scrutiny, speech on 302
Whig party 299, 379, 381
William of Normandy 67
William of Tyre 190
Windom, allusion to 102
Winfrid 182
Winthrop, Robert C. 374

Wirt, William 365
Wit 78
  Attic 146
  Celtic 66, 68, 96, 123, 224, 256, 260, 293, 295, 351, 361, 364
Women, troublesome..157, 185, 202
Words, archaic 65
  exact 362
  desperate 388
  common 74, 76, 341
  single 76
  strong 358
Writers, obscure 80
Writing 79, 221

X

Xenophon 33, 81, 92

Y

Yale College 1, 332

Z

Zarna, battle of 96
Zoroaster 152
Zwingli 218, 222

www.ingramcontent.com/pod-product-compliance
Lightning Source LLC
Chambersburg PA
CBHW022146300426
44115CB00006B/374